POLITICS AND SOCIAL CHANGE

POLITICS
AND SOCIAL CHANGE

ORISSA IN 1959

BY F. G. BAILEY

University of California Press
Berkeley and Los Angeles
1970

UNIVERSITY OF CALIFORNIA PRESS
BERKELEY AND LOS ANGELES, CALIFORNIA

UNIVERSITY OF CALIFORNIA PRESS, LTD.
LONDON, ENGLAND

© 1963 BY THE REGENTS OF THE UNIVERSITY OF CALIFORNIA
SECOND PRINTING, 1970
LIBRARY OF CONGRESS CATALOG CARD NUMBER: 63-19473
SBN 520-00061-7 (CLOTHBOUND EDITION)
SBN 520-01678-5 (PAPERBACK EDITION)

To the memory of

NAGIN PAREKH

PREFACE

This book has two purposes. It continues earlier studies carried out in Orissa (India) between 1952 and 1955, concerning politics. The first of these studies analysed changes in the distribution of power in a village; the second described a struggle for power between the aboriginal Konds and the Hindu settlers in their midst.[1] In both enquiries I learnt a little of the role of Members of the Legislative Assembly (MLAs) and of the working at village level of the modern institutions of representative democracy. In 1959 I made systematic enquiries in this field, and I have attempted to answer the question: What is the relationship between parliamentary democracy in Orissa and the older traditional forms of social and political organization?

My second purpose relates to the theory of social anthropology and, indeed, of all the social sciences which concern themselves with the new and developing nations. Social anthropology has grown largely through research into small, relatively self-contained, and isolated communities. In this book I have tried to see how far the techniques and the conceptual framework of social anthropology can be used in the analysis of a complex and diversified society.

[1] Bailey, 1957 and 1960.

The year 1959 was an interesting one in Orissa politics. After the first general election in 1952 Orissa had a difficult time. The Congress party formed the government, but it never enjoyed a stable majority. Congress was strong in the coastal districts; the main opposition party, Ganatantra Parishad, controlled the hill areas, most of which were Feudatory States before 1947.[2] There were two small left wing groups, the Communists and the Praja Socialists. From the northern hill districts a few members of the tribal Jharkhand Party were returned to the Assembly.

Congress governed, especially after the 1957 election, by allying itself with one or more of the smaller parties, and considerable time and energy were spent in keeping its narrow majority intact. But in the middle of 1959 Congress and Ganatantra formed a coalition, and the three smaller parties were left to be the Opposition.

From my point of view this was a profitable situation. The manoeuvres which preceded the coalition aroused much interest, and I never had difficulty in getting people to talk politics. Furthermore, crisis calls for action, and action is a surer basis than talk on which to found a social analysis.

I attended Assembly sittings almost every day during the first session from February 18th until the first week in April, 1959. I learnt to recognize most of the MLAs, and they got to know me and became curious about my work. I also made contact with the Assembly secretariat and with some of the many hopeful people who sit around the Assembly library and tea room. I learnt about Assembly procedure and the conventions which govern its work. I had little profit from the debates themselves, because my command of Oriya (the language of Orissa), adequate for the villages, did not measure up to the high-flown style used in the Assembly, and because

---

[2] See Map 1. See also Chapter 8, "Hill and Coast."

the loud-speaker system sometimes made even English unintelligible to me.

During the year I interviewed fifty MLAs for times varying from half-an-hour to six hours. I also talked with members of former houses and political workers outside the Assembly. These interviews provided biographical material about the members, their education, wealth, caste, occupation outside politics, and so forth. I gained some idea of what work they did and what organization they had in their constituencies. I also elicited opinions about the Independent Movement, about representative government, and about current political problems and scandals.

I had one direct refusal (from a gentleman refusing on behalf of his wife, who was the MLA), there were one or two polite evasions, and some leaders were very circumspect. Others were helpful. A few (mostly Praja Socialists and Communists) understood immediately what I had come to do in Orissa, and they not only answered questions frankly, but also suggested lines of enquiry which I had overlooked. Some, who had retired from active politics, saw this as their opportunity to put down their record for posterity and talked freely. Men with a grudge, men passed over for office, or men who thought that Orissa's politics had taken a disastrous turn, spoke with a directness that was sometimes embarrassing.

I enjoyed this phase of the work. It provided material from which to reconstruct Orissa's politics over the last thirty or forty years, and it suggested openings for research in constituencies. Moreover, there was an intrinsic interest in hearing men tell what they had done with their lives and in seeing the dramatic events of the last thirty years through the eyes of those who had played leading parts.

Research in the districts and constituencies was done through interviewing politicians and other leading men, through printed material, and by intensive study in selected villages.

PREFACE

x

From interviews with various MLAs I already had some idea of what kind of organization existed in the constituencies. These ideas were tested and amplified by talking with defeated candidates, administrators, and others not directly concerned in politics. I spent six weeks in the hot weather touring in southern Orissa and meeting local leaders. I addressed some small informal gatherings and derived some, but not much, material from the discussions which followed. I had hoped to make a similiar tour north of the Mahanadi river, but floods prevented this.

In these talks I met politicians and reflective members of the middle class; I had little contact with peasants. To fill this gap I returned to the area in which I had worked when I was last in Orissa and where I have friends and good informants. From these people I reconstructed the 1957 election as it had appeared in the villages. I asked how the villagers had been approached, and what was their attitude to politicians and to the new institutions.

Two villages are a poor sample for the whole of Orissa. Moreover they lie in a backward area, where the people are not politically conscious. The tour and interviews with politicians provided some comparative material, but in addition I enlisted people with training in sociology or with special knowledge to write or tell me about their own area. The material varied, but it did correct the parochial outlook I had acquired in my own villages.

I also used printed material about constituency and district politics. The Election Reports were useful, and I gained some insight into the working of electoral machines from analysing judgments delivered in Election Tribunals.

I lacked numerical information about the types of persons who interested themselves in politics and why they did so. I therefore used a census card with such items as age, caste, education, residence, occupation, political activity, and so forth. These cards were completed for all members of the four elected houses in Orissa (1936, 1947, 1952, and 1957). I had intended to include all active members of the different parties, but I could neither collect all the names nor fill in cards for all the names I had.

The readiest response came from the Praja Socialist Party. Their office was efficiently organized, and they had much of the information I required (apart from caste) already in their files. The Communist Party was also well organized. They were suspicious at first, but after three weeks of intermittent discussion and argument, the Party Secretary made their personnel files available to me.

I had a less satisfactory response from the two main parties, Congress and Ganatantra. They controlled larger organizations, but their office work was at a lower standard. This suggested that the two smaller parties were organized in the Western pattern, whereas the larger parties depended less upon an efficient party bureaucracy and more upon ties of tradition (in the case of Ganatantra) and of patronage (in the case of Congress).

Apart from the techniques listed above, I read as widely as the library and bookshop resources of Orissa allowed, but I found little material specifically on the problem which I had chosen to investigate. Throughout the year I kept a file of newspaper cuttings from two local editions of national dailies, a complete file of the Orissa English-language *Eastern Times*, and some cuttings from vernacular newspapers. I endeavoured to collect political pamphlets and various other ephemera, but this material was in fact very ephemeral, and I had difficulty in finding even the pamphlets published during the 1957 election.

Finally, this analysis rests upon events up to the end of 1959 and takes no account of what has happened in Orissa since that time.

My visit to Orissa in 1959 was made possible by a grant of

PREFACE

study leave and funds from the School of Oriental and African Studies.

For hospitality, combined with intellectual stimulation, I thank Professor Aiyappan, who holds the chair of Anthropology in Utkal University; Sri Sachin Chaudhuri, who is the editor of the *Economic Weekly*; and Sri Nityananda Mahapatra, MLA.

I received much practical help from officials both in the districts and in government offices in Bhubaneswar. My ideas were shaped in conversation with many people in Orissa. I cannot mention all, but my especial thanks are due to the following members of the Legislative Assembly: Bankabehari Das, Harihar Das, Prasanna Kumar Das, Gadhadhar Datta, the late Raja Bahadur Kishore Chandra Bhanj Deo, Kishore Chandra Deo, Ram Prasad Misra, Pabitra Mohan Pradhan, Satyananda Champati Ray, and Sadasiv Tripathi. I also benefitted in various ways, intellectual and otherwise, from contact with Harish Buxipatra, Gopinath Das, Nabakishore Das, Nityananda Das, and the young man to whose memory this book is dedicated.

To Professor Aiyappan, his staff, and his students (in particular Uma Charan Mahanti) I owe an especial debt; also to Dr. N. Datta Majumdar. I also thank two men who, in their different ways, provided the detached wisdom of elder statesmen: Professor N. K. Bose and Sri Naba Krushna Chaudhuri. Finally, I acknowledge a debt, now of ten years' standing, to the people of Bisipara, in particular Sri Romes Chandra Mahakhudo, Sri Debohari Bisoi, and Sri Sindhu Sahani.

In writing this book I have benefitted from discussions in Professor C. von Fürer-Haimendorf's seminar in the Department of Anthropology and Sociology, School of Oriental and African Studies, in Professor Philip's South Asia seminar in the same institution, and in Professor Robinson's seminar in the Institute of Commonwealth Studies, University of London. My greatest debt is to my friends who have read and criticized the manuscript: Avener Cohen, Adrian Mayer, Ralph Nicholas, R. L. Rooksby, and Hugh Tinker.

For making the business of publication an unexpected pleasure my thanks are due to those amiable gentlemen who man the University of California Press and to Mr. J. R. Bracken of the School of Oriental and African Studies for sage advice on how to keep them amiable.

For permission to reproduce material verbatim or in paraphrase I thank the editors of the *Economic Weekly*, the *Journal of Commonwealth Political Studies*, the *European Journal of Sociology*, and Professor Philips, the editor of the book *Politics and Society in South Asia*.

I dedicate this book to the memory of Nagin Parekh. His virtues and integrity seem to me to have been distinctively Indian.

School of Oriental and African Studies　　F. G. BAILEY
University of London

CONTENTS

INTRODUCTION. ORISSA IN 1959   1

Part I. THE VILLAGES

1. BISIPARA VILLAGE   13
   The 1957 Election 13
   The Campaign in Bisipara 18
   The Vote in Bisipara 36
   The Bisipara Candidates 53

2. MOHANPUR VILLAGE   69
   The Elections in Mohanpur 71
   The 1957 Campaign in Mohanpur 78
   The Candidates 81
   Village Affairs and State Politics 85
   Bisipara and Mohanpur 99

Part II. THE CONSTITUENCIES

3. THE POLITICIAN'S PROBLEM   107
   The Size of Vote-Banks 109
   Constituencies and Administrative Units 111
   Traditional Groups and Social Change 113

CONTENTS

4. INDIGENOUS POLITICAL UNITS — 114
   KALAHANDI DISTRICT 114
   SENTIMENT AND ADMINISTRATION 118
   CHANGE AND CONTINUITY 119

5. CASTES AND CASTE ASSOCIATIONS — 122
   CASTES 122
   RURAL CASTES AND POLITICS 127
   CASTE ASSOCIATIONS 128
   CASTE ASSOCIATIONS AND POLITICS 133
   CONCLUSION 134

6. MOVEMENTS AND MACHINES — 136
   PARTIES AND THEIR TASKS 136
   THE PARTIES IN ORISSA 139
   THE ELECTORAL MACHINES 141
   THE CONTENT OF MACHINE RELATIONSHIPS 143
   MACHINE PERSONNEL 146
   MACHINE STRUCTURE AND THE PARTY 151
   THE ELECTORAL EFFICIENCY OF A MACHINE 154

Part III. STATE POLITICS

7. ORIYA NATIONALISM — 161

8. THE FREEDOM FIGHTERS — 166
   THE CONGRESS 167
   ORIYA NATIONALISM 170
   THE LANDLORDS 171
   HILL AND COAST 173
   PRAJAMANDALS 177

9. ORISSA POLITICS 1947–1959 — 182
   CONGRESS AND ORIYA NATIONALISM 182
   SOCIAL AND ECONOMIC REFORM IN THE ORISSA PLAINS 186
   THE ORISSAN HILLS 197
   FROM MOVEMENT TO PARTY 206
   POLITICIANS AND VOTERS 217

CONTENTS

xvii

CONCLUSION. POLITICS AND SOCIAL CHANGE	219
REFERENCES	235
INDEX	237

TABLES

1. THE 1952 ELECTION TO THE ORISSA LEGISLATIVE ASSEMBLY — 4
2. THE 1957 ELECTION TO THE ORISSA LEGISLATIVE ASSEMBLY — 5
3. THE 1957 ELECTION IN PHULBANI CONSTITUENCY — 16
4. THE 1957 PARLIAMENTARY ELECTION IN KALAHANDI CONSTITUENCY — 17
5. SOME BISIPARA VOTERS IN 1957, BY CASTE — 41
6. THE 1952 ELECTION IN CUTTACK RURAL CONSTITUENCY — 72
7. THE 1957 ELECTION IN CUTTACK RURAL CONSTITUENCY — 73
8. CASTES IN MOHANPUR — 86
9. POPULATION, AREA, AND DENSITY OF HILL AND COAST DIVISIONS OF ORISSA IN 1951 — 173
10. VOTES POLLED IN EACH DISTRICT IN THE 1957 ELECTIONS TO THE ORISSA LEGISLATIVE ASSEMBLY BY THE GANATANTRA PARISHAD AND THE CONGRESS PARTY — 198
11. CONGRESS MEMBERSHIP IN THE ORISSA LEGISLATIVE ASSEMBLY 1952–1957 — 215
12. SOME CONGRESS CABINETS IN ORISSA, 1946–1959 — 215

TEXTS

1. CAMPAIGN SPEECHES IN BISIPARA — 18
2. ELECTION PROMISES IN BISIPARA — 29
3. LOCAL ISSUES IN THE BISIPARA ELECTION — 36
4. THE STATUTORY PANCHAYAT IN BISIPARA — 55

CONTENTS
xviii

MAPS

1. THE DISTRICTS OF ORISSA   9

                                                   Facing

2. KALAHANDI DISTRICT. ASSEMBLY
   CONSTITUENCIES, 1952   116
3. KALAHANDI DISTRICT. ASSEMBLY
   CONSTITUENCIES, 1957   117

INTRODUCTION. ORISSA IN 1959

Several of the Oriya politicians to whom I talked in 1959 said that the present form of government in India did not suit their country's needs. Parliamentary institutions, they argued, had developed in Britain through a long process of trial and error and were adapted to the social organization and cultural standards of the British people. These institutions were transferred and imposed upon a society of a very different kind, where they did not fit.

Furthermore, they said, India had difficulty in maintaining national unity and in controlling demands for regional and linguistic autonomy; she was also faced with a formidable task in raising her standard of living. These tasks, some of them argued, could be better accomplished by a form of government more incisive and less given to delay and compromise than democracy based on free elections.[1] China and Russia were there to prove the point. Parliamentary democracy was a luxury which should take third place behind national unity and economic development.

The merits and failings of parliamentary democracy are problems for others; my questions are less difficult, for they

---

[1] For an illuminating discussion of this term, see W. J. M. Mackenzie, 1958.

INTRODUCTION

2

concern facts. What, in fact, is the relation between the new institutions and the traditional society in Orissa? What is the link between the candidates for the Orissa Assembly and their voters? What effect does this link have, if any, on traditional social relationships? Conversely, how does it affect the working of parliamentary institutions?

Framed in this general way, the problem does not appear difficult. One examines the behaviour of politicians or of ordinary people acting within the framework of representative institutions and asks how far this behaviour seems comprehensible in the light of indigenous customs, levels of cultural attainment, and membership of such traditional social groups as villages or castes, or in the light of traditional roles like landlord, tenant, prince, priest, and so forth. But at an operational level—planning the enquiry and presenting the results—there are many difficulties.

These difficulties arise because a diagram of behaviour cannot be drawn to one scale only, but must take into account units of varying dimension. For practical reasons of time and resources I have excluded the level of the Parliament and the Indian Union, and I deal only with one of its constituent states, Orissa. Within Orissa I have made three major divisions between political behaviour at the level of the state, the constituencies, and the villages. Obviously, these divisions are not exhaustive.

There are many difficulties of method involved in such an analysis, and I shall discuss some of them in my concluding chapter.

On the other hand my technique of describing political behaviour in Orissa is a relatively simple one. It is like the map of a river. The main stream is State politics; this is fed by the tributaries of political activity in the 14 districts and the 101 constituencies; to stand for the springs and rivulets which feed these tributaries are 51,000 villages. I have begun my analysis with the villages and, so to speak, floated with the current through the constituencies into the main stream of State politics.

Before I set out on this voyage let me give one snapshot of politics as they appeared in the Orissa Legislative Assembly in 1959. The events of that year pose the problem which this book seeks to answer.

When Independence came to India in 1947, the State of Orissa was governed by a Congress Ministry which had the support of a large and triumphant majority in the Assembly. Even before the last results of the 1946 elections were announced the Governor had invited Congress to form a government. The Assembly then had sixty seats. Four of these were filled by nomination. Of the remaining 56 seats, 45 were occupied by Congressmen, giving the Government the support of 75 per cent of the Assembly.

The elections in 1946 were held on a limited franchise. Six years later, in 1952, the first general elections were held on a full adult franchise. In the meantime the Feudatory States of Orissa had been merged with the former British-administered districts, bringing the population of the state up to fourteen and one half million, approximately double that of the old Orissa province. The new Legislative Assembly contained 140 seats.

The results of the 1952 election are given in Table 1. Congress did not win a majority, but it was the largest single party, and it formed a government. It enjoyed the support of a number of Independents (classified with "others" in Table 1).

This Ministry brought in various agrarian reforms, the most important being Zemindari Abolition.[2] In the last year of the Ministry's tenure the report of the States Reorganization Commission was published. The report was received with

---

[2] For details, see Chapter 9.

TABLE 1
THE 1952 ELECTION TO THE ORISSA LEGISLATIVE ASSEMBLY

Party	Seats	Votes [b]
Congress	67 (48%)	39%
Socialist	10 (7%)	11%
Communist	7 (5%)	5%
Ganatantra Parishad	31 (22%)	[a] (45%)
Others	25 (18%)	[a]
Total	140 (100%)	100%

SOURCE: *Report on the First General Elections in India 1951–1952*, Vol 2. Figures for the Ganatantra Parishad have been compiled from the 1952 List of Members of the Orissa Legislative Assembly.
[a] Separate figures are not compiled.
[b] "Votes," throughout this book, unless stated otherwise, means valid votes.

widespread dissatisfaction in Orissa and severely embarrassed Congress.[3] In the following year the second general elections were held. The results are shown in Table 2.

Again the Congress was the largest single party, and it formed a government with the support of the five Jharkhand members. Six of the seven Independents joined the Congress. Before the Ministry was formed one Ganatantra member and four Independents came to the Congress. After the Ministry took office, two more Independents, seven Ganatantra, and one Communist member also crossed the floor.

In April, 1958, four of those who had left Ganatantra and gone to Congress went back again. A few days later three Congress members, including a Deputy Minister, resigned from the party. The following day this Deputy Minister and four members of the Ganatantra, two of them MLAs, were

---

[3] See Chapter 9.

arrested on a complaint of conspiracy laid by one of the Congress MLAs who had resigned a few days earlier. They were released the following day by an order of the High Court. At the same time the complainant and the other MLA, who had resigned, rejoined Congress. Eight days later the Government's Appropriation Bill was passed by a majority of two votes. On the following day, May 6, the Assembly was ad-

TABLE 2

THE 1957 ELECTION TO THE ORISSA LEGISLATIVE ASSEMBLY

Party	Seats	Votes
Congress	56 (40%)	38%
Praja Socialist [b]	11 (8%)	10%
Communist	9 (7%)	8%
Ganatantra Parishad	51 (37%)	29%
Jharkhand	5 (3%)	[a]
		(15%)
Others	8 (5%)	[a]
Total	140 (100%)	100%

SOURCE: *Report on the Second General Elections in India.* 1957, Vol 2. Figures for the Jharkhand Party and "others" have been compiled from the 1957 List of Members.
[a] Separate figures are not compiled.
[b] The 1952 Socialists had by 1957 divided into Lohia Socialists and Praja Socialists. The category of "others" includes one Lohia Socialist.

journed. On May 9, on the advice of the Congress Parliamentary Board, the Orissa Ministry resigned. But their resignation was not accepted by the Governor, and after some parleying between the Governor and the leader of the Ganatantra, the Congress Ministry again took office on May 24.

On February 23, early in the Budget session of 1959, when the Revenue Minister was seeking leave to introduce a bill, the Congress Ministry was defeated by eight votes. But this was reckoned a "snap" defeat, and the Ministry did not resign. The Government's strength at that time was 70 (excluding the Speaker but including the five Jharkhand members) in a house of 138 members. Of the two seats vacant, one later went to the Government and one to the Opposition, making the Opposition vote 68, and the Government vote 71 (excluding the Speaker).

In the course of that session there were several "cut" motions all won by the Government with a margin of four or five votes, the five Jharkhand members voting on each occasion with the Government. On March 16 a man went on hunger strike outside the Assembly to protest against the treatment of persons displaced by the Rourkhella steel plant buildings. The Opposition put several adjournment motions seeking to discuss the affair, but these were disallowed. On March 17 the Opposition walked out in protest. On March 19 the Opposition walked out, again in protest at the Speaker's refusal to allow a discussion of the Rourkhella trouble, but this time they were accompanied by two Jharkhand MLAs, whose constituencies were in the Rourkhella area. The same afternoon the Congress Ministry announced that demolitions at Rourkhella would be stopped, pending an impartial enquiry to be held the following month. The Opposition leader would be invited to attend the enquiry.

On March 18 the Health Minister, in reply to a question, said that Orissa's second medical college would be opened at Burla in Sambalpur district. On April 2, the day on which the Budget Session was concluded, five Congress members submitted their resignations from the Assembly party. They represented constituencies in Ganjam, and they resigned because they considered that the medical college should have gone to that district and not to Sambalpur. On the following day three of the resignations were withdrawn. The Assembly was due to meet again on April 27 to deal with Private Members' Bills and with some official business. How the two members who had not withdrawn their resignations would have voted is not known, for no official business had been discussed by the time the Assembly adjourned *sine die* on April 29. Excluding these two members and the Speaker, the Congress strength was 69 and the Opposition 68.

Several times, while speaking in the House, the Chief Minister had appealed to the Opposition parties to "put the execution of the plan above party interests." He had also held discussions with the leader of the Opposition after the "snap" defeat in February. He made a final appeal when replying to the debate on the Appropriation Bill. The *Amrita Bazar Patrika* wrote "The leader of the Opposition was not taken aback by the appeal. He made a suitable reply." And about this time there began to appear other newspaper reports of negotiations for a coalition between the two main parties.

Six weeks later, on May 15, the Congress Ministry resigned. On May 22 a Coalition Ministry, consisting of the former Congress Chief Minister, the former leader of the Opposition, and one Congressman from the previous cabinet, took office.

The two Ganjam MLAs who had resigned from the Assembly party were expelled from the Congress on June 22.

One may see in these events the decline and fall of the Congress party in Orissa. From a triumphant majority commanding 75 per cent of the votes in the Assembly of 1946, the party's paper support (including Jharkhand allies) in April, 1959, could be shown as a majority only with the help of a decimal point—50.7 per cent. Congress, from having absolute control in 1946, had sunk in 1959 to the point where the maximum energy and ingenuity were required to keep it in office.

The consensus, as I listened to it in the early months of 1959, was that parliamentary government in Orissa was not working well. Government sympathizers said that the Opposition exploited the Ministry's difficulties for party ends, which, given the rules of the game, is to blame the batsman

INTRODUCTION

8

for hitting too many boundaries. The Opposition accused the Government of hanging on to power at all costs and neglecting the proper work of government. Both sides united in diagnosing the disease as "political instability," by which they did not mean a rapid succession of ministries, as in postwar France, but rather a narrow and uncertain majority.

This "instability" led to the unsavoury intrigues of April and May, 1958, of which everyone seems to have been ashamed. It also led to the disproportionate tenderness which the Ministry showed to even the least of its supporters, with the result that narrow local interests were advanced before the general welfare. Without saying where justice lay in the Rourkhella affair, it is at least true that the Government was forced to go back on a decision which it had already taken in the light of what it considered best for the State. With a Coalition Ministry, commanding on paper the support of at least 70 per cent of the Assembly, such pressures would be impossible and a more disciplined obedience could be exacted from the members: as in the case of the two Ganjam MLAs, they could be expelled without imperilling the Ministry's position. At the same time Ministers were freed from party preoccupations and were able to supervise administration more closely and get on with the "implementation of the plan." Thus, from one point of view, the Coalition was a sensible compromise between moderate men in the interests of general welfare.

From the other point of view, that of the left-wing parties who remained to form the Opposition, it was a mere trick to retain power.

Why did the Congress Ministry resign in May, 1959, to make room for a Coalition Government? In the third part of this book I will describe in more detail the difficulties which Congress faced. To some extent these difficulties explain why Congress failed to consolidate its 1947 dominance in the coastal area and to extend its influence to the whole of the new state. But this is not the whole explanation, for the difficulties over Oriya Nationalism, social and economic reforms, and the hill and coast cleavage were all aggravated by a fundamental failing in communication between the political elite and the mass of their electors. This problem of communication occupies the first and second parts of the book.

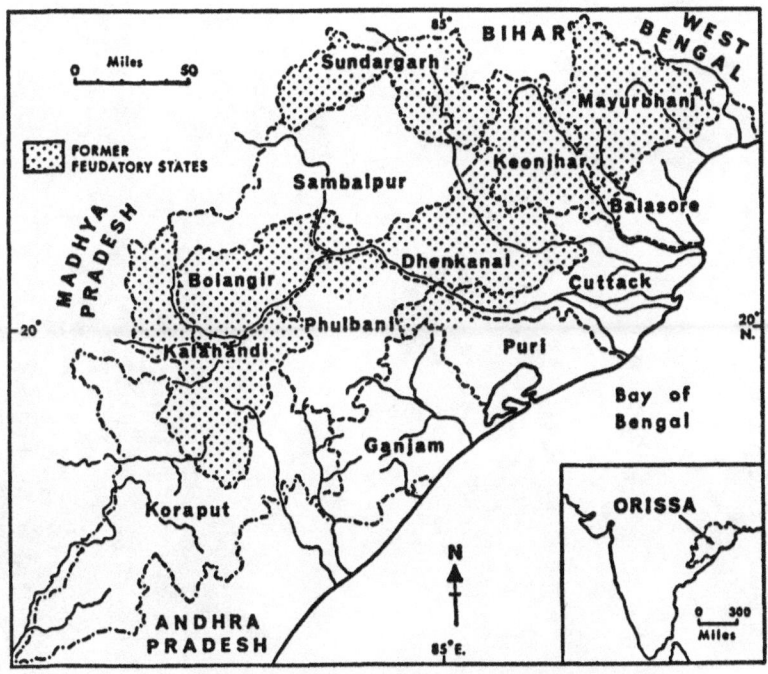

MAP 1. THE DISTRICTS OF ORISSA

I. THE VILLAGES

1

BISIPARA VILLAGE

The 1957 Election

The method of voting in the 1957 General Election was in theory very simple and well adapted to a largely illiterate population. The voter received a ballot paper which he placed in the box of his chosen candidate, the boxes being identified by pictures—a yoke of bullocks for the Congress party, a bow and arrow for the Ganatantra Parishad, a banyan tree or a hand palm forward for Independents, and so forth.

But in the General Election of 1957, when a voter in Bisipara village had come to the head of the queue, had gone inside the booth, had been identified on the register of voters, had passed the scrutiny of the candidates' polling agents who sat there to watch for malpractices (in particular, impersonation), had extended his finger to be marked with indelible ink, had received his four ballot papers, and had listened to an explanation of what he must and must not do when he entered the polling chamber, then, on entering the polling chamber to distribute his four votes, he was faced with an array of no less than twenty ballot boxes.

Bisipara is in two constituencies, one for the Parliament at Delhi, and the other for the Orissa State Legislative Assembly, which meets in the State Capital at Bhubaneswar. Two

BISIPARA VILLAGE

districts, Phulbani and Kalahandi, were put together to make a constituency for the Parliament. The area of this constituency is over 9,000 square miles and for the 1957 election it contained 732,328 voters. Bisipara lies in Phulbani district. Every elector had two votes, for the constituency was represented in Parliament by two members, one of whom had by law to be a member of a Scheduled *tribe*; that is to say, there was one reserved seat and one general seat. Bisipara also belongs to Phulbani constituency which returns two members to the Orissa Legislative Assembly, one to the general seat and one to a seat reserved for candidates from Scheduled *castes*. This constituency contained 125,270 electors and covered an area of 2,000 square miles.

Elections for the Parliament and for the Assembly were conducted simultaneously, so that each elector had four votes and collected four ballot papers when he entered the booth. The papers for the Parliamentary election were of a different colour from those to be used in the Assembly. Parliamentary ballot papers deposited in an Assembly box, or Assembly papers in a Parliamentary box, meant, of course, invalid votes. It was also an infraction to put two votes in the box of one candidate, although I think that some at least of the Bisipara voters did this. Such cumulative votes could be detected by a scrutiny of their serial numbers, and one of the votes would then be reckoned invalid.[1]

The boxes of candidates who belonged to a Scheduled tribe or a Scheduled caste were distinguished by a thick black circle drawn around the symbol. For example, if a voter wished to support the Congress, he would put one vote into the box with the picture of the yoke of bullocks on it and the other into the box which had the same picture ringed around by the black line. But it is to be noticed that a voter with a low

---

[1] A fuller description of balloting can be found in Volume 1 of the Election Commission's *Report* (1959).

allegiance to parties and a high allegiance to persons could, if he wished, vote for two reserved seat candidates, or two general seat candidates. The mechanism which ensured the return of a candidate to a reserved seat in a double-member constituency was built not into the polling, but into the counting. The first person to be declared elected was the reserved seat candidate with the highest number of votes. Once this seat was filled then the distinction of reserved and general seat was withdrawn and the candidate remaining with the highest poll was declared elected. This has occasionally meant that the occupant of a general seat was also a member of a Scheduled tribe or caste.

There were five candidates for the two Parliament seats and fifteen for the two Assembly seats—hence the twenty ballot boxes in the Bisipara booth.

Even in a double-member constituency fifteen candidates for an Assembly seat make an abnormally high figure. Moreover, of these fifteen no less than three came from Bisipara itself, although it has a population of only 700, no history of political activity, and no wealth of political experience.

The Assembly constituency was delimited in 1956 and was sharply divided into a highland and lowland area: the lowland area, in the Mahanadi valley, consisted of Boad, formerly a Feudatory State ruled until 1947 by its own Raja. The upland area was the larger part of the Kondmals subdivision, administered for more than one hundred years as part of British India. At a rough calculation there were two registered electors in Boad to every one in the upland area. The lowland area, contrary to the usual pattern of Princely State and British-administered area, was much the more advanced and more sophisticated of the two, and the Election Commissioners sharpened the division by detaching the more advanced Oriya-speaking section of the Kondmals and joining it to a different constituency.

Six of the candidates belonged to Scheduled castes, and the

BISIPARA VILLAGE

remaining nine were of clean caste. The Ganatantra Parishad and the Congress put up candidates for both seats. Both party candidates for the general seat were lawyers from Boad town. The Ganatantra candidate for the reserved seat came from a village in the Boad countryside, and the Congress candidate for the reserved seat came from Bisipara village in the Kondmals. Eleven candidates were Independents, four eligible for the reserved seat and seven eligible only for the general seat. Three out of these four reserved-seat candidates came from the Kondmals and only one from Boad. But of the Independents eligible for the general seat one only came from the Kondmals, and the other six came from Boad.

TABLE 3
THE 1957 ELECTION IN PHULBANI CONSTITUENCY

Candidate	Valid votes	Percentage of valid votes
GP 1	18,634	28.39
GP 2 (Sch C)	14,900	22.69
Congress 1	7,616	11.60
Ind 1	5,188	7.92
Congress 2 (Sch C)	3,881	5.92
Ind 2	3,028	4.61
Ind 3	2,848	4.34
Ind 4	1,990	3.03
Ind 5	1,797	2.73
Ind 6 (Sch C)	1,535	2.33
Ind 7	1,086	1.65
Ind 8	938	1.43
Ind 9 (Sch C)	835	1.27
Ind 10 (Sch C)	797	1.22
Ind 11 (Sch C)	575	.87

There was a poll of 26.20 per cent in the constituency, and the Ganatantra Parishad (GP) won both seats comfortably. The results of the election are given in Table 3. General seat candidates had paid a deposit of Rs250; reserved seat candidates had paid Rs125. In a double-member constituency deposits are returned only to those who poll one twelfth of the votes or are elected. Therefore, all but the first three candidates on the list given in Table 3 forfeited their deposits.

Five candidates contested for the two seats in Parliament. For the general seat the Ganatantra Parishad nominated the former Raja of Kalahandi, a leading member of their party and an extremely energetic politician. The Congress put up a wealthy industrialist who came from Sambalpur, which is not within the constituency. The GP candidate for the reserved seat was a Kond from the Kondmals. I have no biographical details for the Congress candidate for the reserved seat, nor for the single Independent (who was a member of a Scheduled tribe) but both of them came from the Kalahandi half of the constituency.

TABLE 4

THE 1957 PARLIAMENTARY ELECTION IN KALAHANDI CONSTITUENCY

Candidate	Valid votes	Percentage of valid votes
GP 1	174,920	37.06
GP 2 (Sch T)	151,681	32.14
Congress 1	70,333	14.91
Congress 2 (Sch T)	58,577	12.41
Independent (Sch T)	16,441	3.48

Again the GP won comfortably. Only the Independent lost his deposit (in a Parliamentary constituency Rs500 for the general seat and Rs250 for a Scheduled caste or tribe candidate). There was a poll of 32.22 per cent. The results are given in Table 4.

These, then, are the twenty candidates whose boxes faced the voter in Bisipara's polling booth in the winter of 1956–57.

BISIPARA VILLAGE

In the following section I begin to look at what that voter had learned about the candidates and about the parties and whether what he had learned helped him to decide in which boxes to put his four votes.

THE CAMPAIGN IN BISIPARA

In 1959 I talked to many of the people in Bisipara about the election which had taken place just over two years before. I asked some of them to write down what they remembered of the campaign, and I tried to find out the way in which people had in fact cast their votes. In Text 1 I reproduce one man's account of what took place. Proper names and some libellous statements have been suppressed, and a few obscure references have been cut out or expanded to make them intelligible. Otherwise the text is unaltered.

Text 1. Campaign speeches in Bisipara

When the elections were announced Congress put up four candidates. The Congress Government put up *Congress 2* [2] from Bisipara as its candidate. The Government also allowed four Independents to stand for the Harijan [Scheduled caste] seat, among them *Ind 9* from Bisipara. The candidates began their campaigns on 13.12.56.

Congress 2 fought his campaign with 65 agents, including his own people and some engaged by the Congress general seat candidate in Boad. His agent in Boad was X [a Bisipara Harijan], in the Phulbani area Y [X's brother], and in the Phiringia area Z [a wealthy shopkeeper and contractor of Writer caste].

The Kalahandi Raja [GP 1 in Table 4] put up four candidates for the Harijan seat and the high caste [i.e. general] seat in the Assembly. GP 2 from Boad was their Harijan candidate.

The campaign was conducted with vigour. *Congress 2* and the

---

[2] These substitutes for proper names refer to Table 3, unless indicated otherwise.

Congress Government conducted a joint campaign. About their own candidate the Congress agents spoke like this: "Our Congress Government has put up *Congress 2*, a good, intelligent and educated man to be our MLA. He is a very suitable candidate. He was a teacher for 32 years and did much good work. Having served in all parts of the Kondmals he enjoys the good opinions of everyone. If he is returned then he can do many things that we want him to do. You can be sure that both the clean castes and the Harijans will benefit. If the votes go to *GP 2* or *Ind 9* of the Independent Party, then they will merely sit in Bhubaneswar and look after themselves and their families and draw their pay. Therefore don't vote for them. Vote for the Congress and put your vote in the box with the yoke of bullocks pictured on it. Make no mistake. Make no mistake. Give your votes to the yoke of bullocks box."

When talking of *Ind 9*, they made these allegations: "*Ind 9* has been a policeman for 24 years and done many evil things. He has taken bribes. He has made false charges against the people and imprisoned them. There is nothing good in his record. Even his village brothers will not stand by him. He has an evil mind, and he has beaten people and imprisoned them and profited by his exactions. He cares only for himself and will do nothing for the people. When people see him they fear him as they fear a tiger. He will do nothing for us. If you vote for him then he will treat the people like a wife. No-one will dare to talk to him. Do not vote for him. Vote for *Congress 2*. He is a good man. Vote for the yoke of bullocks. Don't vote for the picture of a banyan tree."

When talking of *GP 2*, they said: "*GP 2* is standing for the Harijan seat. He comes from Boad State. But the Ganatantra isn't the Government. They won't win. If he is elected then he will listen only to what the Ganatantra says and not to what we say. Even with a majority they would do nothing for the people. Don't give a vote to the bow and arrow box. Vote for the yoke of bullocks."

For the Independent Party, *Ind 9* and his agents said: "Look brothers! *Ind 9* is standing as a Harijan to work in the Assembly for the Harijans and the high caste people. Many years ago when Boad and the Kondmals were one, *Ind 9*'s ancestors went to war at Mahasinghi and brought the idol to Bolscoopa, and they were the leaders of the Harijans and in charge of the drummers.[3] They were the right hand men of the Boad Raja. The ancestor who went to Mahasinghi was awarded the title of 'leader' and invested with the *sari*. *Ind 9*'s father also held that title and he journeyed all over the Kondmals looking into people's troubles in his own caste and improving their lot. In the British days the Harijans were short of food and uneducated and they took to thieving. Every day they were going to gaol. Their women were in great difficulties. But *Ind 9*'s father and uncle went to the Magistrate for help and got people educated and taught how to use the plough. Then *Ind 9* took over the leadership of the caste and did much for them. He is educated and has passed out of Minor School (vernacular school).

"With Gandhi's help, he and KS have organized meetings everywhere and tried to get their people accepted into temples and into the hotels. They have won the rewards of being the leaders of their people and making the Harijans a pure caste.

"For the past 23 or 24 years he has done good work as a constable. He has many times been commended for catching criminals, thieves, dacoits, and absconders. Formerly Harijans were not admitted into the police, but by his good qualities he was the first to be admitted, and after his good example others were admitted. During British rule he was working for the welfare of the Harijans in the police. Now he has resigned his job and given up a salary of Rs60 or Rs70 a month and offered his neck as the Independent candidate. Put your vote in the banyan tree box, and then he can go to the Assembly and fight with the Congress on the behalf of the people. He is a man with a good heart and a good mind and is much experienced in the law. Therefore vote for him."

Against the Congress the supporters of *Ind 9* made these allegations: "Congress is putting up *Congress 2* as their candidate for the Assembly in the expectation that he will get votes. But he will not

---

[3] Bailey, 1960, p. 171.

get the votes. At the time when he was a teacher he renounced our Hindu religion and became a Christian. Not even in his dreams did he ever think of the welfare of our Harijan people. Once he became a Christian he was very contemptuous of the Harijans and of the higher castes alike. When the Harijan Minister Santanu Kumar Das came to visit the Government Ashram School at Boida, *Ind 9* and XS made a petition to him, speaking of Gandhi's regard for our people. But *Congress 2* asked to be made an agent for the Depressed Classes League. He got the job and immediately renounced his Christianity and became a Hindu again, for his own profit. Now he is standing for MLA on the Congress ticket. He's a turncoat. When there is a war between the birds and the animals, and the animals win, then he says he is an animal, and if the birds win he'll claim to be a bird. The bat fights on both sides and he is a bat. Therefore don't vote for him, but vote for *Ind 9* who will do excellent work and look after the welfare of our caste. *Congress 2* comes from a bad family, a family of gaolbirds and thieves. Don't waste a vote on him: he will not be elected. The name of *Ind 9* is really Gandhi: he is Gandhi's disciple. Like the Mahatma he will give his life for the people."

This is the kind of lies and deceit they indulge in, so as to get votes.

Against *GP 2* the following kind of thing was said by *Ind 9*'s agents: "*GP 2* is not a Government man. He will just sit in the Ganatantra office and keep quiet. Ganatantra agents are trying to deceive people by saying that he is not a Harijan but really of Herdsman caste. But he is truly a Harijan. The Ganatantra are saying that *Ind 9* and *Congress 2* are Harijans and if they are elected they will do away with caste. But Ganatantra do not want to abolish caste, and therefore they have put up a Herdsman for the Harijan seat. Do not be deceived by these lies."

The Ganatantra agents made the following kind of propaganda: "We are standing for the Ganatantra Parishad. We will lift taxes and cesses from the people. We will give free access to the jungle. The Congress, in order to break the caste system, is setting up Haris and Gondas [the names of two Harijan castes] as candidates. We are setting up a Herdsman and persons of high caste. We will preserve the old caste system. Untouchability will remain. Do not be deceived by Congress propaganda. Vote in the bow and arrow box and put the Congress out of office."

They went to every house in every village secretly by night and deceived the people with talk like this and so they got the votes. Ganatantra won. The Congress Harijan candidate collected from his followers and from people who obeyed the Congress Government about 4000 votes, and lost.

The election was concluded in the second week of February 1957.

This text clearly cannot be accepted as an authoritative and accurate account of what was said in Bisipara during the campaign for the 1957 elections. For example, I asked the writer if he himself had heard Ganatantra agents speaking in favour of retaining the caste system and the practice of untouchability; in fact he had not, but he had, like many other people, heard that this kind of rumour was going around. Nor can one assume that his account of the candidates' campaign speeches is in any sense complete; clearly the record shows only what he remembers, and they must in fact have said much more than this.

However, even if this text—and others like it—is not true to the letter and is in no sense a transcript of actual speeches, it is probably true in spirit. I know the writer well, and he has —considering the area—a record of no little activity on behalf of one of the parties; but this bias does not appear in the text. Secondly, and more importantly, there is a sense in which a text of this kind can tell no lies. What in fact happened in Bisipara in the winter of 1956–57 is, for this enquiry, less important than what the people of Bisipara remember to have happened, or think happened. We are not concerned with the campaign in Bisipara only, but with the people's understanding of the campaign, and of the political institutions which lay behind it. Finally, if it should seem that the conclusions which I draw in the commentary on this text are fetched far beyond the basis of sound evidence, then it must be remembered firstly that these are not so much conclusions as problems and questions, and secondly that these same questions will occur repeatedly in what follows and be tested by different sets of evidence.

The first question for which the text offers some clues is how much the villages understood the significance of the election. The writer of the text is a schoolmaster, a reader (occasionally) of newspapers, and of—for this village—a quite exceptional degree of awareness of the change that was coming over rural India since Independence in 1947. Yet there are some quite clear misconceptions in this text about the limits of Governmental power, and the relation of Government to parties. He writes that the Government puts up candidates and that it "allows" Independents to stand. It is possible that these instances are a slip of the pen. But if they are not, then the first phrase clearly marks a failure to distinguish between the Congress Government and the Congress party, and the latter a failure to distinguish between the Government and the Election Commission. Alternatively, these statements could be construed as a cynical reference to the real seat of power.

Whatever the correct interpretation, these statements are part of a complex idea about what Oriya politicians call the "ruling party." The basic idea in this complex is that the Government is all-powerful and, perhaps, an incomplete acceptance of the idea that Governments may be thrown out by means of an election. Behind this attitude are clearly years of stable authoritarian rule by the British, when the Government was (speaking literally for such places as the Kondmals) in fact all-powerful. The fact that Congress had ruled in India, and at the time this text was written had ruled in

Orissa uninterruptedly since Independence in 1947, must also have influenced the mind of the common man. It is a common phrase to say "I voted for the Raj [Government]," when we would have said "I voted for the Congress party." A third element in this vague idea about the permanence of the Government is the failure to distinguish between the ruling party and the administrative services, which are, of course, permanent. There are very few people in Bisipara who have any conception of the hierarchy which connects the Deputy Commissioner with their MLA.

The complement of the idea of a "vote for the Raj" is the suggestion that a vote against the Raj is a vote wasted, is risky, and has an element of subversion in it. Once again this recalls the days of British rule, when a vote for the Congress party carried the imputation of disloyalty. There is also an ever-present idea that in the distribution of benefits the Raj discriminates between its supporters and its opponents, and therefore a prudent man should vote for the Raj. However, this is only one element in a complex of influences bearing upon the voter, and it was clearly not the strongest influence in Bisipara and Phulbani, since there the vote went overwhelmingly against the Raj.

One of these influences which bear upon the voter, and which is clearly revealed in Text 1, is his assessment of the candidate as a person rather than as the representative of a party. *Congress 2* is commended as "good, intelligent, and educated" and his opponent *Ind 9* is branded as a selfish bully. Both candidates make much of their careers, presenting a picture of disinterested service to the people, with the implication that their future career as an MLA will be no more than a continuation of past good works. The tale of what they have done in the past is offered as proof of what they can and will do in the future. Both present themselves as educated men, and this reflects the voters' conviction that only an educated man will have the skills to intervene effectively in the world of Government and administration. The ex-policeman (*Ind* 9) is recommended for his knowledge of the law, and this is a well-directed appeal since courts of law provide the villager with some of his bitterest frustrations and make it quite clear to him that he is helpless without the aid of an expert intermediary.

This, indeed, is what the voters want: their MLA is not the representative of a party with a policy which commends itself to them, not even a representative who will watch over their interests when policies are being framed, but rather a man who will intervene in the implementation of policy, and in the ordinary day-to-day administration. He is there to divert the benefits in the direction of his constituents, to help individuals to get what they want out of the Administration, and to give them a hand when they get into trouble with officials. This is the meaning which the ordinary villager—and some of their MLAs—attach to the phrase "serving the people."

In short a candidate must present an image of experience and effectiveness, of sincerity, and of a wholehearted and exclusive interest in the welfare of his constituents. When *Ind* 9 and his agents spoke of the noble work of his ancestors with the Boad Raja and with the British officials and of his own work and example in the police, he was testifying to his experience and effectiveness. When he spoke of his Congress rival's brief career as a Christian, he was casting doubt upon the latter's sincerity and imputing motives of self-interest. In his turn, the Congress candidate said directly (according to Text 1) that both *Ind* 9 and the Ganatantra candidate were self-interested—"they will merely sit in Bhubaneswar and look after themselves and their families and draw their pay."

Voters demand that their MLA should be wholeheartedly and exclusively interested in the welfare of his constituents. There are hints of this attitude in the text. The agents of the

BISIPARA VILLAGE

Congress inform the Bisipara electors that GP 2 comes from Boad State, implying that he is an outsider and that his primary loyalties will be elsewhere. Neither *Congress* 2 nor *Ind* 9 make much of the fact that they are Bisipara men. They had no need to do so, for parochial loyalties are axiomatic. The candidates talk as if it is barely conceivable that the voters of Bisipara should not support a candidate from their own village ("*Even* his village-brothers will not stand by him . . ."), and it is equally inconceivable than an MLA from their own village should not work for the village.

In the speeches attributed to *Ind* 9 there are several attempts to compensate for the lonely status of standing for the Independent "party." Neither the Congress candidate nor the Ganatantra man make any play of dropping names, or seeking to associate themselves with well-known personalities. Neither of them need to do so, for the Congress ticket brings with it the electoral bonus of the names of Gandhi and Nehru. For the Ganatantra side, the Kalahandi Raja is a very well-known figure in this part of Orissa, and in any case the mere fact of being a Raja is in itself an electoral asset. *Ind* 9 in fact had none of these advantages, and his agents, apparently, were driven into a crude attempt to get the best out of both sides. Part of the speech brings in the name of the Raja of Boad, to whom the people of the Kondmals owed some allegiance in the distant past, and whose name still figures in many stories about their past, and with whose house they still have some vague ritual connections. He elaborates his ancestors' connection with this royal house, and thus makes some slight attempt to steal some of the glamour which automatically attaches to the Ganatantra Parishad from its connections with the royal houses of Orissa. But this does not prevent him from attempting, at the same time, to take some of the advantage which Congress enjoys through the name of Gandhi. *Ind* 9's name is close enough in sound to "Gandhi" to make possible a play with the word, and to seek to identify *Ind 9*'s image with that of Gandhi. The writer of the text was moved to comment that all this was lies and deceit; and so it is, if taken literally. But the sentences could also mean that *Ind 9* intended to model his life on that of Gandhi and become his disciple.

"Bandwaggoning" is, of course, a familiar electoral technique. But it is of interest to notice the stars to which *Ind 9* attempts to hitch his career, for these say something about the picture of the world outside which is present, or is thought by *Ind 9* to be present, in the minds of the electors. The most direct and compelling invocation is not to policies or principles, or to the parties that hold them, but to persons—to Gandhi and to the local Raja.

Only the final set of speeches recorded—those made on behalf of the Ganatantra—raise questions of the content of policy. These speeches also differ in that they apparently did not contain elaborate eulogies of the Ganatantra candidate and vilifications of his opponents. Perhaps this does not reflect a higher sense of propriety on the part of the Ganatantra candidate (*GP 2* did not, I believe, visit Bisipara) but rather that since the Ganatantra candidates came from elsewhere, their campaign could not so readily be forwarded by raking through the local muck and had to depend more on general issues.

Three of these issues are mentioned in the text: taxes, restrictions on jungle products, and the policies of the Congress about caste and particularly about untouchability.

The promise to reduce or abolish taxes and cesses is more than the politician's standard election pledge. The area in which Bisipara lies had recently come under the statutory panchayat system of local government. These panchayats would eventually have some financial autonomy and would be empowered to make local charges to pay for public services which they organized. The belief got about that in the end the new panchayats would introduce sixty-four new taxes. If there was any basis of reality in this, it must have meant that there were 64 kinds of local service which might be charged against the local taxes. But this is not how the ordinary villager saw it; rather it appeared to him that his present land tax would be multiplied 64 times.

"Free access" to the jungle meant that the villager would be allowed to cut what timber he liked for fuel and for housebuilding. In fact in former days in the British-administered areas the people were allowed access for fuel only to small demarcated areas on the edge of the jungle, and permits were required to cut larger timbers. These rules had been a grievance for many years. Similar rules applied in the small states ruled by Rajas—such as Boad, but the administration was less efficient, and therefore the rules were less burdensome than in British areas. Since 1948 the whole State had come under a uniform administration, and the more rigorous machinery which then applied the forest laws gave the Ganatantra, whose stronghold was in the ex-states and forested hills, a valuable election issue. The change fell with particular severity upon those tribes like the Konds who make part of their living by burning sections of the forest and raising turmeric and other crops in the ash. It did not fall so heavily on the people of Bisipara, and an appeal of this kind probably passed over their heads.

But the third issue—that of caste policy—was a burning one in Bisipara and in the Kondmals generally, and was probably the main reason why the Ganatantra won in the village and why the two Harijan candidates from Bisipara failed so dismally. I return to this question later when I discuss the results of the election in the Bisipara booth.

One cannot judge democratic politics in Bisipara solely on what the writer of Text 1 chose to highlight, and on the four topics—the Raj, the qualifications of a representative, the names with a universal appeal, and policy issues—which I have picked out. Nevertheless, the general content of these appeals, if we leave aside the scurrilities, is not noticeably lower than the content of appeals in other democratic countries in the context of an election. The basis of these appeals —other than the attempt to use the charisma of Gandhi—is self-interest, but this is the enlightened variety of self-interest which concerns itself with the common good or the general weal. Even the alleged Ganatantra campaign in favour of the caste system is, by the standards of elections, a moral issue honestly raised. Apart, again, from the scurrilities, there is no flavour in Text 1 of Eatanswill, of straightforward uncompromising corruption.

But the writer of Text 2, also a Bisipara man, had different memories of the same 1957 election in his village.[4]

Text 2. Election promises in Bisipara

The first candidate (A) to address the village called a meeting in the main street and said: "Brothers, all give me your votes. I stand for the welfare of yourselves and the country. Therefore elect me. If you all, my brothers and sisters of Bisipara, put your votes in my box, then I will give something to all of you. Then you must go round the villages of Besringia and say that everyone is voting for my party. Everyone will obey you and so give their votes to me. If anyone wants to be an agent, then let him speak up and if he goes around the villages making people understand how they must vote, then I will pay him Rs35 a month."

When he said this, MB and DB immediately stood up and said

---

[4] Many of the statements in Text 2 are allegations of practices which the law defines as corrupt. I emphasize that these are allegations, and I do not know which are true and which are false. I have thought it prudent to suppress entirely the names which are attached to allegations of corruption even at the cost of damaging the continuity of this text with Text 1.

they would like to be agents. Then A asked us all: "Well, what do you say? Are you going to vote for me or for someone else?"

Of course, we all said we would vote for him, and he invited us to decide what we wanted and let his agents know next day. When he had gone the men of the village met and discussed it and said: "We'll ask for Rs500 and if he gives it, we'll vote in his box."

Next day his agent, and two local shopkeepers JC and LP called one of our leading men and said: "We'll give you Rs300 if you all vote for A. Even if A doesn't pay up, we promise to pay up ourselves." The leading men passed this offer on to us and we said: "Let's get what we can out of this. If we get the money, we'll put it in the village fund."

MB and DB went to the party office and were given little flags and went around some of the villages telling them to vote for A and on market day they went back to the party office and got Rs5 each.

Candidate B knew all about this and soon afterwards he called a meeting and said, "I am your son and I am standing on your behalf. I touch the ground with my head [a promise of sincerity and a sign of respect] and say that I am giving Rs100 to the village fund. Take it and put your votes in my box." We all said we would vote for him, but we would make no promises definitely until he had paid the Rs100. But when his back was turned we decided that we wouldn't vote for a fellow like him.

The very next day Candidate C called us together and made this speech: "I am your servant. I have never up to this day wronged anyone in the village and I want to work for your benefit as your MLA. Vote for me and our village will be strong. If you vote for me I promise to pave the area in front of the temple." We told him we would vote for him, but we didn't really intend to vote for him.

Everyday the Ganatantra people were coming round and saying, "Brothers, the bow and arrow is our surest weapon. Vote in the bow and arrow box. Vote for the Raja and for my brother and keep the country strong." One day the Raja and the Ganatantra Scheduled Tribe candidate came to the village and made speeches saying things like: "Look brothers, how the Congress government keeps us as if we were all goats for sacrifice. This is a poor area and yet it will be subject to 64 different kinds of tax. Don't vote for them. Vote in the bow and arrow box. If you vote for me I will make it my duty to do many good things for the country. We must cut down the forest taxes and the land taxes and the market dues. If you tell me of your troubles I will fight in the Delhi Assembly to have them removed. If you are frightened to say openly what is wrong, come to the Phulbani office and tell it there." A lot of people, from all castes, went to the office and some of them came back with Rs5, having been taken on as agents. We passed the word that most of our village would vote for the Raja.

Candidate D made several speeches reminding us of what he was always doing for us and promising that if he were elected, then as a mark of thanksgiving, he would put a corrugated iron roof on the Meeting House.

Eight or ten villages in Rasimendi and Sangrimendi [the area in the Kondmals from which the Ganatantra Scheduled Tribe Parliamentary candidate came] prepared a reception and invited the Raja and their brother to meet them. They were garlanded by a Sundi [Distiller caste] from Kerodi, and escorted down the road by drummers and given a seat of honour. Then our spokesman said, "Maharaj, if you stick by your promise we will all vote for you." The Maharaja pledged his word and everyone was contented. Afterwards many of those present went around the villages asking people to vote for the Raja. And the Raja and his candidates won the election for Ganatantra.

This text contains direct accusations of corrupt practices by candidates A, B, C and D, and had any of them been elected, then any elector registered in the constituency could have laid a complaint before the proper authority and brought the accused before an Election Tribunal. If the Tribunal found the complaint justified, then it could set aside the result of the election and either order a new election, or, in certain circumstances, declare the candidate remaining with the highest votes to have been elected. In practice it is far from easy to prove corrupt practices or any other kind of electoral misdemeanour, and I am not here trying to find out whether or not the election in Bisipara was corrupt and in what sense it was corrupt. The relevance of Text 2 lies rather in what it says indirectly about the attitude of the voters of Bisipara towards their politicians and towards the elections.

In their discussion of Candidate A's alleged offer, the writer of Text 2 makes the villagers say, "Let's get what we can out of this." I think this fairly represents the attitude of many voters, not only in this unsophisticated area but also in the more advanced areas of the coast. What lies behind this readiness to be corrupted?

One general condition is the poverty of the electorate. This is, of course, not a total explanation, but neither can it be ignored for, below a certain standard of living, scrupulous honesty is reasonably regarded as a luxury for the wealthy.

Secondly, whatever the law says, many voters in India would consider the purchase of a vote a perfectly legitimate transaction. If one does something for nothing, one does it for oneself, one's family, one's castemen, or fellow villagers. A stranger—and for most electors the candidate is outside this narrow circle of obligation—could reasonably be expected to pay for the favour of a vote.

Thirdly, and most significantly, the majority of the voters do not believe that a free election is the important thing that their educators and politicians make it out to be. To them it seems a remote and academic exercise, even a kind of empty formality which has no effect in the real centres of power. I do not think that the majority, as yet, have any conception of the meaning of "responsible" government; their horizons are too narrow for this. Accordingly a vote is "a little thing"—not a valued and sacred responsibility. In other words, democratic institutions are as yet far from being "legitimized."

They are something which comes from outside, like public money, and they are treated with the same lack of scruple, because their honest management has not as yet become part of the common morality.

An air of cynicism and mistrust pervades Text 2. This, I think, is partly a reflection of the character of its author, but it also reflects a received opinion about most politicians. During the discussion of Candidate A's offer, conditional clauses occur several times: "If we get the money . . ."; "If he pays up . . ." Now, with the experience of two elections behind them, the voters of Bisipara receive the offer of a bribe with the same scepticism that they receive the politician's ordinary protestations of devotion to the public weal. In a sense the offers to corrupt are becoming a formal exercise—offers, at least, to the ordinary voter—and are merely shadowboxing.

Why is this happening, and what is its significance? Undoubtedly its first cause lies in the scale of the elections. Corruption in the Eatanswill manner is not possible with a total adult franchise. There are just too many voters to be bribed by money or by feasting. Many of the politicians to whom I talked in 1959 knew this, and several drew a vivid picture of the difference between the two recent elections on a total adult franchise (1952 and 1957) and the uproarious junketing which went on around some of the urban booths in the 1936 election.

Secondly, neither the would-be corrupters nor their potential beneficiaries had any faith in one anothers' probity, and since the ballot was secret there was no check upon individual voters. The voters did not think that they would get the money; the candidates believed that voters accept money from both sides and vote the way they would have voted anyway, without a bribe. I have no first hand evidence on this, since people do not admit to taking bribes, and, to be fair, I several times heard from middle-class people not themselves concerned in politics, that there was a parodoxical honesty in corruption because the ordinary man, once he has taken money, feels himself obliged to vote for the giver. But the politicians to whom I talked thought direct corruption of the voters quite impracticable because the most that could be expected from a voter who took bribes would be a vote for the side which paid him the largest sum.[5] I heard gleeful stories about important men who marshalled all their tenants and retainers and feasted them and led them off to the local booth, where the results showed quite clearly that most of the tenants and retainers must have taken advantage of the secret ballot to vote against their master. Whether true or not, such stories are an indication of a growing conviction that an attempt to bribe the voter directly is a waste of money.

From the other side, the voters—at least in Bisipara—have despaired of getting direct money out of an election. Those few who became agents made small sums, but none as much as they had expected (except one man who doubled his money by signing on as an agent for both the Congress and the Ganatantra and canvassing indifferently for both sides). None of those to whom I talked admitted receiving money just for a vote, and, more reliably, none of them thought that voters had in fact been paid.

But the same people were quite convinced that money had been paid out to key individuals, with the intention that it should be redistributed to others. If the money was in fact paid, then it went no further. Again, the important point is not to decide whether or not leading individuals were paid, or whether this payment was a legitimate reimbursement of an agent's expenses or was given to pass on as bribes to the voters; the important point is that the villagers believed that

---

[5] A surer method is for the voter to smuggle his ballot paper out of the booth and sell it to an agent, who takes the paper back into the booth and puts it in the appropriate box. I heard allegations of this, but I have no firsthand accounts. Cf. *Report on the Second General Elections in India,* 1957, Vol. 1, p. 80.

at least two people in Bisipara had received in one case Rs200 and in the other case Rs300 for distribution and had kept the money themselves.

This kind of belief is common and quite in keeping with the mistrust and cynicism which are the features of an election campaign. There is evidence of these beliefs to be found between the lines of reports by Election Tribunals. I was also told by a half-amused, half-angry Congress MLA that he had probably lost the votes of several villages which were solidly behind his party through the trickery of an agent of a rival party. This agent dressed in the "uniform" of a Congress worker (Gandhi cap and homespun cloth), carried the Congress symbol, visited the villages, made speeches containing the usual Congress election platitudes, and then, as is usual, took tea in the house of the leading man of the village, through whose influence the voters had been won to the Congress cause. When the agent was leaving, he contrived to get out of earshot of the leading man and then told the rest of the village that he had brought Rs500 from the party funds and given it to the leading man for distribution in the village. Then he left. It may be that this story, too, is part of the folklore that has developed around electioneering, but, true or not, its point is that the villagers are supposed to see nothing unlikely in a party handing out Rs500 to an important man and this important man betraying the trust which the party had put in him.

The voters, in fact, project their own code of morality and obligation upon all but a very few politicians and active political workers. The voters themselves feel no direct interest in the common weal; indeed, few have any conception of the common weal. Consequently they believe that anyone who offers himself as a candidate is out to make money for himself, and they think that those who campaign actively for a candidate do make money. There is an ambivalent attitude towards this money: on the one hand no one in his senses would do the work unless he got some profit out of it; on the other hand the protestations of disinterestedness and regard for the public weal are tainted with insincerity. The few persons whose record, personality, or social background free them from the taint of hypocrisy and self-interest have a long start over the ordinary run-of-the-mill politician.

It is, in short, almost an axiom that politicians—at least those at the lower level whom the villagers know—have dirty hands. But the villagers do not draw this conclusion solely from their experience of election campaigns, but more from their own knowledge of the kind of persons among themselves who enter politics. I turn to this question in later sections in commentaries upon Text 3 and Text 4 and an examination of how people in Bisipara actually voted.

The Vote in Bisipara

Text 3 is a third individual's recollections and comments on the 1957 election in Bisipara. The earlier part of the text, in which he describes the campaigns of some of the candidates, covers the same ground as the two texts already presented and I have omitted it. In the latter part the writer speculates on the reasons why people voted one way or the other.

Text 3. *Local issues in the Bisipara election*

When it came to voting practically everyone voted Ganatantra. Of course, with three people from the village standing, they were able to get some of the votes. But they could not defeat the Ganatantra.

But none of our Harijans voted Ganatantra. The Congress Government had made them "Harijans" when they used to be just "Pans"; that is, they had been permitted to enter temples; no-one could say to them "Chua!" [i.e. "Keep away! You are polluting."]; anyone who refused to let them into temples or said "Chua!" to them would get six months in gaol and a fine of Rs500. With heavy penalties like this no-one is going to stand in their way. Since the Government has helped them in this way, every man and woman among the Harijans, as many as were on the list, were brought out to vote in order that Congress might win.

As for women of other castes, whatever party they sympathized with, most of them didn't go to vote. Women are fools in this, and say, "What does it matter to us who gets the vote? What good will it do us. If we go and vote for them will they make our house rich?" So they didn't vote, anyway not more than half the women.

Whether the ordinary people of the village understand the vote or not, they take the advice of the leading people of the village. Before the poll they hold a meeting and decide for whom they will vote. But if there are factions in the village, then they vote for different parties. They don't take the advice of the rich or the educated. They say, "You are in service. You get paid by the Government. So you vote for the Government. Who pays us? The choice is ours and we'll vote for the ones we like." So they don't listen to people in service. They follow the advice of the people they usually trust.

This is what happens in small villages. But in big villages like Bisipara it is different. The party which says it will do most for them gets the vote. So Ganatantra got a lot of votes by pointing out that Congress had not done for the village what it had promised to do.

In Gumagoro village the leading men are Congress, and that party got most of the votes, but in the nearby Kond hamlets Ganatantra got most of the votes. When the Konds went to vote some of the leading men of Gumagoro were standing around telling them to vote Congress, and they agreed, but they voted Ganatantra just the same. They voted as they wanted.

In a village that has a headman and if he has influence, they vote on his advice. Since Independence, people don't listen much to what Sirdars [6] say. The people who have influence are those whom

---

[6] A chieftain and hereditary official. See Bailey, 1960.

they think can help them. The more educated a village is, the more "party" [i.e. faction] there is in that village.

The Congress Anapurna theatre put on a show at Boida to amuse the people. But the people voted Ganatantra. But some Adibasis voted Congress, because the Government has provided schools for their children who are fed and clothed there, and it doesn't cost the parents a penny. There is even a girl's school at Sankerakhol, where they educate them and teach them how to sew. Also we hear that when Adibasis or Harijans get involved in a case, the Government bears the cost of it. There is an order that no Oriya can buy land from them except with the Government's agreement. The Government knows that Adibasis are poor people. But since Independence, they've gone too far. Harijans and Adibasis get preference for jobs; so they vote Congress. The Government is always saying that Harijans are a depressed caste and that everyone oppresses them. Because they are a low caste, they should not be oppressed; so they are admitted to public places like temples and wells and so forth. And then, naturally, they vote Congress. But in spite of all the favours, a lot also voted Ganatantra.

People say Ganatantra will do a lot of good for Orissa, if it is voted in. But who knows what it will do? No-one knows.

People voted Ganatantra because they thought Congress would impose 64 taxes and would keep a hold on the forest.

MB told me he got Rs10 for a month's work, instead of the promised Rs35. So we can suppose that other Congress agents too did not get their full wage. That is another reason why Ganatantra got votes.

People in service, like Sirdars and schoolmasters and village headmen, all voted Congress.

There are some confusions and inaccuracies in this text, and the presentation is more muddled than in other texts which the same man has written for me. I think that some of this has arisen because the writer, a man of high caste, felt strongly about the favourable treatment which Harijans received from the Congress government, and considered that he and his own people were underprivileged. He returns several times to the theme of the abolition of untouchability and the privileges of being an Adibasi.

The problem is to explain why the people of Bisipara voted the way they did in the 1957 election. There was a booth in Bisipara, but I failed to get any official figures of how votes were cast in that booth. I had, therefore, to ask people themselves how they voted. I was able to do this for the clean castes of Bisipara, but I failed to make the same enquiry among the Harijans. Out of approximately 350 registered voters I have the statements of 216—nearly all of them clean caste—about how they voted (or did not vote) in the 1957 election.

In which box a man chose to put his vote is a relatively simple question. It is much more difficult for him to say briefly why he voted that way, and I did not ask. It would have been useful to have done so systematically, but in fact I discussed this question in Bisipara with only seven people, three Harijans and four clean caste. Among these informants were the three candidates, two of whom gave an informative and balanced account of what had happened. The third remembered only that he had lost his deposit and spent a lot of money to no purpose, and he was preoccupied with present ventures into the different, but allied, field of local government politics.

In some cases it is quite clear why people voted as they did. In other cases their behaviour is inexplicable (to me at least), or else it is compounded from a number of possible motivations, between which it is difficult to distinguish the more from the less important.

Of the 216 registered voters in Bisipara, about whom I have information, 55 did not vote at all, although present in the village on polling day; 12 had forgotten where they put some or all of their votes; and 15 were away from the village at the time.

There is no evidence that any of those absent from the village had gone in order to avoid the embarrassment of voting. Among those who did not remember where they voted the larger part are old men or widows, and in a few cases I think that this reply represents a polite refusal to answer the question. In neither of these categories is there any correlation with caste.

Of the 55 who were present in the village and did not vote, 45 were women and three were very old men. Of the four Brahmin women in the village, none voted. Of the 33 Warrior caste women, eligible to vote, 16 did not, one of them getting as far as the booth and then coming back in a panic. The remaining women who did not vote are distributed in small numbers among the other castes. The Brahmins and the Warriors are at the top of the caste scale, and it is likely that the absence of their women from the poll reflects higher standards of modesty. I think the same would have been true of the Distillers, who aspire to high ritual status,[7] were it not that one of their number was standing as *Ind 4*; in that caste only one out of ten women did not vote. It seems likely, therefore, that the lack of political consciousness, to which the writer of Text 3 attributes women's absence from the polling booth (probably correctly in the case of the Potters—see Table 5) is not the only reason; there is also a convention that respectable women do not visit public places, if they can avoid them.

There are three categories of people, two of them appearing in Table 5, whose vote seems readily comprehensible.

The first are those who put all their votes in the boxes of the Congress candidates. Of the 26 people in this category shown in Table 5, 13 are men and the others are women de-

---

[7] See Bailey, 1957.

pendent on them. In all but one case all the women belonging to the household of a man who voted throughout on the Congress ticket voted the same way. The exception is the man who himself voted Congress and told his wife to do the same,

TABLE 5

SOME BISIPARA VOTERS IN 1957, BY CASTE

Caste	All votes Congress	All votes Ganatantra	Divided votes	Total	X [a]
Warriors	11	27	5	43	20
Brahmin	–	1	2	3	4
Barber	–	3	–	3	2
Herdsman	2	–	2	4	4
Christian	1	–	1	2	1
Fisherman	–	3	2	5	–
Boad Distiller	2	2	14	18	1
Kond Potter	8	14	12	34	13 [b]
Weaver	–	2	5	7	–
Ganjam Pan	–	2	2	4	3
Kond	–	2	–	2	1
Sweeper	2	3	1	6	–
Washerman	–	2	–	2	2
Templeman	–	1	–	1	2
Ganjam Distiller	–	–	–	–	2
Total	26	62	46	134	55

[a] Indicates those present in the village but not voting.
[b] 10 of these were women.

but instructed his mother to vote for Ganatantra. Of the 13 men, two were temporary agents who enlisted when *Congress* 1 (Table 4) spoke in the village, seven were in Government service, one had been dismissed from service but was hopeful of reinstatement, and one was a minor contractor. Of the remaining two, one voted Congress because his late father, a schoolmaster, had been a Congress supporter. I do not know why the last man voted for the Congress. Of the 62 who voted Ganatantra none held any appointment from the Government.

The writer of Text 3 is a schoolmaster, and he voted for the Congress. He said he did so because it would be foolish to risk his job by voting against the Government. I reminded him that the ballot was secret, expecting him to claim that it was not and explain how the votes could be traced. But he replied that probably the vote was secret, but one could never be quite sure and a vote was such a small thing that it was not worth risking his livelihood just to vote for the Ganatantra. He had, however, told his mother to vote Ganatantra. All the men who voted solidly for the Congress, other than the Sweeper, held the same opinions about Congress policy which caused their fellows to vote Ganatantra (see below), and their Congress vote can only be attributed to prudent self-interest. The exceptions are the man who voted Congress because his father would have done so and the two temporary agents, who may have felt obliged to vote for the party which had engaged them—and which, it may be noted, had not paid them in full for their month's work at the time of polling. Finally, no one, among those I have listed, who held a Government appointment, or had business connections with Government agencies (as in the case of a contractor), refrained from voting or voted solidly for Ganatantra. One man (a Sirdar) split his votes between the Ganatantra Parliamentary candidates and the Congress Assembly candidates. In short, there is a clear connection, so far as concerns the clean castes, between a vote for the Congress and economic dependence on the Government.

The second category of people whose pattern of voting seems readily understandable are the Boad Distillers. One of their number was standing for the Assembly as *Ind 4*. Of the 18 people who voted, four (two married couples) voted on a straight party ticket, one couple for the Congress and one for the Ganatantra. The man who voted for the Congress was one of the temporary agents of that party. The man who voted Ganatantra, so far as I know has no strong political convictions and plays no active part in politics, and may have voted Ganatantra because he disliked *Ind 4*. The remaining 14 split their votes. Four voters put their Parliamentary ballot papers in the Congress boxes. Three of these persons constitute one household, the head of which is a schoolmaster and, therefore, in Government service. I do not know why the fourth voted Congress. The remaining ten voted for the Ganatantra Parliamentary candidates; none of them are in Government service. The Assembly votes of all 14 persons, according to their own account, were given to their relative *Ind 4*. (They claim to have given him both their Assembly votes. This means that if the ballot papers were properly checked through their serial numbers, half of these would be declared cumulative votes and therefore invalid.[8])

The dominating influence on the voting seems clear enough in this case. All but four of *Ind 4*'s caste fellows supported him. Of the remaining 116 voters of other caste on my list, only five voted for *Ind 4*. Why the majority did *not* vote for him will be considered at length below. Those who voted for him did so because he was their kinsman.

About the third category, the Harijans, discussion is more difficult since I have no information about how in fact they

---

[8] See Election Commission, 1959, Vol. 1, p. 165. "It is clear that there was deliberate canvassing on the part of some candidates to induce the voters to insert both their ballot papers into the same ballot box." Of the 18 people in the list who voted either for *Ind 4* or *Ind 9*, only two of these did not give their chosen candidate both their votes. Without malice to *Ind 4* and *Ind 9*, it is to be noticed that whatever happens in the checking, the candidate benefits from a cumulative vote. If the checking is slack, he may get both votes: if the cumulative vote is detected, then at least he has robbed a rival of a vote.

voted.⁹ The received opinion among those to whom I talked, both Harijan and clean caste, was that anyone who did not vote on a straight Congress ticket with all four ballot papers (thus voting for their own *Congress 2*) gave one or two votes to their other relative *Ind 9*. In general there are only two possible influences which bear upon the voters of this caste. One is their kinship link with two of the candidates, and there is no reason to suppose that kinship links are any weaker than they were in the case of the Distillers. It would not even be necessary to choose between the candidates, for the voter was free, if he wished, to vote for *both* candidates for the reserved seat. The other influence is the ideological pull (or perhaps one should call it "enlightened self-interest") of Congress policy towards the Harijans. In the case of *Congress 2* this would, of course, reinforce his kinship links; for *Ind 9* it would work against them. The relevance in Bisipara of Congress policy towards the Depressed Castes comes out clearly in Text 3, and it will be discussed below, when I ask why the majority of people in Bisipara voted for the Ganatantra.

Before turning to this main question there is one other characteristic to be noticed about the pattern of voting. Forty-six people divided their votes between different parties or between a party and an Independent. Fourteen of these were Boad Distillers, all of whom split their votes between a party and their own *Ind 4*. Four other people split their votes in the same way, so that 28 split their votes between parties. In all cases this split was between the Parliament on the one side and the Assembly on the other. The division was always, for example, two votes for the Ganatantra Parliamentary candidates, and two for the Congress Assembly candidates. It was never one for the Ganatantra and one for the Congress

---

⁹ This does not mean that the Harijans were reticent—quite the reverse. The failure was mine.

in the Parliamentary seats and the same in the Assembly seats. One can conclude from this that a party's candidates for the reserved and the general seats are regarded by the voters as a team.

I think one might also conclude that those who divided their votes between parties in this way, in fact had parties as much as individuals in their minds. It is, of course, in the end impossible to say what was in a person's mind when he voted. There may have been naive voters who felt that it would be unjust to give all their votes to one party. But I think that there was also the feeling that in some way to vote for both sides was to spread the risk and insure oneself against any risks that might possibly be involved in voting against the Government. In other words, those who split their votes may have been partially affected by the same kind of motive as those Government-appointed persons who voted solidly for the Congress: they thought it safest.

Among the whole 46 of those who split their votes, only four divided them in the pattern of Congress for the Parliament, and someone else (in the four cases it was *Ind 4*) for the Assembly. Forty-two persons voted for the Ganatantra team for the Parliament and either Congress or Independents for the Assembly. This indicates that the majority of the Bisipara voters whose names I listed were attracted by the persons and policies of the Ganatantra Parishad, in particular by the Parliamentary team. In the following section I discuss the factors which influenced the voters of Bisipara in favour of these two men.

Three things favoured the Ganatantra in the eyes of Bisipara voters. The first was the personality of the party's Parliamentary candidates. (I mean here *social* personality, rather than charisma, although the latter too was weighted in favour of the Ganatantra candidates.) The remaining two factors were issues of policy, one being a fear that Congress would impose further taxes, and the other being the acute dislike felt by the clean castes for the Congress policy towards the Harijans.

The Ganatantra Parliamentary candidate was the Raja of Kalahandi. To have been a king is an immense asset for a candidate. Quite apart from his personal qualities and activities, he benefits from the peoples' attitude towards kingship. The people of Bisipara, before the 1952 elections, knew little of the Kalahandi Raja; they themselves had been under British rule for more than 100 years, and before that they had been only nominally under the control of the Boad Raja. Nevertheless they have a considerable respect and affection for the royal houses. They grow up hearing stories about kings and their own connections with the Raj family in Boad (See Text 1); some of their major festivals are ritually linked with the same royal family. Furthermore, many of them trust a member of a Raj family and expect to find in him just those qualities which they assume are lacking in the newer politicians. The king is free, for example, from any taint of personal ambition; the seat of authority, they suppose, is the natural place for him; he does not stand for election to make money, because he already has money; he is not the tool of any local clique, because a king is, supposedly, above that kind of thing.

These advantages were reinforced in this case by the electioneering skill and energy of the Kalahandi Raja and his wife. They toured extensively and continually; they made speeches, held meetings and rallies, contacted local men of influence; and—a tactic which seems to have stamped itself on the minds of one of their opponents, who gave me an awestruck account of the Raja's campaign—they went into the homes of the common people and ate food with them, sometimes arriving after nightfall. In one way or another the Raja's campaign seems to have conjured up a great deal of romance and excitement.

This emotive image was backed by the more solid consideration of trust in the Raja's personal integrity and in his campaign promises. In its turn this trust rested on the Raja's status and on the peoples' ideas about kings and kingship. It was helped in this area—in the Kondmals—by the origins and personality of the Raja's fellow candidate, who stood for the seat reserved for Scheduled tribes. This man, a Kond, came from a village a few miles away from Bisipara. He had just sufficient education to make him acceptable to the Oriya villagers, he was reckoned a moderate and sensible young man, and he did not carry the taint of a murky past in local factions and local intrigue.

To some extent the status and skill of the Kalahandi Raja carried not only his fellow candidate for the Parliamentary seat, but also the Ganatantra candidates for the Assembly seats. But this was not the only factor. There were also two policy issues.

The first of these was the fear that the return of a Congress Government would mean higher taxes. A promise to reduce taxes and a prophecy that one's opponent will increase taxes are standard campaign gambits everywhere, and voters in democracies which have been in existence longer than in India have learnt to discount them. There is some scepticism in India too. "People say Ganatantra will do a lot of good for Orissa, if it is voted in. But who knows what it will do? No one knows." (Text 3). Cynicism of this kind is widespread, but it goes with the idea that it is better to play safe, even though rationally one discounts the danger. There were some, no doubt, who believed that Congress would increase taxes and Ganatantra would not; but even those who realized that circumstances often compel both parties to follow much the same kind of policy, seem to have voted against what they had been told was the extravagant party. The *non-sequitur* is similar to that of the man who believed that the ballot was secret, but it was safer for him, as a schoolmaster employed by the Government, to vote for the Congress party.

And here, as everywhere, the threat of deprivation seemed to carry more weight than the promise of benefits.

In Bisipara this attitude is not surprising, when one considers the view which the people of clean caste (the majority on my list) have of the way in which the Congress Governments have distributed benefits during the past decade. They see themselves as dispossessed, and they put the blame upon Congress.

In Bisipara there is a large and assertive group of Harijans, of the Pan caste and originating from Boad. In early days they were, in every sense, a depressed class. They are untouchables. Formerly they owned no land, and were employed as farm servants in a serf-like status by families of the dominant Warrior caste. As a caste they had no corporate political existence. As individuals they had no political rights except as the appendages of their master's household. They were forbidden to use the village wells, to enter the village temples, and to frequent certain other places, including the village meeting house. They had no voice on the village council and could only make contact with it through their Warrior masters.

But the Pans of Bisipara, and of some other Oriya villages in the Kondmals, enjoyed advantages which the Pans in more advanced areas (like Boad) did not have. These advantages were realised when the coming of the British administration to this area began to change the local pattern of political and economic power. The Warriors were deprived at once of their ultimate sanction of force, at least of its overt use. They and their former subjects became, nominally at least, equal before the courts. At the same time secure and better communications brought new commercial activities to the area. The Administration itself brought opportunities for making a living which had not before existed, both through direct employment and indirectly by creating new wants—lawyers, petition-writers, and other types of go-between.

Although there was a general assumption that citizens ought

to be equal before the law, it was quite early recognized that certain categories of people were too poor and too unsophisticated to look after themselves, whereas cleverer people could make use of the Administration and its courts, to exploit the poor and the simple. A policy of protection was evolved, making illegal the transfer of land between tribal people and non-tribals, controlling rates of interest, giving tribal people preferential opportunities for education and reserving places for them afterwards in Government employment, and, finally, relaxing the full rigours of court procedure to make it easier for tribal people to get a hearing. Since 1947, when India became independent, these measures, both for protection and for uplift, have been extended and intensified.

The Pans of Bisipara were protected and privileged in the same way as other untouchables and as tribal people. But their position in Bisipara (and in a few other large Oriya villages in the Kondmals) gave them opportunities which Pans who lived in remoter villages, particularly tribal villages, did not enjoy. Bisipara Pan boys grew up near the centre of power (Bisipara was for the first fifty years the administrative headquarters of the area) in a relatively metropolitan atmosphere. Above all they grew up with Oriya as their first language, whereas the great majority of other privileged persons had Kui as their mother tongue. Since Oriya is the language of administration, this put the Bisipara Pans in a favourable position in the competition for education and jobs, and in fact a higher proportion of them than of any other caste in Bisipara have jobs as masters in primary schools.

Apart from schoolmastering, some have become traders, a few have had jobs with the Administration, and, most recently, a number of younger men have enlisted in the police and the army. These changes have altered the economic and political status of the Pan untouchables in relation to their fellow-villagers in Bisipara. From being an aggregation of farm labourers, with a status equivalent to that of serfs, they are now, at the lowest, labourers who sell their labour on an open market, and, at the highest, men with a profession (usually schoolmastering), owners of estates, traders, and in general men of substance.

Their growing wealth coincided with Gandhi's campaign to remove the social and ritual disabilities under which untouchables laboured. Inspired by this and under the leadership of their own successful men, the Bisipara Pans have become an aggressive group which combines to force the higher castes, including the former dominant caste of Warriors, to accept Pans as social equals. They are in fact more or less equal economically, and—as recent events have shown—more than equal politically.

Their campaign began about 1948, when they attempted to enforce their right under law to enter a Bisipara temple. They did not in fact succeed at that time, but by 1959 they had gained admission. The years between were marked by a series of bitterly fought conflicts between the Pans and the clean castes of the village, and although the Pans have on almost every occasion lost the battle, there were clear signs when I visited Bisipara in 1959, seven years after my first visit in 1952, that they were on the point of winning the war.[10] At one of the several annual festivals a gantry is erected and from the crossbar is hung a number of small prizes, given by the local shopkeepers. The young men and boys of the village run off the end of a ramp and attempt to snatch one of the prizes from the crossbeam. I watched this sport in 1953, 1955, and again in 1959. On the first two occasions the competition was managed entirely by men of clean caste, it took place in the street of the Warriors, the competitors were all of clean caste, and untouchables were only allowed to try their luck when the others had finished.

---

[10] For a fuller account of these conflicts see Bailey, 1957, Chapter XI, and 1960, Chapter VI.

The audience consisted of everyone in the village, the untouchable Pans sitting apart in a compact group. By 1959 the scene had changed. The master of ceremonies was an untouchable, that same *Ind* 9 who had lost his deposit in the 1957 elections. The competitors were all Pans except for a few young children of clean caste. The sport was still held in the traditional place in the middle of Warrior street, but there was no clean caste audience. A few men sat around watching from the verandahs of their houses, but the audience proper, sitting around the gantry, were all Pans. Many of the men wore shirts and long trousers and shoes, certainly as a mark of status and emancipation, because the normal dress of the villagers is a *dhoti*, and even sandals are worn only when the ground gets unbearably hot in April and May. The Pan women wore blouses and mill-woven saris, and several of the younger ones had put on lipstick and face-powder.

These changes in fashion indicate the source of the change which the Pans have managed to bring about in their social position. Change of both kinds comes from the world outside the village. The initial economic opportunities, which made possible the emancipation of the Pans, came from outside the village. The education, and sophistication, and, above all, the political encouragement and the political techniques and skills which have made it possible for the Pans to combine and compete for power effectively against their former high-caste masters have also come from outside.

The clean castes, in particular the Warriors, are by now slightly afraid of their Pans and are bitterly resentful of the Congress policies which have made it possible for the Pans to become powerful. They consider that the Government is heavily biassed in favour of untouchables, and at the same time they know that such favours become translated into practice through the political experience and contacts of men like *Ind* 9 and *Congress* 2. A Warrior, answering my questions about the changes in the festival between 1955 and

1959, said that they had cancelled another festival that year, because their Pans wanted to monopolize it. "Soon they will run the village. They are the kings now, and we are the subjects."

In these circumstances it is not surprising that any man of clean caste who did not feel personally obligated to the Congress, or believe that his livelihood depended upon the party's favour, voted for the Ganatantra. I do not know whether the rumours that Ganatantra would put the untouchables back in their place originated in fact from Ganatantra politicians; but, even if they kept silent, they must have benefitted automatically from the anger of people in Bisipara, and other similar villages, who felt themselves dispossessed. Text 3 shows clearly that no seed of distrust had to be scattered; the tree of resentment was already fully grown.

In respect of their advancement and their militancy the Pans of the Oriya-speaking communities in the Kondmals and elsewhere in the Kond hills, differ from their fellow untouchables on the plains and from Kui-speaking Pans in the hills. The people of Bisipara believe that there was no "Harijan problem" on the riverine plains of Boad, where Pans and other untouchables knew their place. They were not taken in by the rumour (allegedly Ganatantra inspired) that *Ganatantra 2* (the candidate for the Assembly reserved seat) was really a Herdsman, because he had a lineage name typically found among that caste. That happened, they explained, because some ancestor must have been a Herdsman who had taken a Pan woman, and the issue of such a marriage are Pans, quite unambiguously. Furthermore, they knew that *Congress 2* and *Ganatantra 2* had a distant marriage connection. But they were more inclined to vote for this man from Boad, because they believed that Boad Pans, like the Kui-speaking Pans of their own area, were not Harijan militants.

The difference in the relative sophistication of clean castes and untouchables in Boad, as compared with the same categories in the Kond hills, is also reflected in the origins of the candidates for the two Assembly seats. Four of the six Scheduled caste candidates came from the upland region; eight of the nine general seat candidates came from the Boad plains. This is an indication that in Boad the clean castes dominate, whereas the untouchables remain backward. In the hills the clean castes are backward, and the Oriya Pans, owing to accidents of language and demography, have learnt how to take chances which the new democracy is offering them. This is not, of course, a simple correlation, and I would not claim that future elections will show the same pattern, for there are many other factors concerned in a man's offering himself for election to the Assembly.

In this section I have discussed the reasons which I think persuaded most of the people of Bisipara to vote on the Ganatantra ticket. The most prominent Ganatantra candidate was, in the eyes of the villagers, the best qualified, and they judged his qualifications on the basis of his traditional status, as a king. Secondly, they thought of themselves as dispossessed and blamed the Congress for their misfortunes.

In the next section I ask why the clean castes of Bisipara did not support the candidates from their own village.

THE BISIPARA CANDIDATES

Although the clean castes in Bisipara dislike their Harijans—that word has now become a bitter epithet—and are disliked by them, it would be wrong to think that the village is in a continual state of active feud. From time to time major conflicts blow up near to the point of violence, and both sides become camps of war; sometimes younger men, particularly from the Harijan side, lose their temper or get drunk and set out to make trouble; and there is a continuing currency of bitter comment exchanged within each side. But outwardly the leaders display dignity and restraint, the untouchables observing some of the traditional forms of good-mannered subservience, and the clean castes treating at least the leaders of the untouchables—*Ind* 9 and *Congress* 4 and one or two other men—as persons of consequence.

Furthermore these two men come into their own particularly when the village is trying to manipulate the world outside—an official or a politician, for example. Three instances during a short visit to Bisipara in 1959 come immediately to mind. A delegation attended a visiting official from the Public Works Department to complain about a dam which for seven successive years has broken in the rains and ruined a field area beside Bisipara. Another delegation went off hastily to try to intercept the Chief Minister who was passing a nearby crossroads. A third delegation went to see an official from the Education Department with a request that the local Upper Primary School should be raised to the status of Middle English School. On all these three occasions *Ind* 9 and *Congress* 2 were members of the delegation and played a leading part in the somewhat short-winded oratory by which the villagers try to hold down this type of auditor who is always in a hurry. The men of clean caste, who also went on the delegations, felt that their two Harijan politicians had more skill and more experience in putting a case to an outsider, and that it would be imprudent deliberately to exclude these two men; it might even be dangerous because the two might use their contacts to block what the village wanted. In other words the clean caste people make use, when they can, of those same talents by which they themselves have been pushed from their dominating position in the village.

If the villagers are willing to use these two men to help them manipulate the Administration, it seems strange that they should reject so decisively their candidature for the Assembly. The explanation is, of course, that conflict between the clean castes and the Harijans which I described in the previous section. No doubt the villagers felt, where they were not simply moved by contempt and hatred, that to have one of their own Bisipara Pans as their MLA, would be the final nail in the coffin of clean caste dominance, and that this would more than outbalance the advantages of having a fellow villager in the Assembly.

But the rejection of these two men by the ordinary people of the village was not on a caste issue alone. Another man, *Ind 4*, a Distiller and, therefore, a man of clean caste, suffered the same fate, getting votes in Bisipara virtually only from his own caste fellows, although, so far as the Harijan conflict was concerned, he was on the side of the clean castes.

Text 4. *The Statutory Panchayat in Bisipara*

In accordance with the development plans of the Orissa Government in every district Gram Panchayats are being established. In this way the two *muthas* [11] of Besringia and Balimendi were allotted one panchayat.

There are nineteen members in this panchayat. The members are called "ward members" and they are elected by the votes of the villagers. No-one in Government service was allowed to stand for the panchayat.

The job of the members is to petition in the panchayat, either in writing or orally, for whatever development work they consider necessary in their own villages, and the panchayat is supposed to acquaint the Government with these needs. Then, according to the Government's decision, the panchayat may get on with the work.

In order to run the panchayat one of the nineteen members is selected as head and another as his assistant. The head is called the "Sarpanch" and his assistant is the "Naib Sarpanch." *Ind 4* was selected as Sarpanch and HB of Gerengeli village became the Naib Sarpanch. In the absence of the Sarpanch the Naib Sarpanch is supposed to get on with the work.

---

[11] These are administrative divisions based upon older territorial units. See Bailey, 1960, Chapter IV.

BISIPARA VILLAGE

From our Bisipara village *Ind 4* [a Distiller], DB, MB, [both Warriors], and PS from the Harijan street were candidates. From among them PS got the most votes. Either DB or MB would certainly have headed the poll if they had stuck to their agreement not to contest one another. I think the people would have preferred DB because he can speak well and without fear to Government officials. MB does not have the same kind of spirit; he gets frightened easily.

When it came to choosing a Sarpanch there were meetings night and day to arrange things. BB and SP and other leading men said to DB and HB: "You two stand aside. You won't be able to manage the job. How will you be able to keep going to Phulbani and fighting it out with the Government? But *Ind 4* has a house in Phulbani. They all know him there. He's not timid and he can face up to them. He's the best qualified to be the Sarpanch. If he's there our village has a chance of getting some development work done. You two stand down. We will all give him our vote and make him the Sarpanch." The leading men of the village agreed with this and that was how *Ind 4* became the Sarpanch.

Ind 9 was appointed secretary to the panchayat, and they say he gets Rs40 a month.

The Sarpanch arranged to be in the village every Monday and told the panchayat members from the two *muthas* to come to the meetings on that day.

The panchayat started a weekly market in Bisipara on a Monday. In 1957 and 1958 it ran quite well from October to May, but it was closed during the rains. Then in 1959 it closed down altogether because people just stopped coming to the market: the selection of stuff on sale had become very poor. That was the end of the market.

After that the Government decided to breed fish in the tank near the market in Bisipara. If the Government orders it, how is the panchyat to say no? A sum of money was sanctioned to clear out and deepen the tank. Some excavation was done with this money—that is to say, some earth was shifted, but the tank certainly was not properly deepened. Myself, I thought it foolish to release the young fish in it between August and September, as they did, because they hadn't properly sealed off a *nala* that lets the water leak away. So when the hot weather came the water was nearly gone and they had to catch all the young fish and sell them, and there was no chance for breeding. It was the panchayat's money that bought the young fish.

Then they decided to make a cattle pound. *Ind 4* selected his own cattle-shed for this, and cattle found damaging the crops were to be put into this. How much money they got to build a pound and what they did with it, none of us knew. It is alleged that they put it in their own pockets.

Another matter is keeping the village clean. It is said that they get a monthly allowance for this. We don't know why, because every house is already paying five measures of rice to the Sweeper woman to clean the streets. No-one knows anything about the panchayat giving her wages.

At the moment the panchayat meets in the house of *Ind 4*. But in my opinion they don't do much work. They don't hear many cases: and when they do meet they don't tell us what they talk about. When it's anything important then the Bisoi and the leading men of the village are called and they settle it.

Every panchayat has a Gram Sevak (Village Level Worker). They have to tour the panchayat area and inform the Government of the needs of the people. Where there is a tank or a well to be dug, or a school or a dispensary to be set up, they let the Government know. They teach the people how to do Japanese cultivation and how to manure the rice-plants. They also bring good seed and distribute it. But only one man in a hundred listens to what they say.

The Sarpanch doesn't do what the Government says he should do. The people don't trust the Sarpanch or the Secretary. If there's an election this year, then *Ind 4* won't win it. If the Government permits the Bisoi (the Sirdar) to stand, then for sure he would win. He isn't keen to stand because, he says, there is sure to be some bother about money.

Up to now the people don't know what benefit they can get from the panchayat.

The writer of this text has in effect described a cleavage in Orissa society which fundamentally affects the relationship between parliamentary institutions and the traditional social structure. On the one side is the Government, and, for the writer and his fellow villagers, this means the officials in Phulbani; on the other side of the cleavage lies the village and its traditional leaders. The Government establishes panchayats through the mechanism of free elections, with the intention, as the writer of the text clearly sees, of making a better contact with the villagers, of interesting them in raising the standards of village life, and of discovering what are the "felt needs" of the villagers. If there had been well-established traditional leaders in every village, and if these leaders had proved suitable agents for development and communication, even then ideological considerations might still have forced the Government to institute elected panchayats. The question in fact does not arise because, by and large, traditional leaders in places like Bisipara have not been coöperative, and they have been supplanted, at least in the task of representing the villagers to the Government and the Government to villagers, by a different category of men.

Both sides—the villagers and the officials—are caught in the same dilemma. The officials went to work through men in whom the villagers have confidence, men who can be trusted to arouse public enthusiasm and start the process of development going from within. In other words the officials want to win to their side the real leaders of the village. But in fact they come into contact with quite a different type of person. The villagers are in the same difficulty. They want, as Text 4 says, a man "who can stand up to officials," a man of the world with the right contacts. Yet any villager who acquires these contacts, at the same time, and in the very process of qualifying himself as a man of the world, has forfeited the confidence of the villagers. This is the type of man who is used to bridge the gap between the villagers and the officials. Neither side feel any confidence in the bridge, but they are forced to use it because there is no other.

Ind 4 told me the story of his life. Much of this story concerned his unhappy experience with political parties, how they failed to make him their candidate in spite of what he had done for them, why he was forced to become an Independent and lose his deposit, and how, recently, he had made friends again with the Congress and would certainly be their candidate at the next General Election. Here I give only that part of *Ind 4*'s account of himself and his ambitions, which seems to illuminate the attitude of his fellow villagers towards him.

Ind 4, by the standards of Bisipara, was never a poor man. He is a Distiller, one of those who came from Boad, and he inherited, with his brother, an estate large enough to keep him in moderate comfort.[12] His brother became a schoolmaster. *Ind 4* went to Phulbani when he was nineteen and got a job as an assistant in a Government-run Coöperative organized for weavers. He worked there for fourteen years. In 1936 he left this job, having established himself as a minor contractor in such affairs as collecting market dues, feeding the prisoners in the gaol and supplying rations to the hospital. He seems to have prospered in this, and when I first met him in 1952 he had already launched himself on a career as a public man and a politician. He had stood as an Independent in the 1952 elections and had been defeated. He was also branching out into bigger lines of business, especially in taking Government contracts for building. He owned one of the

---

[12] The story of the Boad Distillers and how they got their wealth is given in Bailey, 1957, Chapter IX.

few brick-built houses in Bisipara, and he had built himself a second house in the market quarter of Phulbani. When I talked to him in 1959 he was established as one of the public men of Phulbani. He was secretary of the Phulbani District Congress Committee. He had twice been an Independent candidate for the Orissa Assembly. He had been chairman of the Ganatantra Parishad in Phulbani. He was Sarpanch of the Besringia panchayat and Sarpanch of a panchayat of a higher grade (the Adalati Panchayat); in other words, he had an active life in local government. He was a life member of the All-India Krishak Samaj (an organization of social and welfare workers). He was president of the Rashtrabhasha Samiti in Phulbani (an organization for the promotion of the Hindi language). He had founded a Lower Primary School in the market area of Phulbani. He was a member of the Hospital Advisory Board and of the High School Advisory Board. Finally, he was the first president and founder of the Phulbani Athletic Association.

But these official positions are only that part of the iceberg which shows above the water. What is visible is his status as a man of affairs: down below, the true source of his eminence, is his role as a broker and go-between. For the people of Bisipara, and for many others, he is the link which enables them to be in touch with officials and official organizations. On the several occasions when I conveyed people from the village to the hospital in Phulbani, there was always a stop in the Phulbani marketplace to send a message to *Ind 4*, or to pick him up, so that he too could go to the hospital and make sure that the hospital menials made arrangements for the sick man to be admitted and seen quickly by the doctor. If a Bisipara man wanted a job with the Administration, he would not think of applying directly, but would work through the contacts which *Ind 4* had with the officials concerned. A place in the High School for a boy, a loan for agriculture, trouble with the police, a grant for development work in the village, a lawyer to be hired, a doctor to be consulted—all these and many others were occasions for consulting *Ind 4* and getting sometimes advice and sometimes active assistance.

Ind 4, justifiably in my opinion, regards himself as a public benefactor. He rests this claim on his public work—on, for example, the school which he has founded, or the cup which he has presented to the Athletic Association, or the time and energy he spends as an adviser for the High School and the hospital, or, finally, on the several extravagant sacrifices which he has financed when astrologers told him that the state of the planets made it necessary in the public interest. But, if we take as given the system of administration under which he and the villagers live, he is also a public benefactor because he is an indispensable contact. Without him the villagers would be even less successful than they are in their encounters with the world outside. They confidently expect his help when they need it, and, from what I heard, they usually got it. They respect him for his skill and his contacts, and they are grateful when these qualities are of use to them. But there has not developed any of that lasting sense of unquestioning and uncalculating obligation which marks the true relationship with a leader. Their attitude towards him is not far above the attitude which the buyer and seller of a house have towards their estate agent.

There are several reasons for the strong element of calculation in the relationship between *Ind 4* and his clients and followers, and for their lack of respect and confidence in him. Firstly, he belongs to a caste which has a very equivocal status in Bisipara.[13] The Distillers are not among the traditional leaders of the village. They are newly rich, and among them *Ind 4* is one of the richest. A mixture of contempt and envy is the standard attitude toward such people in Bisipara as in other places in the world. Secondly, they know that in culture and

---

[13] See Bailey, 1957, Chapter IX.

in attainments *Ind 4* is one of themselves. He has no degree, no matriculation even; he cannot speak English; he is not in Government service. It is true that he has been successful in the world outside the village, and relatively he is very rich, but at the same time he is, so to speak, promoted out of the ranks. Thirdly, although he still has a house and lands in the village, most of his time is spent in Phulbani. Indeed, he could not be a successful broker for Bisipara people if he did not live in Phulbani. But his absence means that he is cut off from the day-to-day affairs of the village, and, little by little, the villagers are beginning to think of him as a Phulbani man, rather than a man of Bisipara.

In a sense the fact that *Ind 4* lives in Phulbani symbolizes the fourth and most important reason for the villagers' distrust. This distrust rests ultimately upon the villagers' idea of human nature and of the limits of moral obligation. This view is cynical in our eyes, or, to put it less harshly, it is realistic. By and large the villagers rank their obligations to themselves and their families first, then to those fellow-caste members who live in the same village, and, at the end of the line, their fellow villagers and fellow castemen in other villages. This sense of obligation of course extends to individuals—relatives and friends—in other villages, but it does not extend to other villages as corporate bodies—much less to our vague notion of the "public interest" or "public weal" which embraces the whole population. For a village leader to be trusted he must belong unambiguously to the village. If his style of life, or his place of residence, or his business, or his social contacts bring him appreciably into relationship with outsiders, then he forfeits the trust of his fellow villagers.

This lack of confidence in the apparent altruism of an outsider is sometimes sufficiently explained by saying: "He is not one of us." More often, nowadays, the broker's ambiguous position between the villagers and the officials—between two sets of relationships and two sets of values, fundamentally different from one another—is translated into aspersions upon his sincerity. In the last resort the villagers do not trust *Ind 4* (the businessman), nor *Ind 9* (the ex-policeman), nor *Congress 2* (the professional social worker and politician) because they believe that when any of these three take on public responsibilities, or do a favour for a man, they only do so because they make a profit out of it. They cannot conceive that anyone should consistently and continually do favours for people who are not his relatives, much less for the general public, unless he makes something out of it. They are probably right, for the brokers themselves—and this is said without malice towards the three men named above—have the same attitude. If they did not I would have found for them a more complimentary term than "broker."

Who, then, are the "real" leaders of the village? What is the meaning to be attached to the word "real"? I first heard it used in this context by an official who had had long experience of village development work in Orissa. He had noticed that when he came to a village for the first time, he encountered three categories of persons. The first to approach him were the "simple" people—the children and others who came to stare at him and his jeep, simply because he was a stranger. After a short time he would be approached by others who escorted him to a house, or the school, or the Bungalow if the village had one. There they brought tea for him and, in the tactful roundabout way of Indian conversation, would find out why he had come and what he had to offer. Any development work which he initiated through these people invariably failed. Successful work had to be done through another set of people, whom he called the "real" leaders. They never approached him; he had to find them. They were reluctant and noncommittal, while the others (whom he called "touters") were coöperative and apparently enthusiastic. But if he managed to persuade the real leaders to follow his advice—to use a new variety of seed, a different cropping technique, to dig a compost pit or a latrine—then the rest of the village, the "simple" people, would follow their example. But they would not follow the example of the "touters."

A man whose technical judgement the villagers respect may be persuaded to make a compost pit or use a new variety of seed. That is one thing and the lesser side of development work; it is quite another thing to persuade the same man to organize his fellow villagers in some common project and to take the responsibility for public money. Towards the end of Text 4 the writer remarks that the man whom the people of Bisipara would really follow would be their traditional leader, the Bisoi, but he was reluctant to take on the job because "there was sure to be some bother about money." The implications of this are that when officials charged with village development search for the "real leaders" of the village, and hope to make use of them, they may be pursuing a chimaera. As soon as a real leader takes active charge in a Government-inspired programme of work in his own village, then he runs the danger of forfeiting village confidence and ceasing to be a "real" leader. He cannot avoid being lined up, in village opinion, with the brokers and touters; and, in fact, he cannot avoid working with these same persons, using some of their methods, and enlarging the range of his contacts outside the village to the point where his fellow villagers may begin to doubt whether he is still "one of us."

This may seem a sweeping, and indeed a very pessimistic, judgement; but, so far at least as concerns villages like Bisipara where the sense of public obligation (and therefore of trust) extends no further than to kinsmen and the village boundary, it is a correct judgement. In 1955 I watched the people of Bisipara pull down an old temple, and, through public subscription, build a better one on the same site. Many of the contributions were in labour and kind, but some money was involved. There was endless trouble about this money, and I have the records of many formal meetings at which accusations of embezzlement were made against several people, including the Bisoi. Feeling ran so high that one faction boycotted the opening ceremony. Nevertheless, these accusations do not seem to have impaired the Bisoi's position as the accepted leader of the village, and he seemed to me to take these accusations in his stride. Yet the same man was reluctant to stand for the panchayat because, if he became Sarpanch, he might be involved in bother about money. It is possible that he feels like this because he thinks that the Government will punish defaulters more heavily than would the village; but I do not think so, because part of the accepted myth about "fiddling" public money is that the culprit nearly always goes unpunished. I think it far more likely that the Bisoi is reluctant to become Sarpanch because it would involve him in the kind of relationships with outsiders that would forfeit him his prestige in the village, and because these are relationships which, like any other villager, he regards with distaste.

This is the crux: the villagers of Bisipara look upon relations with outsiders with apprehension and distaste. Peasant communities are proverbially hard and centred upon themselves; within the boundary there is some degree of trust, some rule of morality; beyond the boundary they expect to be cheated or bullied, as they would themselves deal with a stranger. Relationships with outsiders have not yet acquired "legitimacy." They are not accepted as right and proper, in the same way as relationships with fellow villagers.

To say that these relationships are not yet legitimate is, like any other statement about values and attitudes, no explanation but merely a shorter way of phrasing the problem. A clearer understanding comes from examining the social relations involved. Here the point is that all these new relationships, and the people like *Ind 4* who are skilled at manipulating them, represent a loss of power for many of the villagers, an attack upon their interests—at least, the villagers see it this way. This applies not only to the traditional leaders of village society, like the Warrior caste and the Bisoi in Bisipara; it applies also to humbler people of clean caste, because many of them like things as they are and do not want new responsibilities thrust upon them. In other words, for many villagers the old institutions still have legitimacy, are accepted unquestioningly, and are defended from the attacks of politicians, officials and brokers. Understandably, the Harijans are more open-minded.

In a paradoxical way this attitude is also at the root of the behaviour of the brokers and the lower type of politician and official. For them too the ties of kinship and close personal obligation are all-compelling. The newer relationships, which they have with one another, have not yet acquired the moral legitimacy which exists in more diversified societies. In other words, the allegations of nepotism, corruption, self-interest, and all-round dishonesty are well-founded. On public occasions these men speak the new morality of service to the people at large, but they do not practise it.

In discussing the way in which the villagers look upon the brokers who bridge the gap between the village and the officials, I have used the terminology of values; in effect, I have said that the brokers are rascals. But this is no more than the point of view of the villagers; it is not an absolute judgement.

Firstly, it is not a simple affair of black and white. If *Ind 4* does do well as a broker, it is also true that he is indispensable to the people of Bisipara, and they would be a lot worse off without him. He performs a necessary function as a means of communication. Secondly, it would be entirely unrealistic to pretend that, if it were possible to transform the standards of the brokers overnight by an injection of the appropriate morality, then all problems would vanish. Even if the brokers became honest, they would still be accused of dishonesty and insincerity, because these accusations are a projection of the villagers' dislike of outsiders. At the root of the matter is the fact that the villages are being incorporated into a larger society, and the people who are powerful in this larger society are not always the same people who were powerful in village society.

Bisipara differs from most villages in its vicinity. It is peopled by Oriyas, while the majority population in the Kondmals is Kond. For a time it was a headquarters village. It is a village of part-time traders and middlemen. Accordingly, it is more sophisticated and more advanced than the majority of villages in the Kondmals. On the other hand, seen against the background of the whole of Orissa, Bisipara lies in a backward area, far from the main lines of communication and cut off from the centres of power and influence. It had no part in the two major events of recent years—Independence and the merger of the Feudatory States—which have shaped Orissa politics since 1947. Seen from Bhubaneswar, the capital of Orissa, villages like Bisipara are backwaters and politically irrelevant.

It is also clear that the issue which more than anything else decided how the people of Bisipara voted in 1957—the conflict with their own Harijans—is, in many ways, peculiar to itself and to a few other Oriya villages in the Kondmals. This issue was not important even in the plains area of the same constituency.

A village of 700 people which fields three candidates in a General Election is clearly exceptional, and it might be argued that the account of the people's experiences in this election and the conclusions I have drawn from it cannot be typical of rural Orissa. To make but one point, it might be the case that in villages which do not themselves have a candidate in the contest arguments turn on party and policy issues, and personalities play a much smaller part than they did in Bisipara. It must, indeed, be true that the content of sheer calumny in the campaign is lower when the candidate is not personally known to the electors. This was the case in Bisipara with the Scheduled caste candidate for the Assembly. Yet, on the other hand, the story of Bisipara brings out most clearly that what the villager sees most directly in politics is the nearest politician and that his acceptance of the new institutions as legitimate does not rest only on the efficiency with which they work, but also on moral judgements about the persons associated with the new institutions.

2

MOHANPUR VILLAGE

Cuttack, the old capital of Orissa, is built on an island between the river Mahanadi and one of its effluents, the Kathjori. The site is considered unhealthy, and space for new building is restricted. Since Independence in 1947, the seat of the Government is being removed to a planned township built on the open plain beside the old temple town of Bhubaneswar, eighteen miles to the south of Cuttack. By 1959 the MLAs and all but a few departments of Government were provided with living quarters there. But Cuttack remained the centre of commerce. The principal markets were there. Some industries were built on the island itself, and a big industrial development was taking place on the northern bank of the Mahanadi, across from Cuttack Island. All the main Oriya newspapers were still published in Cuttack and the University, although the major part of it would eventually move to Bhubaneswar, was still in Cuttack.

The two places are eighteen miles apart and are connected by a trunk road and by the railway, a section of the main line between Calcutta and Madras. The road carried a heavy traffic. Bhubaneswar was still largely an Administrative settlement, a town of officials and politicians; for many goods and services these people still depended upon Cuttack.

MOHANPUR VILLAGE

Close to the connecting road, on the southern bank of the Kathjori, lies Mohanpur, a village of about 1,300 inhabitants. Its houses are built along the line of the river, and none of them are further than one hour's walk from Cuttack. There is a frequent bus service, and the journey from the village to the centre of Cuttack takes hardly ten minutes. From Bisipara to Cuttack is more than a day's journey. Not many people from Bisipara have been to Cuttack, and those who have made the trip remember it as an event in their lives. For the people of Mohanpur a visit to Cuttack is an everyday occurrence.

Geographically, and administratively, Mohanpur is a distinct village and is not merely a suburb of Cuttack. But its economy is very closely linked with the town. Some of its land grows market crops for sale in Cuttack. Some of the landless people in the village make a living by carrying vegetables to market, either hawking the goods themselves or selling them to wholesalers. The artisan castes in Mohanpur, smiths and carpenters and potters, sell their wares or ply their craft in Cuttack and in surrounding villages and get only a part of their living from work in their own village. Men of the Confectioner caste own businesses, some in catering and some in other trades, both in Cuttack and in other towns in Orissa. More than 40 men from the village are "in service"—that is, in salaried employment for the Government or for commercial and industrial concerns in Cuttack and elsewhere, some as far afield as Jamshedpur, the Tata steel town in Bihar. Scheduled caste people get an important part of their living working as labourers, maintaining the roads and the river embankments. There is a regular daily exodus, my informant estimated, of at least one hundred people from the village to jobs in Cuttack.

THE ELECTIONS IN MOHANPUR

In Bisipara there were two elements in the lack of popular political sophistication: an active distaste for politics and politicians, as interpreted by and revealed in the actions of the local brokers; and, secondly, a plain ignorance of everything to do with the wider stage of Orissa politics. Mohanpur is different. Its people know much of what is going on, and they have had a long experience of representative politics. In this section I describe the content and extent of this awareness; but I emphasize that these were issues about which Mohanpur people talked, and they were not, necessarily, the issues which influenced the majority of voters in Mohanpur to favour the Congress.

In the 1952 election, the people of Mohanpur displayed a great deal of enthusiasm. This enthusiasm was partly political. The party workers had managed to create an atmosphere of almost millenarian expectation. This was the first election on a total adult suffrage. Many promises were made, both of specific benefits for individual groups and individual villages and of a general well-being that was to come about as the result of the election. Similar hopes had been aroused by the Independence Movement, and there was a vague idea that the blessings which Independence had failed to bring would follow upon the first General Election. The enthusiasm did not derive entirely from the political or social expectations but also from the accessories of campaigning—meetings, loudspeakers, gramophone records, processions, and so forth. In other words, for many people the 1952 election was a *tamasha* —an entertainment.

By 1957 this feeling was gone. Most of the specific promises made in the 1952 election had proved to be the politicians' empty campaign pledges, and for every one voter who felt he had got what he wanted there were a hundred who felt that their trust had been betrayed—not so much their trust in particular leaders or parties, but rather their faith that the way they voted would have an important influence upon their lives after the elections. There was no millennium in sight in 1957. Secondly, in the constituency in which Mohanpur lies, the politicians themselves lowered the temperature of the campaigning. Compared to 1952 their campaign in 1957 was mild and relatively unexciting. Both parties contesting—the Congress and the Communists—spared themselves because they believed that, whatever they did, this constituency was a safe seat for the Congress.

TABLE 6

THE 1952 ELECTION IN CUTTACK RURAL CONSTITUENCY

Candidate	Valid votes	Percentage of valid votes
Congress 1 (Sch C)	20,718	24.54
Congress 2	18,565	21.99
Communist 1	10,005	11.85
Socialist 1	8,100	9.59
Communist 2 (Sch C)	7,956	9.42
Socialist 2 (Sch C)	7,685	9.10
Ind 1	4,311	5.10
Ind 2	4,153	4.92
KMPP [a]	2,908	3.44

[a] Peasants, Workers, and Peoples Party.

The constituency is Cuttack Rural, a double seat with one place reserved for a candidate from the Scheduled castes. The 1952 election returned both Congress candidates comfortably, out of a field of nine. The results are given in Table 6. The poll of valid votes was 35.7 per cent.

The boundaries of the constituency for the 1957 election had been considerably changed, but the result was still a comfortable victory for the Congress. Neither Independents nor the Socialists tried their luck again, and there was a straight fight between the Congress and the Communists. The poll of valid votes was 31 per cent. The results are given in Table 7.

Mohanpur has had a much longer experience than Bisipara of representative democracy and voting. It experienced the general elections of 1936 and 1947, although these were conducted on a restricted property franchise. It has also seen a number of Local Government elections, for Union Boards and District Boards. Elections apart, it has had nearly forty years

TABLE 7

THE 1957 ELECTION IN CUTTACK RURAL CONSTITUENCY

Candidate	Valid votes	Percentage of valid votes
Congress 3	24,958	32.75
Congress 4 (Sch C)	21,952	28.79
Communist 3	15,997	20.98
Communist 4 (Sch C)	13,328	17.48

of the Independence Movement. The majority of the voters had lived through one or more of the great campaigns of this movement—Non-Coöperation, Civil Disobedience, and the Quit India movement. In the last of these, in 1942, three members of the village had been detained as political prisoners by the British.

Their own direct experience apart, the people of Mohanpur are in a much better position than the people of Bisipara to know what is going on—or is rumoured to be going on—in the world of politics. The hundred people who go daily to Cuttack, and others who work in different towns in Orissa, bathe in the tides of rumour and gossip. They read the newspapers and bring them back to the village. Three people were employed by one of the Oriya-language dailies. At the junction where a track leads from the main road to Mohanpur and beyond it to other villages, some Mohanpur men of Confectioner caste had set up tea stalls, and these were gossip centres where the villagers and people travelling to and fro sat and talked about the affairs of the day, often about politics.

On the eve of the 1957 election they talked about politics and about the prospects of the different parties. In particular, according to my informant, they talked about the performance of the Congress party in office and about the internal state of the party.

Much of what the Congress had done in office between 1952 and 1957 aroused adverse comment. Three events in particular were talked about, and the general opinion was that none of these helped the Congress cause. These events have been mentioned earlier. Here I describe them in more detail because they illustrate the wider political horizons of Mohanpur people, compared to the narrower horizons of Bisipara people.

Sharecropping tenants had been protected by a bill in 1947. By this bill the landowners' share of the crop was limited to two-fifths, and no sharecropper could be evicted. But the provision against eviction only applied when the landlord had 33 acres or more. Those who had become sharecropping tenants after 1947 were not protected. In 1954 a Tenants' Relief Act was passed, and it set the maximum share for the landlord at one-fourth, and allowed landlords to resume up to seven acres for personal use. On all sides the provisions of this bill and the efforts to implement it caused dissatisfaction. Firstly, it was not easy for a tenant to prove that he had been cultivating a field at a particular time. No documents are signed in these agreements; there are no receipts. The tenant is usually a poor man and has neither the skill nor the resources to fight through the courts for the rights the acts gave him. Secondly, since it was difficult or impossible for the tenant to prove his occupancy right and therefore protect himself against eviction, the landlords, by using the threat of eviction, were able to extract more than the amount of rent laid down by the statute. Thirdly, many of the landlords were not big landowners, but men who were in service or employed in an occupation which kept them away from the village. Many of these panicked when the news got about that there would be a second, and probably stricter, measure for the protection of sharecroppers, and withdrew their land, arranging for it to be cultivated by hired labour. The sharecropping tenants, by and large, were people who had a little land of their own, but not enough to keep themselves, and they were then faced with the alternatives either of going short or of demeaning themselves by taking work as day labourers, alongside landless people, many of whom were untouchables. In short, although the framers of the bill intended a more equitable distribution of wealth and greater security for the less well-off, in practice the bill satisfied no one and made everyone feel less secure than they had felt before.

It is interesting that this issue should have provided one of the main talking points in the period before the 1957 election in Mohanpur, because in fact the problem scarcely arose in Mohanpur itself. Very few sharecroppers—my informant estimated the number at five—lost their lands in Mohanpur. The problem was of direct concern more in those villages which were far enough from Cuttack to make the daily journey onerous and make it more difficult for a landowner who was employed elsewhere to manage his own land and more difficult for the small farmer to live by market crops. But the Tenants' Relief measures—and the associated agrarian reforms of Agricultural income tax, Zemindari Abolition, and later a ceiling on landholding—became major points of conflict among the politicians and the elite. The somewhat inarticulate right wing in the Congress itself and outside the party was ranged against a vociferous and active left wing under the guidance of the two rival radical parties, the Socialists and the Communists. The tenants' issue was one of the talking points in Mohanpur not because it was a burning issue in that village, but because Mohanpur people were in touch with State politics. In Bisipara the sharecropping system went on as it had always done, with half the crop to the tenant and half to the landowner, and no security whatsoever for the tenant. No tenant invoked either of the tenant protection statutes, nor did tenants talk about the measures because none of them had heard of it.

A second set of events which could hardly fail to affect the Mohanpur people was the outbreak of disorders which followed upon the publication of the report of the States Reorganization Commission in 1956.[1] Many of the people in Mohanpur had first-hand experience of the trouble in Cuttack: some witnessed or took part in the riots; shops and offices were closed; and the bus and rail services were suspended. Through their own elite, the humbler people of Mohanpur were kept in touch with the larger issues of Oriya nationalism, which lay behind the troubles. In Saraikella and Kharsawan, the two small states which were the cause of the trouble, they had no direct interest whatsoever. In no sense was this a parochial question; it was an issue concerning the Orissa State and Oriya patriotism. Once again, this was an issue in which the people of Bisipara took no interest whatsoever.

A third issue about which there was some concern and interest in Mohanpur, although it had nothing to do with their own village affairs, was the change of leadership in the Orissa Congress on the eve of the 1957 election.[2] The Chief Minister resigned and went to work for the Bhoodan Movement. He was replaced by a man who had been the first Chief Minister of Orissa in independent India, had then gone to the Central Government, and who, in 1956 was Governor of Bombay. The change was connected, according to opinions

---

[1] See Chapter 9.
[2] See Chapter 9.

expressed to me in 1959, with the predominantly left-wing policies followed by the 1952–1956 Ministry, with the rising strength of the Ganatantra Parishad and Congress misgivings about its own strength, with internal struggles for power between factions within the Congress party itself, with the disturbances of 1956 and Oriya Nationalism, and with many other events, trends, and personalities. It was, in other words, the type of happening about which all kinds of plausible explanation can be advanced, and all manner of speculations about its significance and effect entertained; and the leadership of Congress became one of the talking points in the tea shops in Mohanpur. This, once again, is not a parochial issue and it cannot be tied in any direct way to the fortunes of the Mohanpur villagers; but they—at least some of them—were interested in the change. In Bisipara a few people knew the names of the two men, and that one had replaced the other. But there were no speculations, so far as I know, about the reasons for or significance of the change.

These were not, of course, the only issues talked about in Mohanpur. Other and more parochial questions were raised. For example, there was a disastrous flood on the Orissa plains in 1955, and the main river dyke, close to Mohanpur, was breached. This is a not uncommon occurrence on the Orissa plains, and the organization of relief and rehabilitation is by now almost a matter of routine. But there are inevitably frictions and delays, and these are exploited—or sometimes quite justifiably condemned—by opposition politicians. There is often some kind of scandal about the distribution of rehabilitation funds—for example, allegations that Congress supporters are favoured—or there are accusations of embezzlement. Inevitably flood relief and rehabilitation becomes a subject for gossip and scandal.

The talk about agrarian reform, about the border question, and about the leadership in the Orissa Congress are examples introduced to show that, in some sense of the word, the people of Mohanpur had a political consciousness which the people of Bisipara lacked. It was, of course, a consciousness of a particular political system and of the issues with which it was concerned and of the people who played a prominent part in it. The people of Bisipara, too, were politically conscious in the sense that they were interested in who held power, but they were, on the whole, ignorant about all parts of the new representative system of politics, except where it impinged immediately and directly upon their own lives. In other words, they were interested far more in who would hold power in the village, rather than in who led the Congress party, or whether tenants or landlords would call the tune, or whether Orissa could stand up for her rights against the central Government.

THE 1957 CAMPAIGN IN MOHANPUR

The 1957 election in this constituency was a straight fight between the Congress and the Communists. Several of the leading men in the village were Congress supporters of long standing and had worked voluntarily for the party for many years. The Communists had no equivalent local support on which they could rely.

In Cuttack both these and the other parties held frequent meetings around election time, but in the village itself and in its close vicinity, only the Congress held public meetings to which leading politicians were invited. Before the election campaign started some local men from Mohanpur and other villages had banded together and organized two welcoming meetings for the new Chief Minister, at both of which he spoke, and both of which were considered successful. The Scheduled caste candidate, *Congress 4*, who came from a village in the vicinity of Mohanpur, held a meeting in Mohanpur itself. It was not accounted a great success by the Mohanpur people. The untouchables of Mohanpur turned up in force, but very few people of clean caste went to hear what he had to say. No one seems to have remembered what was said at these meetings, but an incident which is alleged to have taken place at a third meeting, in a village two miles from Mohanpur, became a minor scandal. A few Mohanpur people went to the meeting, but most of them seem to have got the story secondhand. The meeting was addressed by a prominent Oriya politician. A rival party had sent a band of expert hecklers who worked with such success that the speaker lost his temper, and eventually the meeting broke up in disorder. But before it broke up the prominent man was heard to say (or so it is alleged) that if his rivals won, the people who voted against his party would feel the weight of the party's displeasure. Admitted that they could not tell how individuals voted, but they could find out the vote in each booth; and villages which had failed to support them could not expect to get any preference in development work.

If true, this would be a flagrant example of intimidation, and it is interesting that my informant and other people in Mohanpur thought it a plain abuse of the rules of the game. But at the same time they looked upon it as a piece of truth that had slipped through the curtain of hypocrisy, because the man was angry. Questions in the Assembly reveal that politicians think the same way, and there are frequent accusations that the party in power favours its own supporters. I think that most people believe that such favouritism does take place. The Bisipara people would think it a normal piece of political realism. So, probably do the people of Mohanpur. Nevertheless, they had sufficiently absorbed the principle of free elections to be shocked at the open utterance of threats.

There were, then, four meetings in or near Mohanpur. Two of these (those to welcome the new Chief Minister) seem to have been successful by *tamasha* (carnival) standards. Of the remaining two (already described), one failed to cause a ripple on the pool of village life, and the other ended in disorder and gave rise to a scandal. Neither party made any sustained attempt to make a "mass contact" with the voters of Mohanpur.

A number of pamphlets and broadsheets were distributed in the village both by the contending parties and by others. In 1959 I was unable to recover any of these, but from what my informant said, and from such pamphlets elsewhere, they consisted of two parts: first an exposition of the party's policy and achievements set against an exposure of their rival's malice; secondly a glorification of their own candidate and a vilification of his opponent. The mud, apparently, stuck closer than the rose petals but on the whole it seemed unlikely that anyone was much influenced by what he read in, or had read to him from, the propaganda leaflets.

Both parties canvassed in the village. The Communists had stationed an experienced worker from another part of the constituency in the village six months before the election. He held no public meetings but he canvassed actively among the Cultivator caste. When the election came near, Congress appointed a young Brahmin to canvass for them in the village and allowed him two assistants as messengers and bill-stickers. The postmaster and an employee of the Depressed Classes League both canvassed for the Congress, but discreetly, since both were disbarred from active politics by their appointments. Both parties made an attempt to capture the women's vote. The Communists sent in a young woman party worker; the two daughters of *Congress 3* canvassed some houses in the village.

The Congress alone had voluntary workers from among the permanent residents of the village. One man of Writer caste, a wealthy shopkeeper with a business in Cuttack, had been a party member for many years. He had taken a hand in organizing the meetings to welcome the new Chief Minister. He made an attempt to get the Congress ticket, but, by his own account, he did not have wealth enough to organize a sufficient following and make an impressive case for his own nomination. However, in spite of this disappointment, he continued to work in the Congress cause. He was assisted by the leader of the Washerman caste in the village. On polling day a well-to-do man, who had been in the service of a rich industrialist in Delhi, and now held a catering contract in a railway town in northern Orissa, organized and paid for a band of youths to march around the village carrying Congress posters and shouting Congress slogans.

No one seems to have extended themselves much in the campaign in Mohanpur in 1957. There are several reasons for this. Firstly, as already noted, both parties believed that whatever happened the Congress would win, and neither side wished to waste propaganda resources which might be more effectively employed elsewhere. Secondly, since the village is very near to Cuttack, and since many of the villagers go there daily, its propaganda "needs" were to some extent met by the meetings and processions which took place in Cuttack.

These are elements which originate outside the village. Why did the campaign not develop along the lines of internal cleavage in the village? Why were the bigger issues of state politics not translated into local rivalries and conflicts? To this question I will return after examining the qualifications of the four candidates, as seen from the village.

The Candidates

What, then, were the characteristics which commended or disqualified the various candidates in the eyes of the voters of Mohanpur? In the simplest idea of representative systems and free elections the voters are supposed to measure up each candidate's qualities as a potential representative, or delegate, and vote for the one who, they think, will do the job best. At a more sophisticated stage, the voter takes the personal qualities of the candidate as given and supports a party, making his decision rationally according to the policies proposed by the different parties.

This picture of a rational voter applies only rarely. Most people in the older democracies vote by habit. In Bisipara, however, it did seem that the voters made their choice through rational, or at least quasi-rational processes, and, secondly, that the majority had their eye upon the person of the candidate as much as upon his party. Moreover, what mattered was not so much the personal qualities of the candidate—not in every case, at least—as the status which he already possessed outside the system of representative democracy. This way of thinking is clearly shown in their rejection of "brokers" from their own village, and in their confidence in an ex-Raja.

A similar set of questions can be asked about the voters of Mohanpur. Did they look to the caste of each candidate? Or to his locality? Or to the way he made his living? Finally, did they vote more for the person or for the party?

Caste and locality seem to have been of importance only in the case of the Scheduled caste candidate, *Congress 4*. He came from a village nearby and he was well known in Mohanpur. *Communist 4*, also a Scheduled caste candidate, came from the same constituency but he was not closely identified with its interests nor did he have many personal contacts there. The home of *Congress 3* was in another constituency. He too had spent most of his life away from his village, and was generaly considered a man of Cuttack town. He had no particular regional affiliations with Mohanpur. He was of Bengali extraction and, therefore, not identified with any group in Mohanpur on the score of caste membership. No candidate, therefore, with the partial exception of *Congress 4*, enjoyed any significant advantage over the others through caste membership or through local affiliations in Mohanpur.

All four candidates were relatively experienced politicians. *Communist 4* (Sch C) had been ten years in the party. He was a matriculate, which, for an untouchable, is still a relatively high educational qualification. He had been gaoled in 1949 during the rising in Andhra, like other Indian Communists, and therefore had the renown of having been a political prisoner. *Congress 4* (Sch C) had taken part in the 1947 Quit India movement. He had held a seat in the 1947 Crissa Assembly, and again from 1952 to 1956. He was a member of the District Congress Committee. *Communist 3* was one of the leaders of the Orissa Communist Party. He had been a politician since his student days and had taken part in the Freedom Movement from the middle of the 1930's onwards. He joined the Communists in 1940. He had been imprisoned on several occasions, first as a Congressman by the British, and later, in 1949, by the Congress Government as a Communist. *Congress 3*, at the time of the election in his later fifties, had spent a lifetime in the Independence Movement and was one of its original leaders in Orissa. He too had been gaoled several times by the British. He had been an MLA in all three Assemblies in Orissa, 1936, 1947, and 1952. He had held high office in the Orissa Congress Party and was at that time a member of the District Committee and the Pradesh (Provincial) Committee and was a past-President of the Orissa Congress. He had held minor offices in an earlier Government, and in the 1952–1956 Government he was Minister for Public Works.

This brief description of the careers of the four candidates in the 1957 election in Cuttack Rural constituency is enough to show a striking difference between them and the people who stood for the constituency in which Bisipara lies. In Mohanpur's constituency the candidates were all professional politicians. Three out of the four of them had a history of political activity in the Nationalist Movement going back beyond the granting of Independence in 1947. In so far as they were known, they had made their name in modern politics. Of the candidates in the Bisipara area all had come recently to this form of politics, and, if they were known before, then their reputation rested on activities and achievement outside modern politics.

To have taken part in the Independence Movement is, in many respects, a hallmark of political respectability. There is a strong feeling both among the electorate and the politicians that many of those who have entered politics since 1947 have done so for what personal profit they can get out of it. This brick is thrown particularly frequently at those who are old enough to have taken part in the National Movement, but who either held aloof or—worst of all—supported the British. But most of those who went into politics before 1947 can point to an impressive list of personal sacrifices for an ideal. On the other hand, it is also alleged that many of the most illustrious Freedom fighters have done more than enough, in the decade following Independence, to wipe away their credit balance in the bank of public approbation. It is also true that to have been a Freedom fighter is no longer a crucial qualification for electoral preferment. In Orissa that issue has been quite decisively settled against the members of the Freedom Movement (see Chapter 9). Nevertheless a little of the old glory clings to the Freedom Fighters, particularly in those coastal districts which were a centre of Congress activity.

On this score by far the best-qualified of the candidates was *Congress 3* and he had the additional advantage of being a renowned orator. But this was not his only advantage. He had also proved himself a man capable of getting into the higher seats of power; he had been a minister. The voters look to their MLA not for his record and performance as a legislator, but expect him to be their representative, a man who can stand up for them against the local administrators and win favours for them in the distribution of development money or other favours. They look to him partly to dispense patronage, and a minister, particularly the Minister of Public

Works, rates particularly high on this score. If the electors vote him in, they hope he will be willing and know he would be capable of doing something for them. If they voted against him, and for the Communist candidates, then, supposing he won and learnt of their defection, they would have thrown away the chance of patronage.

The assumption was that the Congress was going to win. To some extent the vote for the two Congress candidates was not only a vote for them as persons, but also a prudent vote for the Raj, of the same kind as the votes given by Government employees in Bisipara. In 1957, from a place like Mohanpur, a win by the Congress seemed a reasonable expectation. The party had won in 1936, 1947, and, albeit more narrowly, in 1952.

But I think, although I cannot prove, that Congress support in Mohanpur in 1957 rested on a deeper foundation than the self-interest implied in a vote for the Raj. Voting for the Congress had become a habit, that same fundamentally irrational—one might call it "moral"—identification with a party which characterizes party support in the older representative democracies. Support for a party had been divorced from parochial issues and even from personal interests—at least far more so than in Bisipara. This will become clearer after a discussion, in the following section, of the lack of connection between village affairs and state politics.

VILLAGE AFFAIRS AND STATE POLITICS

It is at first sight a paradox that Mohanpur people, many of whom are, by Bisipara standards, politically sophisticated and equipped with a much better knowledge of how politicians and administrators work, should nevertheless refrain from using this knowledge and these skills to manipulate politics within their own village. In Bisipara, state politics were only comprehensible to the people in so far as they could be translated into issues within the village—for example, the tax burden or the conflict between clean castes and untouchables. The relatively low degree of parochialism in Mohanpur is an index of political maturity—measuring maturity from the standards of parliamentary democracy—and of the degree to which Mohanpur is integrated into the larger society of Orissa. In Bisipara the reverse position holds. The village has a high degree of internal integration and is very little connected with the world outside; and representative politics have not yet achieved any considerable legitimacy, as things which exist in their own right and not merely as one of several weapons used to achieve dominance in the village.

An estimated breakdown of Mohanpur population by caste is given in Table 8. The lists have been abbreviated so as to make clear the categories which are or could be relevant to a discussion of cleavages and conflict within the village, and which, from the experience of Bisipara, one might expect to be translated into the categories of State politics.

TABLE 8

CASTES IN MOHANPUR

Brahmin	9%	Cultivator	20%	Confectioner	8%	Un-	
Writer	10%			Other specialists [a]	23%	touchables [b]	30%

[a] Herdsman, Carpenter, Barber, Blacksmith, Cosmetic vendor, Bell-metal vendor, Goldsmith, Gardener, Fisherman, Oilman, Potter, Painter.
[b] Washerman, Drummer, Bauri, Kandara.

Thinking back to Bisipara one would expect firstly that there would be some antagonism between the clean castes and the untouchables in Mohanpur, that they would be ranged against one another as corporate political groups, and secondly that this antagonism would have been expressed in the elections and generally in State politics as they appeared in the village. This is what happened in Bisipara where there was a more or less direct identification between the Congress and the untouchables on the one side and on the other side the clean castes and the Ganatantra Parishad. Furthermore, the policies which have encouraged the untouchables of Bisipara—preferences in education and reserved positions in the employment of the Administration and Harijan "uplift" in general—are not confined only to Bisipara but apply over the whole of India. One would also expect that the untouchables of a village within walking distance of the old capital of Orissa, and in an area which is as advanced as any in rural Orissa, would have a better standard of education and a higher degree of political sophistication than the untouchables of Bisipara who live in one of the most backward districts of Orissa and whose village is one hundred miles away from the railway.

I was told that the untouchables of Mohanpur all voted for the Congress candidates, and that few or none of them voted for the Communists. The reasons given were that the Congress candidate for the reserved seat was a man of the locality, and a proved and experienced politician, and that untouchables in any case would have favoured the party which had promoted Harijan uplift. The Harijans of Bisipara voted in just the same way. But in Bisipara the clean castes were moved by the same issue to vote against the Congress and for its rivals. In Mohanpur the clean castes voted for the Congress, and there is no evidence of any significant or systematic conflict between the Harijans on the one side and the clean castes on the other.

There are two reasons for this: firstly, the Mohanpur Harijans are, relatively to the higher castes in their locality, very poor; secondly, their economic and political interests (in so far as they are conscious of any political interests) lie not within but outside the village. The village is no longer, in the case of Mohanpur, an arena for conflict between the untouchables and the clean castes. That conflict, in so far as the Mohanpur untouchables are able to contend at all, takes place in the wider arenas of Orissa or all-India politics.

The Mohanpur Harijans are relatively poor, because they have not had the advantage under which the Bisipara Harijans started the race. Bisipara Harijans live in a vast hinterland of tribal ignorance, and have benefitted from an absence of competition. Secondly, and more generally, for most of the past hundred years Bisipara has lain in a "frontier" area, an area of expansion and opportunity for those who are lucky or energetic. In Mohanpur conditions have been more settled—so far at least as concerns opportunities for small entrepreneurs. There have, in fact, been spectacular opportunities for advancement in the Orissa plains, but these have demanded much higher qualifications than untouchables could hope to command and went mainly to the Brahmins and the Writers and to some of the specialist castes. Most Harijans in Mohanpur have remained landless labourers who work on the farms of other people and who get temporary employment from the Government in maintaining roads and the river embankments.

Of their own accord very poor people do not take part in politics, nor is it easy to organize them for political action. They remain interested in the welfare of themselves and their families and will not spare time or energy to work for the collectivity. Nor have they the independence, in some cases, to work politically against those who employ them, although this last factor is probably only of marginal importance in Mohanpur. All the left-wing party workers emphasized that it was almost impossible to organize the very poor, except occasionally for a short time over a particular grievance; and these organizers usually tried to recruit support from among people of at least some substance. The Communists made no effort in Mohanpur to organize the untouchables, but concentrated upon the Cultivator caste.

The second reason why there is no conflict in Mohanpur between the untouchables and the clean castes, is that in the village there is little or nothing over which to compete. It follows that even if the Harijans had obtained that edge of wealth to make them want to cut their way into local politics, they would be unlikely to stage the fight within the village. Both they and the clean castes get a significant part of their income from sources outside the village, either in Government service or from commercial sources in Cuttack. The centres of power for Mohanpur villagers are in Cuttack. The proximity of Cuttack has another significance too. An untouchable with ambition can cut his ties with the village much more easily than his fellow in Bisipara could. The relative isolation of Bisipara puts two limitations on the tactics of the Harijans in their struggle with the clean castes. Firstly, if there are any victories to be won, they have to be won in Bisipara: secondly, the Harijan group has to preserve solidarity, for, since very few individuals go away to work, the ambitious man can only rise by taking his fellows along with him on the upward path. In Mohanpur neither of these conditions applies so strongly. A large number of untouchables can and do go outside the village to make a living, and by going away the ambitious men among them may be able to jettison their local caste fellows and improve their own status.

Both these factors—that there is little left in Mohanpur for which to compete, and that there are better opportunities outside both for the clean castes and for the Harijans—are instances of what is meant by saying that Mohanpur is more closely integrated into the larger society than is Bisipara. It so happens that Harijans in Mohanpur have not yet reached the level of wealth at which it is possible for them to make claims to a higher political and social status, but when they do reach that level they are likely to fight not as the Harijans of Mohanpur but within the larger framework of State politics. In short, the Harijan issue which played so crucial a role in the 1957 election in Bisipara was of no significance in Mohanpur, because Mohanpur has come to that degree of integration with the larger society where parochial issues no longer are of sufficient importance to be the medium through which State politics are understood.

Some six months before the 1957 election the Communists had put a worker into Mohanpur with the intention, according to my informant, of winning the support of the Cultivators by exploiting their differences with the dominant Brahmin and Writer (Karan) groups. The hostility between these two groups is of long standing and is commonly found in villages of the coastal districts, in particular the three northern districts of Balasore, Cuttack, and Puri. Broadly speaking the conflict arises from two differences. Firstly the Brahmin and Writer castes are, or were, the landowners and zemindars; the Cultivators were tenants and farmers. Secondly, the Cultivators have by and large remained peasant-farmers while many Brahmins and Writers have made striking use of the opportunities offered by the presence of the British administration and occupy a very high proportion of posts within the administration and form the greater part of the professional classes. The middle class in eastern Orissa, and to some extent in western Orissa, is drawn largely from either Brahmin or Writer caste. They dominate all the political parties in Orissa with the exception of the Ganatantra Parishad, and in that too the Brahmins form a significant part of the leadership.

The agrarian policies of the Congress, both before and after Independence, were, almost without exception, favourable to the small man and against the wealthy. A heavy agricultural income tax was imposed, so adjusted that it fell on the wealthy and left the small farmer alone. Zemindari holdings were abolished. Tenants were given security. During 1959 a measure was introduced to limit the size of all agricultural holdings and to distribute surplus land among the landless.

The policy was, in short, entirely in the direction of the proclaimed Congress goal of socialism in agriculture.

In so far as the Brahmins and Karans (Writers) are landlords and wealthy men, whereas the Cultivators are small farmers, one would expect them to be ranged on opposite sides over agrarian issues. One would also expect the issue to be a live one in Mohanpur, and to have had some effect in the 1957 election. If the Communist agent in the village took the line that Congress policies had not fallen heavily enough on the landlords, or that the implementation of socialist policies had been defective (as happened in the example I have already mentioned, over the Tenant Protection legislation), then it was entirely sensible to try to work through this grievance to gain the support of the Cultivators. Yet, in the end, the campaign was a failure, and the Cultivators voted Congress like the rest of the village. How is this to be explained?

Firstly, although there is a cleavage of interest between the Brahmin-Writer category and the Cultivator groups in many parts of the Orissa plains, this has not yet fully emerged in party politics. No party is clearly identified with one side or the other. There is no alignment of parties and caste interests in this case, as there was in Bisipara between Ganatantra Parishad and clean castes against Congress and untouchables. This is partly because the Cultivator interest is not homogeneous, is widely spread, and is imperfectly organized. There are a few leading politicians who originate from one or other of the Cultivator castes, and from time to time some of them have made use of Cultivator caste associations to build up a political following. But these links are, as yet, links of sentiment rather than links of common interest, and, once elected, the Cultivator politicians do not promote measures which favour Cultivators as a collectivity, although they do, of course, distribute favours among their fellow Cultivators when they are in a position to do so. Again, there are too few politicians of Cultivator origin to form any compact and effective block in State politics, and they are distributed between the parties.

From the other side the Brahmin and Writer interest is sufficiently represented in State politics to be a power. But once again they form a category within politicians rather than a group with a self-conscious identity and explicit common interests. No other interest in the State—neither clean castes like the Cultivators nor the Harijans—represent a serious threat to their dominance, and even within the Ganatantra Parishad, which is led by princely families of self-styled Rajput origin, the Brahmins at least are adequately represented. Secondly the elite group is itself divided into hostile groups of Brahmins on the one side and Writers on the other. This hostility is not so live an issue in contemporary politics, but at one time it caused a major cleavage within the Congress and the Independence movement,[3] and it is still strongly felt within the ranks of the Administration. Thirdly the leadership of the Congress, the Praja Socialist Party and the Communist Party, is recruited from both Brahmins and Writers, so that there is no question of any party becoming identified either as the party of the Cultivators or the party of the Brahmin-Writer category.

Coming down to the immediate issue of the election in Mohanpur, there was no candidate in this constituency of Cultivator caste. The General seat candidate for the Congress was of Bengali origin and a Writer by caste; the Communist candidate was a Brahmin.

In the village itself, although there is a broad correlation between Brahmin-Writer and landlord on the one hand, the division is not so clear-cut that caste hostility can be easily translated into conflict between economic classes and between parties. In the Brahmin-Writer category there is a proportion of poor men, small landowners, tenants, even landless peo-

---

[3] See Chapter 8.

ple. From the other side there are a few rich Cultivators, and there are some very prosperous men of specialist castes, in particular the Confectioners. Secondly, the same factor as in the case of the Harijans operates to remove this conflict from the arena of the village. Wealth is not got by economic activity within the village, but by having a job or a business outside the village. Political and economic energies are directed towards Cuttack and the world outside.

In short, although there were potentially two caste conflicts which might have become the carriers in the village of conflicts between political parties in the State, neither was of significance because Mohanpur village is no longer a main locus of political and economic activity for its people. This is one reason why the electoral campaign did not develop along the lines of internal cleavage in the village.

Mohanpur is not, however, merely a suburb of Cuttack. It is more than an aggregate of households connected only by proximity. For purposes of administration Mohanpur is a distinct village and quite separate from Cuttack. It has its own ritual and ceremonial life, and its people organize a series of festivals through the year. A traditional village council arranges these festivals, and also serves as a court to hear disputes within the village and arbitrate between the disputants. The village also has a Statutory panchayat, set up at Government behest and charged with some of the functions of local Government and with certain judicial responsibilities. Mohanpur people also manage, and to a large extent finance, two schools, a primary school and a Middle English school, the last of which is a particular object of village pride.

There is, of course, a political and an economic aspect to the running of a school or the organization of the festive life of the village. Someone has to make the decisions, and some means of providing the finance has to be organized. It is also true that institutions of this kind can give rise to violent conflicts and sharp factional divisions. Yet these fields of activity are secondary; they are not of the same order as control over men's livelihood and over economic resources.

In some situations and in some villages, control in these secondary fields of power symbolizes the possession of "real" power. This was the case in Bisipara. When the Harijans attempted to gain a fuller share of the ritual life of the village by demanding access to the village temples, they were, in effect, proclaiming that the clean castes and in particular the Warriors no longer were the masters. In the same way, before the conflict began, denial of access to the temples together with the whole paraphernalia of untouchability, were symbols of the real dominance which the Warriors exercised within the village.

In Mohanpur the locus of real power is outside the village. What then has happened to the secondary institutions of power—the village council, organization of festivals, and the management of the schools? Do they fade away, and does the village cease to be a community and become merely an aggregate of households? Do these institutions too tend to be involved in wider groupings and come to depend upon State and Administrative bodies, rather than upon local initiative? One would expect this to happen, particularly with the expansion of welfare activities by the State and the increasingly common feeling that "they" will provide (or at least "they" ought to provide). One would also expect this development to take place with the emergence of political parties and free elections, for, as I show later, the difficulties of making a "mass contact" drive politicians into attempting to capture every conceivable kind of existing congregation of people, from castes to village councils to trade unions to learned societies, and to influence every person who himself has influence, down to the village headman and the village schoolmaster.

In the more isolated villages one expects resistance to this development and attempts to preserve village integrity; and our discussion of Bisipara has provided examples of this attitude of suspicion and hostility on the part of the villagers towards the world outside. But Mohanpur is in many ways a part of the world outside, and it would seem likely that any resistance which the people of that village might have felt towards the final and total integration of their village with the larger society—which would be symbolized by the collapse of parochial initiative in the secondary fields of power—would by now have vanished.

Yet it has not. The final and total integration has not taken place. Those same people who make the greater part of their living in the world outside, and who have a sophisticated appreciation of how politicians and administrators work, and who, therefore, could easily involve these secondary institutions of power into the wider society (possibly to their personal advantage), not only deliberately refrain from doing so but take active steps to see that this development does not take place through default of their own precautions. They insulate secondary institutions of power from contact with State politics. Two examples will show how they do this.

Mohanpur has a traditional village council to which every adult male has access. This does not mean, of course, that everyone plays an equal part in the work of the council. Some are more active than others. But it so happens that those who do take a leading part in the council are not confined to any one caste or clique but are drawn from a wide spread of castes and contain both educated and uneducated people, both rich and relatively poor.

The Statutory Panchayats, set up at Government order, are representative bodies, chosen by election, with a system of reserved seats for untouchables. In some villages these elections have been occasions for different factions to try their strength against one another, and these factions have aligned themselves with political parties, so that conflicts in State politics have emerged on a small scale in the villages. Sometimes the conflict is between the traditional leaders and those who wish to displace them, often people with strong contacts outside the village. In Bisipara, for example, there was a general foreboding among clean caste people that if they were not careful then the next Chairman of the Statutory Panchayat might be a Harijan.

But in Mohanpur there was none of this. There was not even an election. The traditional council met and chose the men who would stand for the Statutory Panchayat, and these men were returned without a contest.

It seems indeed that the people of Mohanpur regard the Statutory Panchayat not so much as an organ of local self-government, but as a means of liaison between the actual organ of self-government—the traditional council—and the Administration. The new panchayat is at the same time a means of manipulating the Administration, where that is possible, and of keeping officials at arm's length and, most of all, of preventing secondary institutions of power in the village from becoming entangled with party politics. Meanwhile the traditional council continues to run the village. The Chairman of the new panchayat is a man with a business in Cuttack, not so very often in the village, and the new panchayat does not meet very frequently. The real work is still done by the traditional council. The chairman also happens to be a prominent supporter of the Congress—the man who offered himself as a Congress candidate but failed to get the nomination—and it is to be presumed that one reason for his nomination as Chairman of the Statutory Panchayat by the traditional council was his good relationship with the ruling party, through which he might obtain favours for the village.

The majority of both the new and the old councils are Congress sympathizers. Nevertheless, they make every effort to keep party allegiances from influencing village affairs. This is particularly clear in the management of the M.E. (Middle English) school. The villagers could have got much more outside aid for this school than in fact they have done; they prefer to do most of their own financing. Grants of any kind usually mean an obligation to a politician and this gives him some measure of control in the village. The village prefers to keep its own control of the school, and, therefore, has not sought grants which, with its many connections with politicians and administrators, it might have obtained without much difficulty.

Schools also can become involved in politics through the teachers. Teachers, on the average, are more sophisticated and more politically conscious than the ordinary villagers. Furthermore, particularly in the remoter villages, they are men of standing to whom the people turn for advice. They are, therefore, useful allies for a politician seeking votes, and such a man often makes his first approach through the headmaster of the local school. The senior boys, too, can be used with good effect in election campaigns and are commonly so used, and have been since the early days of the Nationalist movement. But the Mohanpur school is different. At the time of the 1957 election the headmaster was a distant relative of the would-be Congress candidate and was himself a Congress sympathizer. But he was ordered by the village to take no active part in the campaigns, and to repulse any approaches which political agents might make to him. In 1959 the headmaster was a member of the Communist Party. The attitude of the village council and the school management towards him was that he was entitled to hold what political opinions he liked, and to work for the party in his own time, so long as he did not involve the school in politics. My informant took a particular pride in the efficiency of the school, and in the fact that it had been kept entirely clear of party politics.

The insulation of the school and of the village council from party politics is not done by excluding from these institutions people who hold political opinions or even those who play an active part in politics. This solution occurred to the people of Bisipara, who were determined that not *Ind* 4 but one of their own men would be the next Sarpanch. In Mohanpur village integrity is preserved by a convention that party politics are not an all-embracing activity but can be kept as a separate segment of a man's life. This is a profoundly important point because it means that in Mohanpur, but not in Bisipara, one can be interested in party politics without thereby offending the canons of good behaviour.

In fact the Mohanpur people have a mixed view upon party politics and representative institutions. On the one hand there is a fear of contagion and a feeling that party politics, when they come to direct village affairs, are undesirable. But, unlike Bisipara, one can take part in party politics and still be respectable, providing one does so within—or rather outside—prescribed limits.

There is not much need to ask why it should be respectable to show an interest in State politics. Such activity is one among many aspects of an involvement in relationships outside the village. In Mohanpur there can be no automatic and unthinking condemnation of too close a connection with the world outside the village, as there is in Bisipara, because the greater part of the population have such connections. Party politics, in other words, share in the general legitimacy of outside relationships.

But this does not explain why the legitimacy should stop short at involving the remaining secondary institutions of village power into the larger power system. Two things might be involved. On the level of values, one might argue that village integrity is a positive moral value, as it is in Bisipara. But in Bisipara we traced this value back to the interest which the majority of the village had in stability and in the *status quo*, and their fear that outside relationships would entirely dispossess them of the power they held over their untouchables.

One cannot use the same argument for Mohanpur, because there the decisive arena of power has already shifted outside the village and the shift has, presumably, been recognized and accepted as legitimate. But it might be argued that village integrity does in fact achieve a moral status, and become something valued in itself and apart from interests which may once have lain behind it. Mohanpur, in what I have been calling the "secondary institutions of power," does have the remnant of village integrity, and these institutions may be valued as symbols of a largely vanished real integrity.

There is an alternative and more realistic explanation, and one more flattering to the perspicacity of Mohanpur leaders than an explanation resting on blinkered sentiment. These people know that there is a high price to pay for the use of party or Administrative resources. The price is not only the reciprocal favours which must be done for givers, but also the paralysing faction disputes which the competition for control of a Statutory Panchayat or of the management of a school can bring about. The right explanation for the determined hold which the Mohanpur people keep upon their remaining community institutions may simply be that they think this is the more efficient way of getting their children educated or managing the affairs of their village. This is another reason why the electoral campaign did not develop along the lines of internal cleavage in the village. This is the explanation which the villagers themselves offer. In its essentials this attitude is the same as that of the people of Bisipara.

Bisipara and Mohanpur

The secondary institutions of power in Mohanpur—the council, the festive organization, and the Middle English school—are, to use a metaphor, the last citadel of village and community integrity (or, if you take a wider view, they are the last ditch of reactionary parochialism). In Bisipara the ramparts have only recently been breached, and the people have not yet got used to the idea that they are about to live in a more open society and that it would pay them to set about learning how to do so.

In more technical terms, Mohanpur is more closely integrated with the larger society, whereas Bisipara has a high degree of internal integration and externally is isolated. This means no more than that in Mohanpur more people have more frequent dealings with men and institutions of the town or of other villages than in Bisipara. Whether or not there is any absolute standard by which we can say whether this development is good or bad (and value judgements are heavily implicit in the phrases "community integrity" and "reactionary parochialism" which I have used above), I do not know, and it is not a question relevant here. I want only to try to pick out appropriate social categories, which help understanding of the difference between Mohanpur and Bisipara and the process of social change in which they are both involved.

The situation in Bisipara is relatively simple, for only three actors, basically, are involved in the drama: the village, the Administration, and the "brokers." The village and the Administration represent sets of values which are usually different and sometimes in conflict with one another. They also represent relatively closed circles of social relationships, with few crosscutting ties. In other words, there are relatively few people who have roles to play in both systems, and this fact makes conflict between the two the more probable, and, when it does occur, less restrained than it would be if there were more people with a foot in both camps. Only the brokers bridge the gap between the two sides.

The brokers are the people who subvert the integrity of the village community. ("Integrity" here is used in the sense of "wholeness," but, as it happens, the sentence would for a

Bisipara villager and for many officials too, be just as meaningful if "integrity" were used to mean "honesty and probity.") But the brokers are also the people who have transcended the narrow parochialism of village life and have accepted the responsibilities of belonging to a wider community. They are the agents of social change, and they are the means by which Bisipara is becoming integrated into a wider society. In particular they are linked, both in fact and in the minds of the villagers, into a common category with the politicians who operate and hold power in the system of representative democracy.

Mohanpur presents a much more complicated picture. The village here is represented by a group of people who live near one another, and are known as Mohanpur people, but who make their living and fulfil their political ambitions as much or more outside Mohanpur than within it. Village activity, in the strict sense, is not the comprehensive activity that it is in Bisipara, but is confined to managing the school and running the festive side of village life. Neither is the outside world the simple homogeneous unit that it appears to be when viewed from Bisipara, where the outside world is the Administration with a fringe of brokers (including politicians) attached to it. For Mohanpur people the world outside the village means not only the Administration, but also commerce and industry. Furthermore a good part of the Mohanpur people can make a quite clear distinction between the Administration proper, and the politicians. Some of them are themselves politicians in a small way, and some of them are in service.

Where, then, are the brokers in Mohanpur? The broker is a person with special knowledge and special contacts who can help the villager to get in touch with or manipulate the Administration or who can perform the same service in the other direction for an official. Clearly such persons exist also in Mohanpur. The chairman of the Statutory Panchayat, for example, has special contacts with the ruling Congress party, and one may presume that those employed in Government departments are available to help their fellow villagers in dealings with those departments. But there are two linked differences in the role of the broker in Mohanpur and in Bisipara. Firstly the broker in Bisipara is a jack-of-all-trades. Very few brokers operate in Bisipara, and they must deal with all matters. In Mohanpur the business has become specialized into brokers with particular kinds of knowledge and particular contacts. Secondly to be a broker in Bisipara is, so to speak, a specialized occupation. In Mohanpur it is a side activity, a by-product of an appointment in the services or the management of a business in Cuttack. There are more brokers in Mohanpur, and brokering takes up less of their time.

Once again, this is a way of saying that Mohanpur is more closely integrated with the world outside than is Bisipara. Many more people in Mohanpur have ties with outsiders and outside agencies. The clear and sharp division between the village and the Administration does not exist in Mohanpur to the same extent as in Bisipara. In Mohanpur people can and have made their own contacts with the Administration and with the world of commerce. If the word "broker" is still appropriate, there has grown up a class of people who are their own brokers.

This class of people—they are the middle class—are the category whose existence sharply differentiates villages like Mohanpur from villages like Bisipara, where the middle class does not exist. If the brokers are the agents of social change the existence of this middle class is the sign that change has taken place—that the village is no longer a tight world of its own, that village integrity has gone and that parochial horizons have been transcended.

These are the people who are interested enough to discuss and sometimes even to take action about political issues which do not immediately concern their own material interest. This is not to say that they are selfless and concerned only with the public weal; to claim that would be to swallow uncritically the myth which the middle class commonly puts out about itself. But it is to say that their conception of the public weal is radically different from that of the peasants of Bisipara, and it is seen against a background of all-Orissa interaction rather than against the narrow social system of a group of villages.

In the following section I continue to look at the relationship between the politician and the voter, but this time from the politician's point of view: downwards upon the aggregate of villages that make up a constituency. We no longer stand beside the peasant, looking to the past for guidance and reacting passively to innovations, but beside the new men, the manipulators, the agents of change.

II. THE CONSTITUENCIES

3

THE POLITICIAN'S PROBLEM

The politician wants power. Whether his intention is public service, or private gain, or both, the first step is accession to a position of power: to be elected a Member of the Legislative Assembly. Broadly speaking there are three ways in which he can do the job. He may try to make a "mass contact"; he may use existing groups, nonpolitical as well as political; or, thirdly, he may build up an organization of new groups.

To say that a politician has a "mass contact" is, in Orissa, to pay a high compliment. Such a man—and there are very few—has risen above the ordinary run of politicians who rely on cliques and factions for support. If a constituency consisted exclusively of the members of one caste and they all supported a candidate because he came from their caste, then, in the opinion of those with whom I discussed this question, it would be wrong to call this "mass contact." An essential part of this relationship seems to be that it should transcend traditional loyalties.

Many difficulties stand in the way. The candidate who has a message for every household in his constituency has, in most cases, no means of delivering it. Secondly, even if he had the means, it would be difficult to compose a message which seemed constructive to everyone, still less a message that would please everyone.

Orissa has a population of over fourteen and one-half million (1951 Census) and an Assembly of 140 members, one member to every 100,000 people. The area of the State is 60,000 square miles. Some constituencies are very large in area, particularly the rural double-member constituencies. The Assembly constituency in which Bisipara lay in the 1952 election covered 2,000 square miles; Keonjhar, in the district of the same name, covered 1,256 square miles; and Malkangiri in Koraput covered 2,288 square miles. The first two are double-member, and Malkangiri is a single-member constituency. Only in those very few constituencies which consist of towns (for example Cuttack City covering 22 square miles) or which contain towns (like Puri) is the area small.

Size is not the only obstacle. Communications are bad. Even the ubiquitous jeep cannot reach many places and candidates must walk or, at best, use a bicycle. In western Orissa there are mountains and thick jungle; in the coastal plain there are many unbridged streams. A successful candidate in Cuttack district canvassed all the major villages in his constituency. He travelled on foot and on cycle. He arrived in the afternoon in a village; addressed a meeting in the evening; in the morning he talked with those who showed interest and then moved on to the next village. His constituency is not large—about 140 square miles, but the task took six months.

In more developed countries a politician can "put himself across" through the press, radio, and television. There is no television service and there are few radio sets in Orissa. As yet newspapers hardly reach the peasant. I have no figures for newspaper distribution, but one may make an estimate of their impact by looking at literacy figures. For the whole State literacy in Oriya is 15 per cent; the highest rate is found in Cuttack (23 per cent); the lowest is in Koraput (5 per cent).

THE POLITICIAN'S PROBLEM

Literacy is, of course, not a perfect index of the influence of the press. A literate man in a village may share his pleasure by reading aloud to an audience. On the other hand not every literate man reads newspapers; nor are literates evenly spread through the population, for they tend to be concentrated in the few towns. At least this may be safely said: up to now no politician in Orissa has been made or broken by what voters have read about him in the newspapers.

In short, a candidate who decides to treat his electors as a socially undifferentiated mass of rational minds, to be contacted and persuaded of the rightness of his cause, is not being realistic. He must find other means of communication.

THE SIZE OF VOTE-BANKS

The candidate, therefore, has to take his electorate in groups. In a system which employs universal adult franchise it seems obvious that the larger the groups of voters, the better for the candidate who commands their allegiance. But quite small groups can become important through the electoral system and the way it works in Orissa. When many candidates stand and victory is gained on a minority vote, a small number of voters may have decided the issue. This may also happen when the parties are evenly balanced. Finally, when there is a very low poll, a few resolute voters may win an election for the man they support.

In the 1952 election 56 out of 140 seats were won with less than 50 per cent of the votes (less than 25 per cent in a double seat). In the 1957 election 65 seats were won in this way. In 1957 in single-seat Khallikote, the winner polled 25.32 per cent of the valid vote in a field of seven candidates. In the same year in Jharsuguda (double-seat) two men were returned with 16 per cent and 14 per cent, respectively, of the vote in a field of eleven candidates. In Khallikote the 25.32 per cent of the valid vote in fact represented 4,892 votes out of 46,889 electors of whom 19,324 (41 per cent) cast valid votes. In Jharsuguda, with a poll of 31 per cent, the winners received 11,000 and 9,700 votes respectively, in an electorate of 112,262 disposing of 224,525 votes. If, then, a man can be elected on less than 5,000 votes, quite small votebanks become significant.

A small poll has the same effect. A high percentage may in fact be a very small number of votes. In 1952 in Udayagiri-Mohana, a single seat with 48,337 electors, only 4,907 people (10 per cent) cast valid votes. In a straight fight the winner received 58 per cent of the votes, but these represented only 2,851 votes, against his opponent's 2,056. This poll was the lowest for an Assembly constituency in India, and Udayagiri is exceptionally wild and thinly populated. Nevertheless, it is not entirely misleading to point out that only 800 votes—the voters in four or five medium-sized villages—separated the candidates. The Orissa poll for the Assembly in 1952 was 33.7 per cent; in 1957 it was 34.29 per cent against a national average of 46.49 per cent, Orissa having the lowest poll in India.

Given that only 35 per cent of the electors vote, then, even in a straight fight, a successful candidate needs the backing of less than 20 per cent of the electors. Khallikote in 1957 was won on the support of a little over 10 per cent of the electorate. So long as the poll remains at 35 per cent, then the firm support of about 10,000 people will provide victory with 80 per cent of the votes even in a straight fight. Several men, when more than two people have stood, won with the help of 5,000 or even fewer voters. Therefore, units which provide the reliable support of even 1,000 electors—a single large village if everyone there casts a valid vote—are worthy of a candidate's attention.

If this were the whole truth then campaigning for an assembly seat would not be so difficult, and, incidentally, the safeguard against bribery which total adult franchise provides (because no one has the means for large-scale direct bribery) would not operate effectively.

But campaigning is still a baffling problem. The size of the poll is not an independent variable, and the candidate has to allow that his opponent may conduct a vigorous campaign and bring more people to the booths. Secondly, it is not easy to find out who are one's own supporters.[1] Voters by habit are not common in rural Orissa, and it is, therefore, difficult to concentrate upon known supporters and marginal voters. Thirdly, in constituencies where there are many candidates, especially Independents, the situation is immeasurably complicated.

In fact, the apparent simplification offered by the small number of voters required for victory, seldom results in the candidate working out how much support he needs and where he can best get it. Rather they seem to follow a catch-all tactic or seizing upon any and every group and congregation. It does, of course, remain true, whether the candidates realize it or not, that in courting a group which commands as little as 1,000 votes, they are not wasting their time.

CONSTITUENCIES AND ADMINISTRATIVE UNITS

In the absence of efficient means of mass communication, the politicians try to make contact with their electors through existing groups. It is therefore important to know what relation these groups bear to constituencies.

Orissa has 13 districts, divided into 48 subdivisions, and into 306 police stations (1955). Most constituencies consisted of an aggregate of police stations. No constituencies lay across district boundaries. By and large, therefore, the boundaries of

---

[1] Cf. Text 2, p. 30. "Of course we all said we would vote for him. . . ." Identifying supporters and opponents is clearly difficult.

constituencies followed administrative boundaries. What is the relation of these units to social units?

A village is both an administrative and a social unit. The villages, which the Administration recognizes and uses, are also communities with a strong sense of identity and with institutions which regulate internal affairs and allow the village to act as a corporate unit in situations of which the Administration takes no cognizance, or even in opposition to its wishes. But to win over a village, is obviously not the same as winning a constituency.

Every man knows under which police station, subdivision, and district he lives, for, whenever he comes into contact with the Administration—a petition, trouble with the police, business before the courts, and many other things—his name must always be identified by the four administrative units: village, police station, subdivision, and district. Beyond this the people derive some sense of identity and fellow feeling from their common experience under the same administrators —a sense, perhaps, of being all in the same boat. This feeling may be strengthened if the administrative unit coincides with cultural or ecological boundaries. In the eastern Kondmals traditional tribal divisions coincide, very roughly, with the boundary between the police stations of Phulbani and Khejuripara. In Kalahandi district Jaipatna and Kasipur police stations were small kingdoms, feudatories of the Kalahandi Raja.

These examples are exceptions to the general rule that no orthogenetic social framework exists inside administrative divisions. In general administrative units offer the politicians no corresponding social units which would be rallying points and networks of communication for their election campaign. The only such network is the Administration itself, which the candidates cannot, legitimately, use.

The district does command strong loyalties from the middle class, and, even for the peasant, a candidate from another district is a foreigner and, therefore, to be rejected. (Or so it is believed; very few candidates have tried their luck away from home.) But, once again, there is no indigenous mechanism for corporate activity other than that of the Administration itself.

TRADITIONAL GROUPS AND SOCIAL CHANGE

There is—with rare exceptions—no group in the traditional society which regularly corresponds to the modern constituency. But some traditional groups, recruited on principles which have nothing to do with representative democracy, nevertheless influence its working. Candidates may try to capture traditional groups and use them as vote-banks. The traditional group itself may take an active part in representative politics. It may, for example, become a pressure group. Thirdly, the structure of traditional society may become the mould within which representative politics operate at constituency level. Old loyalties and allegiances may continue within the new framework of representative politics.

It is not always easy to make these distinctions on the ground. Nevertheless, they are important as indicators of social change, of the adaptation of traditional society to representative democracy. I take up this problem in the following two chapters in relation to different types of indigenous groups. In the final chapter in this section, I describe the efforts which politicians make to create new groups and new ways of communicating with the electorate, and, once again, ask what is the effect of these innovations upon the traditional society.

4

INDIGENOUS POLITICAL UNITS

In 1952, out of 17 candidates whom I can identify as members of one or another of the Princely families, 13 were elected to the Assembly, most of them with comfortable majorities. In 1957, out of 30 such candidates, 22 were elected; of the eight who failed, five were defeated by another royal candidate. Most of those defeated were subordinate members of the family, and in only one case known to me, in either election, was a former ruler (the Raja of Talcher) defeated by a commoner candidate.

At first sight these successes are a clear case of an indigenous sociopolitical institution being used to win an election. In this chapter I examine one example in order to see just what is being used in such a situation.

KALAHANDI DISTRICT

In the 1952 election in Kalahandi there were four constituencies, three double and one single. Congress won the single constituency, Kasipur, which was reserved for a Scheduled tribe candidate, and it won the double seat of Nawapara. Ganatantra, under the leadership of the Kalahandi Raja, won the other four seats.

For the 1957 election the boundaries were changed and one seat was added, making Kasipur a double constituency. In this election Congress retained Nawapara, and Ganatantra won the six remaining seats.

The old state of Kalahandi included all the present district of Kalahandi, except Nawapara, which was a zemindari within Sambalpur district. All the other ex-zemindars who live in the present Kalahandi district are former feudatories of the Kalahandi Raja. Nawapara (i.e. the zemindar) was not. I was told that relationships between him and the Kalahandi Raja were not good before 1952, but I do not know whether this is true, nor, assuming it is, why they were enemies. Whatever the cause, the Nawapara Raja was induced to offer himself as Congress candidate and won both elections comfortably. I have no first-hand knowledge of Nawapara, but my informants insisted that there was no worthwhile party organization in the constituency. The people supported their Raja, and only through him had Congress won and retained the two Nawapara seats.

Kasipur is a small hill zemindari on the border of Kalahandi and Koraput districts. In the 1952 election it was put together with the neighbouring zemindari of Jaipatna to form a single-member constituency, the seat being reserved for a Scheduled tribe candidate. (Both these estates coincide with police stations of the same names. It was these, of course, and not the zemindaris that were delimited as Kasipur constituency in 1951.) Jaipatna had a population of almost 49,000; Kasipur had 53,000 (1951 Census). Kasipur, I was told, voted Congress, whereas Jaipatna voted Ganatantra. Congress got 11,000 votes; Ganatantra polled 8,000. (See Map 2.)

In the 1957 election the police stations of Koksara and Thuamul Rampur were joined with the original two, and Jaipatna-Kasipur became a double-member constituency. Ganatantra won this election. Since I could not get voting figures for booths, I cannot say for certain how votes were distributed. The combined vote of the two Congress candidates was 21,000. My informants said that Kasipur alone provided these votes. The man returned in the Ganatantra interest for the general seat (the Jaipatna zemindar) said that he received about 1,000 votes from Kasipur and the rest from the other three areas.

The change of boundaries accounts for the Ganatantra victory in 1957. The core of Congress voters, a majority in 1952, were submerged in the larger double-member constituency of 1957. Victory was not due to any change in the relative efficiency of constituency parties. The voters chose Congress or Ganatantra not, for the most part, because they were loyal to either of those parties, but for other reasons.

Congress support in Kasipur, like the support of both parties elsewhere in Kalahandi, rested upon loyalty towards the ex-ruler. The Kasipur ruler chose Congress and his people followed him. Moreover he chose Congress not—so everyone believed—because he was attracted by their policy, nor because they could offer him the inducement of office (the 1952 seat being reserved for a Scheduled tribe candidate), but because he had a longstanding feud with his lord, the Raja of Kalahandi, a leading figure in the Ganatantra party.

Here the skeleton of feudal relations is clearly visible. Originally Kalahandi possessed one feudatory, Thuamul Rampur. Many years ago the Raja of Jeypore (now in Koraput district) was attacked by the Raja of Bastar. Kalahandi, in response to an appeal, despatched a force under Thuamul Rampur to help Jeypore. Bastar was defeated, and, for a reward, Kalahandi received from Jeypore the territories of Kasipur and Jaipatna, which he handed over to Thuamul Rampur. The latter had three sons: one stayed in Thuamul Rampur, one became Kasipur, and the third Jaipatna.

Kasipur, in the generation of the present Kalahandi's father, married a daughter of the Jeypore zemindar and received a part of the Jeypore estate as his dowry. Some quarrel, the

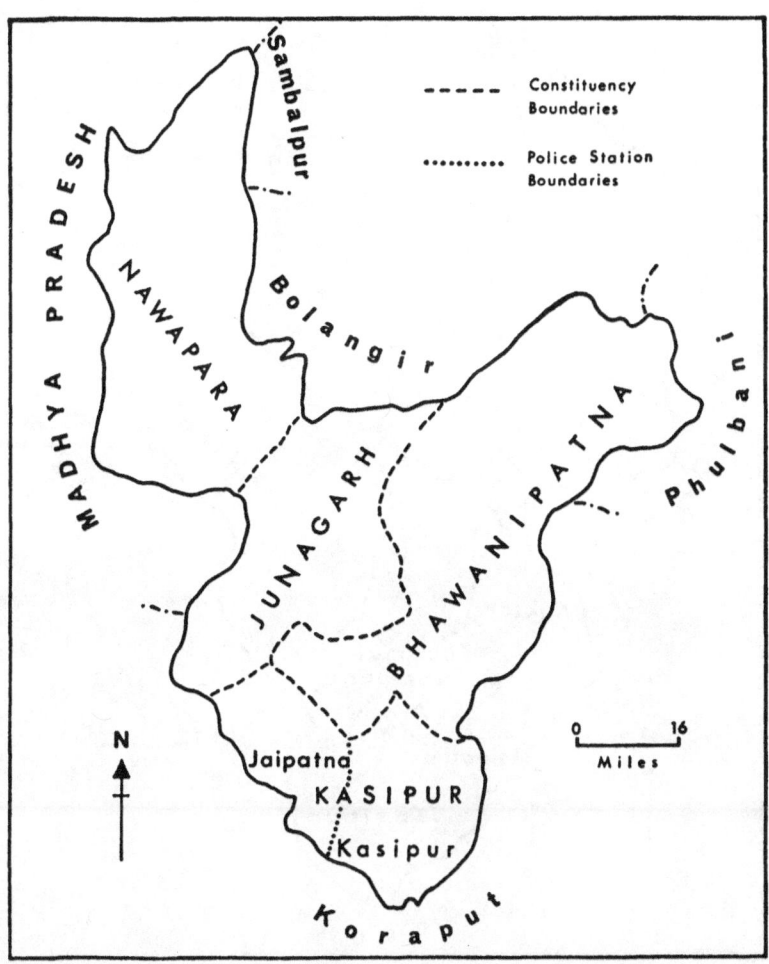

MAP 2. KALAHANDI DISTRICT. ASSEMBLY CONSTITUENCIES, 1952

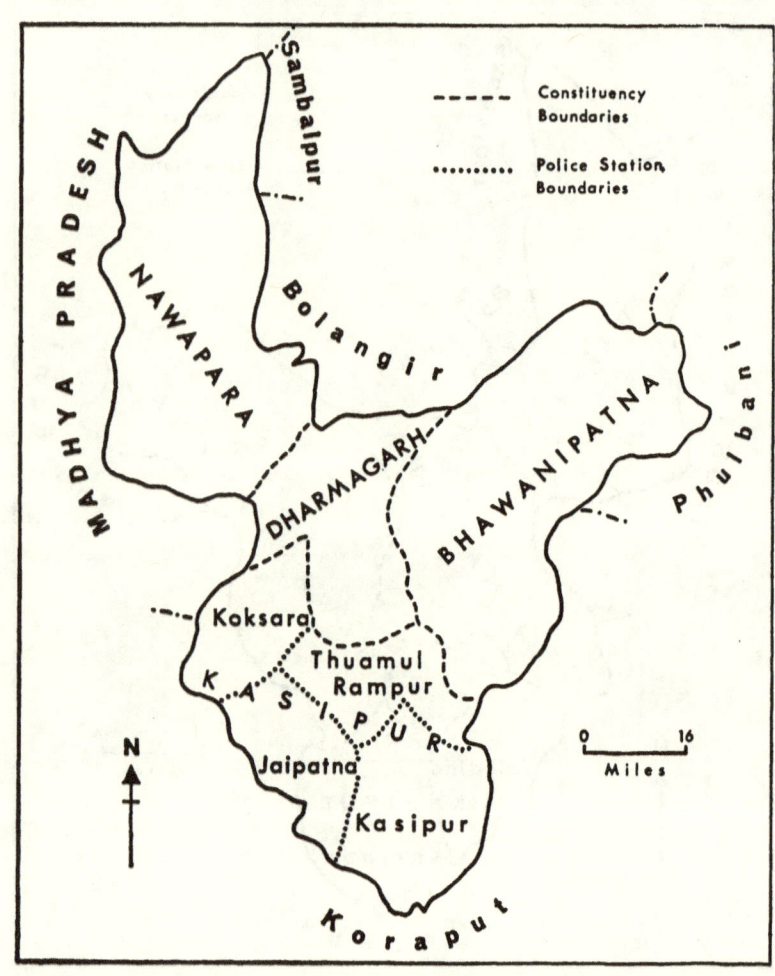

MAP 3. KALAHANDI DISTRICT. ASSEMBLY CONSTITUENCIES, 1957

cause of which I do not know, blew up between Kasipur and his lord at Kalahandi. Kasipur thereupon declared himself a vassal not of Kalahandi, but of Jeypore, citing both the origin of his estate and the land that came in his wife's dowry. At this Kalahandi caused Kasipur to be declared unfit to rule and had his estate put under a Court of Wards, which meant in effect that Kasipur was governed by officials in the service of Kalahandi. These officials, so it is said, were heavy-handed, and drove the people of Kasipur, already indignant at their zemindar's downfall, to stand even more solidly behind him. Kasipur eventually was restored, but the bad feeling persisted, and when party conflicts gave the Kasipur Raja a chance to restate his dislike of the Kalahandi royal house, he took it; and his people backed him.

In the 1957 election the zemindars of Jaipatna and Kasipur were rival candidates for the general seat, standing, respectively, for Ganatantra and Congress. Jaipatna told me a story which neatly, if comically, underlines the way in which the past appears to live on in present politics. For many years his house and Kasipur's, although both vassals of Kalahandi, had been enemies and used to raid into one another's territories. This went on until the British pacified the area early in the nineteenth century. In the 1957 campaign Jaipatna took it into his head to go across the hills to Kasipur and hold a public meeting under the walls of his rival's palace. It so happened that Kasipur had the same idea for the same day. One went round by road to Jaipatna; the other crossed the hills to Kasipur; and neither knew where his opponent was until he arrived. Both, Jaipatna said, without a second thought abandoned the meeting and hastened home—no doubt with an atavistic dread of finding their lands ravaged and their strongholds given over to fire and the sword!

There are other examples of an older structure seeming to provide not only the framework but in a large part the content of modern political activity. Both elections in Jeypore, for example, have been decided largely on a dynastic quarrel within the zemindari family. Congress has the backing of one line; the other line, evidently the one which commanded popular support, backed the Ganatantra candidates, and on both occasions Ganatantra won.

SENTIMENT AND ADMINISTRATION

The larger Feudatory States had two levels of administration: a professional bureaucracy and a system of minor hereditary officials who controlled territories rather than offices. These chiefs were found throughout the western hills and were variously called Gaontias, Nayaks, Bisois, Dolobeheras, and so forth. Their precise status varied in different areas, but this variation is not significant here.

The higher officials, the bureaucrats proper, vanished in 1948. Some retired; others found different occupations; some were taken into the Orissa Administrative Service or the Indian Administrative Service. These were transferred from the areas where they had served before 1948, and their place was taken by officials transferred from coastal districts.

The Congress planned to remove hereditary officials and put in their place a system of local self-government through elected panchayats. But the influence of these local chiefs waned much more slowly than that of their superiors. Firstly, the change was slow, and the introduction of panchayats has gone forward only with difficulty. In many areas hereditary officials are still used by the Administration to collect tax and as agents of law and order. Secondly, they are natives of the areas which they governed and could not, like their alien superiors, be transferred elsewhere. Thirdly, many of them have an influence which did not rest solely on their official appointment; they were relatively wealthy, had strong personalities, and possessed the habit of command.

Congress politicians complained that these were the men who won elections for the Ganatantra. The Kalahandi Raja was said to know the name of every chief in his own district and many outside. These men did support the Ganatantra since they, like their Rajas, were being dispossessed of their power by the Congress. But I do not think that they did anything more, as a class, than lend their influence to candidates supported by the royal houses. It did not seem that the old structure was at hand, ready to be mobilized as an electoral machine, but rather that chiefs stood alongside other men of influence—schoolmasters, caste leaders, and so forth—who commanded small vote-banks.

It was, in short, a matter of sentiment rather than administration. The former ruler did not have the sanctions which he once possessed to galvanize these men into action. His support rested on their affection for him and their nostalgia for the days when their influence was supported, rather than undermined, by the ruling power. In other words, what survived out of the older structure was not a complete network of command, but rather a number of small groups which acted as vote-banks. The network of administrative and judicial relationships which once linked them lingered on only as a sentiment of affection for the former ruler and the society which he symbolized.

CHANGE AND CONTINUITY

What is the place of these indigenous political groups in representative politics? Are they pressure groups? Are they passive and unthinking vote-banks at the command of a politician qualified to use them? Is the old society here surviving unchanged in the modern democracy?

None of the indigenous groups, considered in this chapter, are pressure groups. They operate only at election times. What binds them together is not an immediate mutual interest which they wish to promote, but only the sentiment of past allegiances. Admittedly the line is difficult to draw, and they could have aims which would make them a pressure group. They might, for example, want to restore the Rajas. But no such end is made explicit for them. By and large the members of such groups are politically ignorant and apathetic; they vote on the instructions of their leaders.

Vote-banks of this kind will disappear quite rapidly as a new generation grows up, unless they are consolidated and fortified by other means. The old structure has gone and it no longer regulates power relations. Only sentiment remains. These groups can only survive if their members are bound together again not by sentiment alone but by ties which are seen to serve some practical end. At the moment people give their vote to their ex-rulers, partly because, as I so often heard, "a vote is a small thing," partly because their lives have been made difficult by a change of regime, and partly from a habit of allegiance. But they do not give more than their vote, unless stimulated by new goals and taught that they can achieve these goals in the new democracy by acting as a group.

Some candidates, whose hold upon the electorate is strongly out of the past, nevertheless build an organization to strengthen the corporate feeling of the group and their hold upon it. Jaipatna provides a clear example. The zemindar, since his election as an MLA in 1957, has played a leading part in four agitations. The least spectacular of these has been a campaign to improve the road which connects Jaipatna village with the world outside. He has worked mostly by parliamentary means, by asking questions in the House, inviting Ministers to drive down and visit him, thus giving them first-hand experience of the cavernous potholes, and so forth.

The other three agitations were concerned with the sale to non-Oriyas of licences to exploit jungle produce and the very small benefits which local people are able to derive from this trade; the allocation of contracts in development work to outsiders instead of to local persons or local panchayats; and State aid for a high school which had been constructed and maintained out of local resources. All these agitations, except the road, had been fairly successful and they were conducted (in addition to parliamentary means) in the manner perfected by the Congress during the Freedom Fight: fasts and hunger strikes, prayer meetings, processions, telegrams to prominent persons, and some violence.

The significance of this is not in the success or failure of the agitations, but in the fact that old ties, which had been reduced to mere sentiment, were now reactivated in the new form of democratic action. From conversations with this zemindar I have the impression that he saw himself still as the leader of his people, helping them in a fight against the world outside. And perhaps they saw him in the same light. But, however they looked upon the situation, in fact this group was in the process of making what seemed to be a successful transition into a new structure. When the generation which has a sentimental attachment to this zemindar and the institutions which gave him power has died out, the group may still continue in active existence.

Is this change or continuity? I think it is change. The boundaries of the new group may continue to be the same as those of the old. More probably, they will expand to take in the whole of the constituency, perhaps even bridging the old cleavage between Jaipatna and Kasipur. But even if the boundaries remained the same, the structure of relationships within the group will have changed. Indeed, they are changed already, for the men who worked in the agitations with the Jaipatna zemindar were not for the most part his old feudal subordinates, but new men. The zemindar himself, when he leads these agitations, is no longer a zemindar; he has become a politician.

5

CASTES AND CASTE ASSOCIATIONS

To what extent do politicians make use of castes and caste associations in order to win an election? Does this result in social change?

Castes

An outline of the rural caste system is necessary for readers not familiar with Indian society. I take as an example the village of Bisipara (Bailey, 1957 and 1960), which contains twenty-two caste groups, varying in size from one person to over 150. Two principles unite these groups into a system: segregation and hierarchy.

Segregation is achieved in several ways. Each caste (*jati*) has its own name—Washerman, Herdsman, Warrior, and so forth. There are differences of occupation. Brahmins are priests; Washermen wash clothes; the Barber cuts hair; untouchables are scavengers and music makers. But this mark of identity is not uniform throughout the system. Many occupations are not caste-defined. Anyone, for example, may be a schoolmaster or a lorry driver. Most castes may cultivate the land. A third form of segregation, also partial, is residence.

Bisipara has a Warrior Street, a Pan Street, a Distiller Street, and a Potter Street, but men of other than the eponymous caste may live in the street, except in the case of untouchables. Fourthly, there is a variety of diacritical customs. Some castes are vegetarian, some eat meat; some eat chickens, others will not; some drink milk, others refuse it. Castes have their own patron deities. Some festivals are common to everyone in the village, but transition rites (at death, birth, puberty, and so forth) vary in details from one caste to another.

These four fields of activity—names, occupation, residence, and customary distinctions—are an everyday reminder of difference, but they are not the fundamental source of segregation; this is kinship. A man is born into a caste. He may contract a valid marriage only with a woman of the same caste. All his relatives by descent and by affinity belong to the same caste as himself, and he has no kinsmen beyond that group. A caste is a group of actual or potential kinsmen.

A man has a place in two systems: he belongs to his own caste, which is a kinship system, extending to other villages besides his own; secondly, he has relationships with people of other castes, mainly (in the present context) in his own village, and these cannot be ties of kinship. I now describe these "vertical" relationships.

The castes stand in a ritual and secular hierarchy, expressed in rules of interaction. One may take certain forms of cooked food only from members of the same caste or of a higher caste. To accept food, and in certain castes water, from a man of lower caste, is to be polluted. In some situations, and between untouchable and clean castes, mere touch pollutes. The hierarchy is also symbolized by various attributes. Some customs degrade. For example, only lower castes permit widow remarriage. Occupations are graded, and, by and large, those which are considered more polluting rank low: the untouchable who flays dead cattle and eats the carcase is very low; the Washerman who handles clothes soiled by bodily emissions is also low. On the other hand cattle herding or cultivation are not polluting (except in a few cases), and those who have these *as their traditional occupations* are of higher ritual status.

There is a partially separate secular hierarchy. The Bisipara Brahmins, who stand at the top of the ritual hierarchy, never had much political power, and the village was ruled by the Warriors, who stand second (speaking roughly) in the ritual hierarchy. Nevertheless, except at the top and the bottom of the ritual scale, the places of the Brahmin and the untouchable respectively, ritual rank tends to match political and economic power. It is important to remember this, since social mobility and the ritual signs in which rank is expressed, are main interests of the caste associations to be considered in a following section.

Finally, in most villages one caste dominates. In Bisipara it was once the Warrior caste. They owned the land; they ran the village. They do not do so now, and, as the attitudes revealed in Chapter 1 show, this loss of power affects their vote.

The "horizontal" organization is a means of regulating kinship links which pass between individuals in one village and another. In some cases these links are of unilineal descent, but this category is very much smaller than the category of "in-law" and "mother's brother."

For a time I kept a record of visitors from other villages to selected households in Bisipara. Relatives from other villages were in almost all cases from the families of women born in Bisipara and married elsewhere, or born elsewhere and married into Bisipara: the sisters (and descendents of these sisters) of ego's father and sometimes grandfather, his own sisters, and his daughters, on the one side; on the other side the families from the natal home of his daughters-in-law, his wife, the families of his mother's brother, and sometimes his father's mother's brother.

Such people form a man's kindred, that is, an ego-centred category of kinsmen. No two persons have exactly the same set of relatives. Given that a caste group in a village usually consists of one or two main descent groups and that no new marriage can be contracted with families linked within five generations in the maternal line, most of the families listed in the preceding paragraph came from different villages. Depending on the size of the sibling group of themselves, their fathers and grandfathers, and the number of their own married sons and daughters, nephews and nieces, Bisipara Warriors may list cognatic kinsmen in anything from three to thirty or more villages. And a chart of cognatic relationships for all the adult Warriors in Bisipara would link them to every other village where there is a Warrior caste group within a radius of about thirty miles.

Marriages give rise to disputes, not merely between the spouses but also between their descent groups. Within each caste, councils settle or try to settle these disputes. These are often *ad hoc* assemblies meeting to settle a particular case. But some castes have formal policy-making bodies which meet not only as courts but also as "legislatures," laying down, for example, the amount of bridewealth that should be paid, restricting dowries, prescribing conditions for divorce, and so forth.

These bodies also regulate relationships between their own group and other castes. They are particularly concerned with behaviour that may lower prestige. They punish illicit liaisons with persons of lower caste; they penalize anyone who takes up an occupation associated with a lower caste; and so on.

In Bisipara, Warriors, Herdsmen, and Distillers have caste legislatures of this kind, and one caste of untouchables has recently followed suit. Other castes settle their disputes through *ad hoc* councils, but have no general assembly. The assemblies of the three castes mentioned meet at long intervals—usually between two and four years. They elect officials, and recently they have begun to keep a record of proceedings, and accounts of the small sums of money of which they dispose.

How far is this type of organization typical of the rest of Orissa?

The two organizing principles of segregation and hierarchy and a body of customs through which they are maintained are found everywhere. All but a very small part of the small intelligentsia observe the rules of caste endogamy. For everyone caste fellows are kinsmen, actual or potential, and there are no kin links across caste boundaries.

I am less confident about the universality of caste legislatures. Only three of the castes represented in Bisipara had such assemblies. There are no figures for other parts of Orissa, and, as will become clear later, it is difficult nowadays to distinguish them from caste associations.

I also have no systematic information about the size of castes. But there are good grounds for assuming that castes (in their present definition of endogamous groups) must always have been small (Marriott, 1955:190). Among the peasants, cognatic kinsmen for the most part live within a day's walk—roughly fifteen miles at the most. Beyond that distance it becomes difficult to observe the obligations of kinship and men do not like to send their daughters far away, nor do women like to lose touch with their brothers. Secondly, as Marriott observes, it is difficult to imagine the elaborate system of avoidance and pollution working except between people who know one another and who know one another's background. Caste is not based on any visible criterion of difference. It is not like a colour bar and one can only avoid an untouchable, if one already knows that he is an untouchable. The same fact appears when one hears a Bisipara man discussing marriage prospects for his son or daughter. There is always an informed person within reach who can vouch for or deny the respectability of the family of the proposed bride or groom. The world of the traditional caste can only be a small world.

Rural Castes and Politics

Being a small world it is of less advantage to a politician trying to build up a following; conversely, it is—or would be, if it cared to do so—less able to put pressure on politicians. An appeal through the assembly of even the largest caste will reach only a small part of the total electorate in most Orissa constituencies. The caste may lie across constituency boundaries. Even when it is contained within a constituency, it is unlikely to cover the whole area.

However, since quite small congregations may matter in an election, one may ask whether politicians can capture the votes of a caste through its assembly and officials.

There are many difficulties. By no means all castes have such assemblies. Secondly, caste assemblies have a narrow range of interest. They meet to punish misbehaviour in the fields of kinship and ritual propriety. What appeal, then, can the politician make to them, or what can they ask from him? Thirdly, to be identified with one caste may forfeit the support of others; and, in the same way, factions within the caste itself may make it impossible to capture the whole organization. Fourthly, caste leadership rests on persuasion rather than authority, and leaders have no ready sanctions, except in the contexts specified by tradition. Fifthly, castes are not easily mobilized. The assembly meets at long intervals. The members are dispersed through different villages. Finally, to make a systematic appeal to the electors through caste or community prejudices is illegal; and if a successful candidate is convicted on such charges, then the election may be declared void, the offending candidate barred, and the ballot held a second time.

This happened in Berhampur constituency in 1952. The election of two Independent candidates was declared void on the grounds that the Scheduled caste candidate was under age, and that he had used undue influence and coercion over the members of his own caste, the Bauri. I have no first-hand knowledge of this case and had no means of discovering what proportion the Bauri form of the total electorate. It is not likely that they were more than one fifth. Evidence was given, purporting to show that the Bauris of this area were convinced supporters of the Congress. But, shortly before the election the Independent candidate was elected leader (*Behera*) of the local Bauris. Later, it was alleged, Bauris were taken to a temple and made to swear an oath that they would vote for the candidate, on pain of ostracism. It was also alleged that the "religious heads" of some other untouchable castes did the same on behalf of this candidate.

The traditional caste is not an effective means of getting votes, nor can it function as a pressure group. To be effective such a group has to change its aims and change its form; it has, in fact, to become a caste association. The importance of the traditional caste is that it can become a building block for a larger edifice, the caste association, and these larger structures can still use the automatic and unreflecting loyalty which the smaller groups command.

CASTE ASSOCIATIONS

For more than fifty years there has been visible in different parts of India the beginnings of a process which seems likely to change the caste system. The smaller units (*jati*) which I discussed above, are being amalgamated into larger groups which, although commonly called "castes," seem to me to be arranged in a system which is not in the least like the traditional caste system. There is, as yet, very little systematic information about these new units—caste associations. I do not know how many caste associations exist in Orissa, how large they are, nor how important a part they play in the lives of their members. But there is enough information to demonstrate that these units have emerged in response to political and economic changes in the larger society, and perhaps to suggest that these new groups are the harbinger of a much wider form of social stratification, in place of caste.

Members of the same caste (*jati*) are actual or potential kinsmen. The *jati*, therefore, is a group, membership being defined by actual or potential interaction. The members also have common attributes: the same caste name; the same traditional occupation; often a collection of myths relating their place and circumstances of origin and giving them a role in the general myth of Hinduism; the same patron deities; a way of conducting rites and ceremonies that partially distinguishes them from other castes; and, in a rather nebulous fashion, a "reputation" (for hard work, idleness, dishonesty, cunning, stupidity, bravery, and so forth). Most of these attributes are shared with a limited number of other castes (defined on the criterion of interaction). For example, the Sundi (Distiller) caste, in the sense of *jati*, is bounded, so far as the Bisipara Distillers are concerned, roughly within Phulbani district and the northern parts of Ganjam district. But there are Distillers elsewhere—in Orissa, in Bengal, and in other parts of India. These people, too, are called Sundis, and they have a common traditional occupation—the manufacture and sale of liquor. Within the area of the Bisipara Herdsmen (Gauro) there are other Herdsmen, also with the same traditional occupation, but not intermarrying with the Bisipara Herdsmen and bearing a different name.

Those castes (*jati*) which tend to unite into one caste association have, in a rough and ready sense, approximately the same position in the hierarchy of caste. This, emphatically, does not mean that everywhere throughout India or throughout Orissa, each with their innumerable local systems of caste interaction, any caste can be immediately given a place in the hierarchy, once its name is known. There are many examples where this is not the case. In Bisipara the Washermen are ranked among the clean castes, but in neighbouring Boad, in the same district, they are considered untouchables. Nevertheless I would argue that over the kind of area in which a caste association is formed, those who think themselves eligible to join this association, by virtue usually of a common name, will be found to occupy a more or less similar position in the traditional scales of prestige. Indeed, as will appear later, the aims and purposes of these associations seem to rest on the assumption of a fairly common rank and prestige experience in local caste systems. Over wide areas and in some cases over the whole of India there is a rough agreement about the prestige attached to certain occupations and certain objects.

These, then, are the bases on which caste associations are formed. Those castes (*jati*) which form a category by virtue of a common name, a common traditional occupation, and a roughly common status position in their respective caste systems, tend to transform themselves from a category with common attributes into a group defined by interaction.

The transformation is achieved by a series of federations until one association covers the whole area. Usually this is the linguistic area or the State, as in the example of the All-Orissa Oilmen-Vaisyas;[1] but it may extend, nominally at least, to the whole of India, as in the case of some untouchable organizations.

To judge from the example of the Orissa Oilmen, these associations have two main interests. One is to extend their membership as widely as possible. There are frequent resolutions that contact should be made with other Oilmen, not as yet in the association, with a view to establishing ties of marriage and bringing them into the association. The second aim is to establish uniformity of custom throughout the caste, and in particular to do away with customs which lower the caste's prestige, and to encourage customs which add to its prestige. This aim is also pursued in a secular fashion by en-

---

[1] N. K. Bose, N. Patnaik, and A. K. Ray.

couraging education and providing scholarships for children of their own caste. The second aim, in short, is to raise their status.

These new wide caste associations are not simply the old caste assemblies much enlarged. The two are genetically connected, and, most importantly, the sentiment of kinship which pervades the smaller unit is also found in the larger unit. But there are important differences. In the older organization the leader is a *"Pradhan"* or *"Behera."* In the newer he will be a "President" and will be assisted by a secretary and a treasurer and work through a committee. These structural differences indicate a difference in scale between the two types of organization, in the social milieu in which they work, and in their intentions.

This difference is made clear if one examines what the two types of organization consider "proper" ritual behaviour. The older and smaller organizations enforce an accepted standard of behaviour. The caste associations want to bring in new standards. (This is something of an ideal distinction. Even the "primitive" assemblies of, for example, the Warriors in the Bisipara area, interest themselves in new standards of behaviour.) The older type of caste accepts the *status quo*, including its own position in the prestige hierarchy, and enforces behaviour which other castes would acknowledge as appropriate. The caste associations do not accept the *status quo* but claim equality with the highest. The new system provides an arena in which caste associations compete with one another for precedence, whereas in the old system castes by and large accept their position in the hierarchy.

The differences can also be expressed in terms of the total society. In the older system society was divided vertically—that is, competition lay between territorial units. In the new system appears the beginning of a system of social stratification proper; competition is between horizontal and not territorial segments of the society. Once again, these are ideal distinctions, and in fact the new horizontal development is, in Orissa at least, relatively slight.

The change in caste is to be associated with improved communications and the centralizing over larger areas of political and administrative power. The older type of caste belongs, if one may put it that way, to a small-scale, nonbureaucratic, political organization—the system operated within a kingdom or chiefdom, where rule was personal and relations more or less face-to-face. Kinship and caste relationships came to an end at political boundaries, and these boundaries were culturally marked by differences in custom between two castes which bore the same name. There is an excellent analysis of this system in eighteenth century Malabar by Miller (1954), one which is almost the ideal type of what I mean by the "older system." These same cultural boundaries are visible even to the casual traveller to-day in Orissa. To cross the traditional border from Kalahandi to Koraput reveals a different world: the saris are of different weave, they are worn differently, loads are carried differently, the dialect changes, the women are tattooed differently, and so forth.

These diacritical differences between castes (*jati*) with the same name and the same function, differences which the old political divisions enforced, are just the differences which the new caste associations seek to remove. They can do so only because the older political divisions are no longer significant; they no longer mark off from one another competing political groups. Competition now takes place in a larger arena, and those groups which are best able to compete are numerically large. In such a competition the Warriors of the Kondmals do not count; neither do the Distillers or the Oilmen of the Kondmals. But the two latter, if and when they become part of an effective Orissa-wide association of Oilmen or of Distillers, will count; so too could the Warriors if they were to link themselves with the large Chasa and Khandayat cultivating castes of the Orissa plains.

It seems a paradox that groups which, if my argument is running correctly, seem destined to play a part in the wholly secular arena of democratic politics, should be so concerned with the symbols of ritual purity and respectability. The reason may be that these are all-India symbols of respectability (Bailey, 1960:190). It may also be that only the leaders of the new associations, and not all of them, truly appreciate in what arena they are competing, whereas the rank and file still "think little" and see ritual symbols as an end in themselves. Perhaps the new associations can only gain a following through their parade of ritual symbols.

The genesis of the new associations remains obscure in the absence of case materials. N. K. Bose (personal communication) has suggested that in Calcutta the lead came from men of humble caste who had risen into the professions and there found themselves socially handicapped by their origins.[2] Unable to throw off kinship links with their fellows, as they might have done in a society where kinship was of narrow range, they formed caste associations with the object of raising their collective status.

Caste Associations and Politics

I found no evidence that in Orissa caste associations are systematically used by candidates in promoting an election campaign. Nor, in the reports of Election Tribunals, did any candidate, either in 1952 or 1957, appear to have used such an association. One MLA, I was told, made a donation to a caste association (not his own) which held a congress in his constituency, but MLAs make donations to any congregation that meets in their constituency. The Oilmen, at their conference in Puri in 1959, are said to have censured an Oilman politician who held cabinet rank, because he did not do enough for his caste fellows.

[2] A similar point is made by Ghurye (1950, p. 194).

As in the case of the caste assemblies (*jati*), discussed earlier, caste associations are not sufficiently well organized to be of predominating interest to the politician. Nor are they ubiquitous. Also, especially when an association is large (as in the case of the Oilmen) it is likely to split along party lines, a progressive section emphasizing secular sources of prestige like education and jobs in the services, and a conservative section more concerned with ritual respectability. The former associate with left wing parties, the latter with Congress. The association then becomes not a block vote at the behest of a politician who can win it, but yet another arena where he has to compete with rival politicians.

There is as yet no caste association in Orissa so well organized as the Nair Service Society in Kerala or the wealthy caste associations of Gujarat. Such associations as exist are poor and indifferently organized. They cannot cut decisively across cleavages of territory, or, for that matter, across the newer cleavages of party. Neither of the two castes dominant in the coastal plains, the Karans and the Brahmins, have associations of this kind, so far as I know, and the associations which exist are of castes which have not yet tasted power in the new arena of democratic politics. The significance, however, of the caste associations is that, if we may judge from what has happened in some other States, the associations may be the means by which hitherto submerged sections of the population become politically articulate. Caste in the form of associations, but not of the older *jati*, may become, for a time, a main organizing factor and a main cleavage in the new political system.

CONCLUSION

So far as the constituencies are concerned, caste is not usually a dominating influence in the relationship of the politician and the voter. There are signs that inasmuch as what are now reference categories become groups—that is to say, they become caste associations—then caste may become of greater importance in the electoral contest.

The politician is seeking to find some form of organization that will transcend small territorial groups and ease the problem of communicating with his voters. One solution to this problem is the party. But this is difficult, because the ordinary voter has an extremely narrow range of public responsibility and is not willing to give time and effort without the promise of immediate material reward. Parties have no moral appeal. The importance of caste is that this alone has the possibility of providing the politician with a ready-made *moral* element on which he can draw to form associations, without the members of those associations calculating at every step what they are going to get out of it.

6

MOVEMENTS AND MACHINES

The politician's problem is to get in touch with his electorate. He cannot, as I have explained, reach them as an undifferentiated mass and must try to work through groups. But the groups into which they are already organized are small, parochial, and elusive. He therefore seeks to create new groups, one of which is the political party.

PARTIES AND THEIR TASKS

Broadly speaking there are two kinds of political party.[1]

Parties of the "python" type attempt to swallow the entire lives of their members. Such a party runs its own newspapers, its own schools and centres of adult education and indoctrination, its own recreational and welfare organizations, regulates working time through the control of trade unions and, in short, attempts to provide its members with a complete way of life. The intention, of course, is one-party government, and such parties are more formally called "parties of integration." Com-

---

[1] See S. M. Lipset, 1960, p. 86.

munist parties are examples; the pre-1947 Indian Congress tended towards this model.

Parties of "representation" (or "horse-trading") interest themselves much more exclusively with politics, and seem to lie relatively dormant between elections, at least so far as concerns the general public. The parties in Orissa, with the partial exception of the Communists, are all of this kind, whatever their aspirations, for they do not have the resources to be anything else.

The distinction is, of course, a theoretical one, and python elements are to be found especially in the Congress and the Communist parties in Orissa. Nevertheless our discussion in the main concerns what may be called "democratic" parties rather than python parties.

A party of the former kind has two main tasks: one is education; the other is adjustment of interests. The parties help to keep the electorate aware of what the Government is doing, and of what alternative policies exist. They educate the voter about his rights, about the method of casting his ballot, about when and where he should vote, and about what is likely to be the result of voting one way or the other, and so forth.

In the older democracies the task of presenting the party's "image," of saying what it stands for, is largely done through mass communications and through the prominent personalities who lead the party. This is no easy task in Orissa because the kind of issues for which parties stand as yet mean nothing to the peasant voter, and even if they did, there is still the physical barrier of poor communications.

The second task of a party is to adjust interests. Various disparate interests, through the skill of party managers, find a common platform in the party's policy. This is not only a question of finding a common denominator in a varied pattern of interests, but also of identifying similar interests and reducing their number by uniting them. In older democracies this task is not done by the parties alone. For example, the workers in different factories or in different industries are associated in a trade union: the party, in adjusting interests, then deals with the unions, and not with the numerous factories. One reason for the parties' difficulties in Orissa, in so far as they attempt to perform this task, is that the middle belt of associational activity is largely missing. The parties are then faced with the impossible task of handling thousands of small units, and so meet, once again, the problem of communications.

In the districts a party has a small body of paid officials who advise and sometimes direct a corps of voluntary workers, who are, relative to the total population, not numerous. These people persuade the voters that theirs is the best party, and they may try to adjust interests at a minor level, but these are secondary activities. Their main function is that of intelligence, of finding out who are their supporters, of alerting them, and of seeing that they turn out on election day.

There are two models for ground organizations of this kind, the distinction resting on the means of persuading voters and recruiting workers. One model is that of the "machine," in which workers and sometimes voters expect some tangible reward, not necessarily a bribe, but assistance of exactly the kind which brokers provide (see Chapter 1). In the other model, the "movement," this element of calculation is absent and the voluntary workers give their services because they are in the habit of doing so, and in the last resort because they are morally (that is, without calculation of immediate personal material gain) convinced of the rightness of their party's policies.

In this chapter I shall describe the "movement" and the "machine" elements in constituency parties.

THE PARTIES IN ORISSA

All five parties in Orissa—Congress, Ganatantra, Praja Socialist, Communist, and Jharkhand—have, broadly speaking, the same form of organization. Ordinary members, who pay a low subscription and may vote for officials, are distinguished from active members, who pay a larger subscription and who alone may stand for office.

The party framework is a hierarchy of elected committees: at the top is a State Committee, from which is drawn an Executive Committee. Below this are District Committees, one for each of the Administrative districts, and these too have Executive Committees. Below these are Committees for each constituency, and, often in theory only, committees for each polling booth and each village. In the upper parts of the hierarchy full-time party workers guide and assist the work of the committees.

Beside this local framework, and consisting largely of the same people, is a bureaucratic organization. All parties work on different "fronts"—labour, student, women, *kisan* (peasant)—and all active members must specialize in one or another front. At the top, coördinating the work of the local organizations, the specialist organizations and the party in the Assembly, is the Head Office.

In fact this is a poor description of the reality. In 1959 no party had an organization throughout the State. The Jharkhand was confined to the northern hill districts adjoining Bihar. Ganatantra support was limited to the western hills. The two left-wing parties were well-organized on the coastal plain, but not represented in the hills except partially in the districts of Mayurbhanj, Koraput, and Sambalpur. Congress had the widest organization, but even that was poorly organized in the western hills, hardly at all, for example, in Kalahandi and Bolangir. Where parties were poorly represented, at best they might count on finding an *ad hoc* district body to fight an election; even where they were well-organized, many constituency committees might be *ad hoc*, raised only to fight the election and disbanding afterwards.

The largest party in Orissa is certainly the Congress. Out of a universe of some seven million voters, *active* workers in Congress—those eligible for office—in 1959 numbered 1,381. I would be surprised if other parties put together could have matched this number of active workers.

The parties, in short, have not been able to find workers in their rivals' territory. What difficulties stand in the way of party organization?

One immediate obstacle is poverty. Volunteers who work without payment are more readily found in a prosperous country. A low margin of economic security, chronic undernourishment, and universal underemployment are not the best conditions for vigorous party activity. Moreover parties which rely on rank-and-file subscriptions cannot afford competent salaried organizers.

Secondly, the peasant sense of moral obligation does not go beyond family, village, and caste. If peasants work beyond those limits they expect to be paid, and they look with suspicion on those who do such voluntary work, and believe they are in fact being paid.

The party's other task—that of identifying local interests, combining them and so reducing them to manageable numbers—is equally difficult, for the same reason: parochialism. Here and there parties managed to capitalize on peasant hostility towards landlords or the Administration. But these successes always proved temporary: no unified and self-conscious peasant class emerged. Once the immediate crisis was over and the heat of the agitation had died away, the peasants again divided into countless small groups of families, castes, and villages.

MOVEMENTS AND MACHINES
141

In short, the creation of widespread groups, held together by a sense of moral [2] dedication to a common purpose, is a task quite beyond the resources of the politicians and sometimes beyond their imagination. Moreover, their attempt to create such groups is often not wholehearted, since they have found an easier way of muddling through elections; they have learned to operate electoral machines.

THE ELECTORAL MACHINES

A machine is fuelled, so to speak, not by moral fervour, but by calculations of profit and advantage. This distinction is an ideal one, and any group of people working to win an election will certainly show both the moral element and an element of calculation in their activities.

The distinction is not merely one of motives. The type of relationships found in a group largely unified by moral feelings (a "movement") differs from a network mainly based on calculation. There are different limits of possible action in the two cases, and a difference in the nature of their probable future development.

There are also more immediate differences. The movement is open about its aims and intentions and is not secretive or apologetic about its methods. The machine, on the other hand, resents publicity. For the movement there are handbooks and reports explaining not only its intentions, but also its framework of organization. None of this is made clear for the machine. One reason for this—and a factor which makes research doubly difficult—is that there is no standard pattern for a machine. It is, so to speak, craftsman-made to suit local

---

[2] I cannot emphasize too strongly that *nowhere* in this book does the word "moral" imply my judgment of rightness or wrongness. It is used for actions done without calculation of profit and advantage.

demands and conditions. Its strength lies in the maximum adjustment which it makes to the existing local structure of society and to the demands of individuals. A movement is the opposite of this: it is mass-produced (to continue the metaphor), and it seeks to make existing social facts fit into it, rather than adapt itself to them. It has to do so because it cannot afford to temporize over its ultimate aims, which have the status of moral imperatives, and allow these to be watered down because they do not fit the demands of the existing society. The machine recruits its workers by giving them what they want. The movement teaches its workers what they should want.

The fundamental task of a machine is communication. It puts the candidate in touch with his voters. This is not, of course, mass contact; it is a means of establishing ties between the candidate and specific groups or networks within his constituency.

Votes are the ultimate profit which the politician expects to get out of the relationship. But this is seldom a relationship directly between the politician and the elector. The machine recruits workers of various kinds and at various levels, who then persuade electors to vote for their man. But they may also do other things. A politician has not only to win votes at the general elections; he has also to make a prominent place for himself in his party and to get himself chosen as candidate. This involves both campaigning among party members and a very complicated process of bargaining and putting pressure upon rivals and other influential people. This work, too, can be done by the machine. In short, the machine exists, so far as the politician is concerned, to win votes for him (or to dispose of rivals in other ways) both inside his own party and in the contest with other parties.

MOVEMENTS AND MACHINES

The Content of Machine Relationships

The complexity of the system and the cloud of secrecy and double-dealing make identification of those involved in running a machine very difficult. I enumerate some types of persons and some activities mentioned by judges in their summing-up at Election Tribunals, and then I attempt to systematize. (Some statements impute improper electoral behaviour, and I have, therefore, not given a sufficiently close reference to make identification possible.)

1) A bribe was paid to the secretary of a Lower Primary School so that he would use his influence to get votes for the defendant.
2) A man with a licence to deal in controlled foodgrains canvassed customers in his shop. He was obliged to the politician on whose behalf he worked, for support in getting the licence which gave him a local monopoly in these commodities.
3) The manager of a group of professional actors touring the villages made propaganda for one of the parties.
4) A young man, who was called to give evidence, seems to have worked at first for both sides, and eventually to have settled down with the Congress. After the election he received a minor appointment in Government service.
5) The judge drew attention to the fact that one of the Congress workers had received the licence for a paddy-purchasing agency.
6) Three polling agents (the men who sit inside the booth to protect a candidate's interests) were identified as a relative of the candidate, one of his tenants, and a man prominent in the statutory village council (*gram panchayat*) of the candidate's village. Although there is nothing improper in employing such men for this purpose, the judge drew attention to their status in order to indicate that their testimony could not be accepted as unbiassed.
7) "It is evident that the candidate had many relatives in the area who worked for him honorarily."

8) It was alleged that a candidate received help from Government servants.
9) Two shopkeepers, who had a hotel near one of the booths, provided free refreshments and supported one of the candidates.
10) A sum of money was paid to the Abbot of a local monastery to get votes in the nearby villages.
11) Money was given to a Harijan leader for the same purpose.
12) A Minister visited the constituency and promised an increase in local development grants.
13) It was alleged that a Government servant induced a man to "preach for" the Congress.
14) It was said that police officers and village watchmen of X Police Station had assisted in organizing the candidate's meetings and had asked people to vote for him.
15) An MLA had a bad name because he had been "taking contracts in his own name and the names of his henchmen and making illegal profits out of the contracts."
16) The conduct of a man petitioning on behalf of a defeated MLA was doubted since this same MLA had been instrumental in getting him appointed trustee of an endowment fund.
17) The MLA "supplied relief to people in the floods, for which they were obliged to him."
18) The MLA had a number of workers who were indebted to him for "recommending their names for licences to operate retail-controlled commodity shops."
19) The testimony of a witness was doubted because he belonged to a *jatra* party (theatrical company) which "owes its patronage to [the MLA]."
20) A man had obtained "some contribution for constructing a dramatic pandal [stage] from the Socialist candidate."
21) X was "seeking a job with the help of the MLA." He was later appointed to the Agricultural department.
22) X was "obliged to the MLA for being appointed teacher."
23) "The secretary and head pandit [Headmaster] were obliged

to the Congress candidate" who, as the sitting MLA, had helped them to get Government contributions for construction of the school building.

24) "The MLA has recommended his name [the secretary of a school] for getting the relief fund for the school and a sum of Rs1,150 was sanctioned for the excavation of a tank at village Y, which was entrusted to him for excavation. For all these matters he is obliged to the MLA."

25) "Several projects were granted in the names of X, Y, and Z on the recommendation of the MLA, as they were his supporters."

26) ". . . his colleagues in the Congress threatened to withhold his dues from the Government outstanding in connection with the paddy-purchasing agency by using their influence with the Ministers, unless he retired from the contest."

27) "As the Congress party is the ruling party in power . . . when a person becomes a Congress MLA he wields large influence with the officials . . ."

The content of these relationships is almost always a material transaction of some kind. In return for electoral work, a man gets a job, or a licence to deal in controlled commodities, or a grant of money from development funds, or a contract to carry out development work. Sometimes no specific benefit is mentioned, but the judge indicates that the worker has a status (tenant, debtor, and so forth) from which he may expect preferential treatment, or through which he may suffer deprivation if he does not toe the line. Nor are these favours once-for-all affairs: the beneficiary may expect further awards, or he may be kept in order, as Example 26 shows, by the threat of deprivation. There are also examples of relationships which *prima facie* may be of a moral kind and not based on calculation of immediate benefit. Candidates are assisted by relatives, and I have other examples, not given here, in which people are bound into the network by ties of caste, by the pious attachment of a former pupil to a teacher, and so forth. Such a relationship does not, of course, rule out expectation of material benefits as well.

In few of these cases was the boss or the politician clearly shown to be paying money out of his own pocket. Almost always he dispenses patronage of one form or another. He finds jobs, he allocates contracts, relief money, and licences, or, to put it correctly, people believe they are allocated on his advice. Patronage of this kind up to 1959 was very largely in the hands of the ruling party, the Congress, as the judge observed in Example 27. This is to some extent true even in constituencies which return members of other parties, and I have listened to bitter complaints, particularly from Independents, that their constituents fare better if they make application to the defeated Congress candidate than if they come to the Independent MLA. This, in turn, may explain why left-wing members and Independents express impatience at having to play the role of broker. It might also explain why voters often refused to return the sitting MLA from left-wing parties: he had been unable to do much for them.

MACHINE PERSONNEL

Given the difficulties of communication described earlier, the person whom the politician wants in his machine is the man who can transcend traditional groups. Conversely, the people willing to enlist in a machine and who see this as a major opportunity are those whose horizon is no longer limited to their own village. The ordinary peasant may be grateful for assistance from men like the brokers described in Chapter 1, when he gets into trouble or wants a favour from the administration, and he may well give a vote ("a small thing") in return. But he also views the whole business with distaste and apprehension and does not see it as his golden opportunity to make his way in the world.

Several kinds of men are attracted. Some are reaching up into what—with a considerable extension of the word—may be called the professional field. Others have ambitions in the world of commerce. Both find it advantageous to take part in politics, and both, as I shall describe later, may eventually be recruited as full-fledged politicians.

A man has learned to read and write in Oriya, a man who knows English and perhaps has a degree or has passed one of the examinations on the way to a degree, or even a man with the humble qualifications of primary schoolmaster, mechanic, or driver, does not find it easy to get a job. Even now, with the expanding development programmes and India's great need for experts, there is still competition for jobs of this kind, which are secure, often pensionable, relatively well-paid, and of immense prestige value. All these jobs are mediated through patronage, because the great majority of them are in the service of Government, or in institutions indirectly controlled by the Government. I was assured by a man whose son-in-law had been appointed Assistant Technical Storekeeper in an industrial plant, that no less than three cabinet ministers had taken a hand in the negotiations, and that he had won the day only because he had the backing of the Chief Minister. Even in those few cases where jobs in private commercial concerns for skilled or white-collar workers exist a politician's support can be helpful, since the owner of the concern is himself dependent on the same support, as I shall show below. Seen from above, India is no doubt short of qualified people; from below the reverse sometimes appears to be the case.

In commerce and manufacturing, entrepreneurs have the same dependent relationships upon politicians. A number of commercial activities are monopolies, farmed by the Government. There are licences for extracting timber and other forest products, for manufacturing and selling liquor in "wet" districts, for the purchase of paddy at controlled rates and its guaranteed resale to the State, and for the retailing (at various times since Independence) of cloth, foodgrains, and some other commodities. It is not difficult to make a profit, both legitimate and otherwise, since a partial monopoly is guaranteed. Naturally there is competition for such privileges, and a man who knows an official, or knows a politician who knows an official, stands a better chance than the rest, even when the licence is formally auctioned.

Development funds are controlled by the Government. Where a building is involved there is a potential source of benefit for two sets of people. If a school is to be built, then this is a favour for the people in that area. But the school building has to be erected, and since this is often done by contract, there is a second favour for the man who takes the contract, organizes the work, and makes his profit. It is the intention that public work of this kind should be done through public bodies, like panchayats, and that they should handle the contract. But much is still done by private individuals, and, in any case, there are many types of project which require the supervision of an experienced man and could not be handled efficiently by a committee. There are examples of such favours being used to enlist political support in the cases quoted above, and there are many others which could have been quoted.

To digress, this is, of course, an economic problem in that it involves the distribution of scarce resources. The electoral machines are in fact a hidden cost on this distribution, for they pay people to do election work which ideally should be done by voluntary unpaid workers. Relief monies, development monies, and contracts are not distributed on the basis of economic rationality alone, but are also used to plug deficiencies in the political system.

The type of relationship found within a machine is the same from top to bottom: calculation of profit. But this does not mean that the same type of man is found all the way up and down the machine. The boss or broker is not a person, but a role, and this role may be combined with other roles. As one moves from the bottom to the top of the machine, the roles associated with being a boss change significantly.

At the bottom a distinction is made between a "broker" and a "touter." A man who was pointed out to me as an "out-and-out touter of the worst kind" later said, when I asked him what he did for a living, "I am trying to do business without having any capital." But a broker, like the man described in Chapter 1, is a man of substance, furthering his business interests by making contacts and recruiting followers for politicians. The touter is merely a man who lives on his wits. "Touter" is a piece of Oriya-improved English, used originally to designate a man who acted as agent for a Pleader or Advocate, persuading people to go to law. From this the term has been extended into the political field to describe people who have a nose for trouble, and the knack of making trouble worse while pretending to restore order, and who profit from the trouble. To be a "touter," however, is not the same as being an "agitator." The latter word, in the way that it is used in Orissa, does not have the same degree of condemnation that it carries in English. One may speak of "good agitators" but to talk of a "good touter" is to contradict oneself. An agitator is a man seeking to redress a public grievance in the only way possible; a touter is a man exploiting or inventing a grievance so that he or his patrons may profit from it.

Above the brokers are notionally many levels of "bosses." The defining characteristic of the boss as distinct from the broker, is that the former has other bosses or brokers dependent upon him. But the distinction which I wish to introduce here is that between the boss, at any level, and the politician. The boss does not have politics as his vocation: he is a businessman, and he is engaged in politics as a necessary accessory to his business. His goal is power through money, not office. For the politician, on the other hand, office is its own reward, and he may be willing to lose money in order to get it, although such an investment is by no means always unprofitable.

This is clearly an ideal distinction, and when one surveys the politicians in Orissa, it is not always possible to say for certain what are their ambitions. Nevertheless one can discern, in some cases, a shift in their aims. This seems to coincide with the achievement of a certain level of financial success. This level is not the same for everyone and depends on their environment and their imagination. There were some men in backward areas like Phulbani, who there appeared to be men of wealth and substance, but who would have appeared on the plains to be very small fry indeed. In such districts these men are likely to feel that they have gone as far as they are likely to go, and as far as they want to go, in the world of business. They may then turn to politics, and this turn is usually marked by the acceptance of party membership and of office within the party, and ambitions to become the party's candidate in the next election. They continue to work as brokers and bosses, for without the machine they have no standing, but their business now tends to become an accessory to political activity, and not, as was the case before, the reverse.

This brief and sketchy analysis of the personnel of an electoral machine, identifying the roles of brokers, touters, bosses, and politicians, reveals two ways in which the political elite may be recruited. One road is through the touter and agitator, the other through the broker and the boss. Both may eventually become politicians. In both cases there is a continuance of the initial activity which brought them into contact with the ordinary man. In both there is a point in which political activity, from being an accessory to making a living, achieves the status of a legitimate end. Whether or not the element of calculation and self-interest, present in the roles of brokers, bosses, and touters, then becomes suffused with the moral purposes of the party and with unthinking loyalty to its leaders and its central ideas, is impossible to say in general terms.

There are, indeed, signs that the recruitment of politicians through the electoral machines, and their continued use of the machine relationships which initially brought them to prominence, impede the development of morally-united political groups. I turn now to this question.

MACHINE STRUCTURE AND THE PARTY

In theory a machine is a pyramid of people, with the politician at the apex and the ordinary villager at the bottom, linked together by relationships of mutual profit. As one goes higher up the pyramid each boss is bigger than the one below him, in the sense that he deals with affairs involving more money or has contacts with the more important administrators and politicians.

But the "pyramid" metaphor is not accurate. The bigger bosses, whose names are mentioned with respect and who are called "influential men" also deal directly with the common people. The machine is not like the modern army, in which only the junior officers directly handle troops of men. Every boss and broker has what might be called his "home farm," just as a feudal king had his own estate. The existence of many small self-sufficient units is a structural fact inclining towards instability.

I did not succeed anywhere in tracing out what seemed to be a full and rounded picture of the local machine networks. Such rounded networks may not in fact exist. The network is not a formal administrative structure, with defined offices. The job is not waiting there for the man; rather the situation is there and the man with the right sense of opportunity must come along, create the job, and fill it. It is no one's business to see that the job is filled. Therefore electoral machines have a random and irregular existence. Again, this is a highly competitive world, success being a condition of continued existence; it does not have the ordered security of a bureaucracy. We can make more sense of the machine by regarding it from the top almost to the bottom as a battlefield, rather than as an association of like-minded people.

Machines, in other words, belong to individuals rather than to parties. The focus of loyalty is a person: those who work the machine are loyal—if that is not too flattering a word—to a man and not to an idea. The machine consists, in fact, of a network of key individuals, hierarchically organized, but undisciplined and unstable. It is reminiscent, as I suggested, of the upper levels of a feudal organization. In the ethics of the system the higher bosses deal with the lower bosses and not directly with their followers, and, conversely, if a man at the lower end wants something which only the MLA can get for him then he does not approach the MLA directly but through his own, or an ascending series of, bosses. The supreme loyalty—again as in a feudal system—is to your own boss, and this means that the system is apt to work like its older counterpart—whole units being detached from one boss and attached to another.

Any generalized analysis of a feudal system always makes it seem much tidier than it was in fact. The same is true of a machine: allegiances are apt to change rapidly and there is a quite bewildering degree of impermanence at the lower levels, a constant stream of new recruits coming in, while others drift away to different bosses or out of the system altogether.

The handling of such a machine is not a simple affair. In some ways the word "machine" is most inappropriate. The activity is not routine but is very much an art and is bound

MOVEMENTS AND MACHINES
153

to be so because there is never enough loot to satisfy everyone. For every man who gets a contract and for every village that gets its school, there are ten who do not and they are potential recruits for the rival machines. This is probably what had happened in Example 15, quoted above: contracts had gone to the MLA's "henchmen," and those who were not favoured became his enemies. The boss of a machine is faced with the continual problem of judging who, if offended, is likely to do the least damage. This, of course, is a problem which faces any leader, but it is doubly dangerous for the boss since his whole edifice rests on benefits conferred. The leader of a movement has at least the chance that a disgruntled follower, disappointed for office, will be kept in line by moral attachment to the movement.

The party does not have a single coördinated and unified machine. At elections it must rely on a vast number of machines, of different sizes, each attached to a person in the party or in temporary and uncertain alliance with the party. The boss is not a man who has politics as his vocation. The full-time party organizers have a corps of agents under them, and these are centrally organized and controlled, after a fashion, but these men are not bosses as I define them. They are messengers and negotiators, and they are in no sense in immediate control of the machines.

An organization of this kind is a mercenary army, with both eyes fixed on the loot. It is true that without a victory there is less loot, and to that extent the various contingents are steered into some kind of common and coördinated action; but it is also true that the army will not fight if there is no prospect of loot, and will readily change sides if prospects look better from the other camp. There are countless examples of this. A boss who has entered politics and loses the race for the party's ticket may quite suddenly appear in the ranks of the opposing party. A change of allegiance, both before and after the election, is not uncommon. In Phulbani district, after the 1957 election, of four members returned in the Ganatantra interest, three crossed the floor to join the Congress.

The explanation of such behaviour in terms of values is that, as yet, parties have achieved a low standard of legitimacy, or, as I have been phrasing it, they do not command moral allegiance. The machines are partly to blame. The machine structure facilitates a change of allegiance and so contributes to party instability. The boss is not a "subject" of the party leaders; he is a subordinate ally, and, if he decides to shift his allegiance, he takes his followers with him.

In short, some of the party politicians, and many people on the lower edges of formal political activity, are in command of private armies and in that way are less amenable to party discipline. In turn, a great part of the energies of politicians goes not into educating the voter and building up an association which transcends parochial loyalties, but into conciliating adherents and fighting one another.

THE ELECTORAL EFFICIENCY OF A MACHINE

I want now to bring the discussion of electoral machines into perspective, for it is possible that their importance as one of the recruiting agencies for politicians, and the part they attempt to play in bringing voters into the party's fold, has made them seem more important than they are in fact.

My starting point is the immense gap in communication between the elite who rule and the mass who are governed. The ordinary business of administration, more particularly the present development programmes with their insistence on self-help and their need for popular enthusiasm, and finally the mechanics of democracy with its periodical appeal in free elections, all make it necessary that the elite should establish communication with the mass. There are three ways of doing this: agitations, which are attempts to create new groups on a basis of moral indignation over particular injustices; political parties, which attempt to do the same thing in a more generalized and permanent fashion; and electoral machines, which by-pass moral considerations, and attempt to create groups on the basis of individual self-interest.

To the sceptic the last appears to be the most effective way of doing the job. I do not know whether this is so or not, but there seems to be some contrary evidence and some general factors which limit the effectiveness of an electoral machine.

The contrary evidence is both general and particular. Given that the Congress has for most of the time been the ruling party in Orissa and therefore has had the most effective control over patronage, if machines are the only key to electoral victory, we have no means of explaining why the Congress has not won more striking victories, why its control of patronage in the Ganatantra areas did not enable it to beat Ganatantra candidates, and why a score of left-wing candidates have managed to keep their end up in the coastal plains. Coming down to the particular, what happened in Bisipara (see Chapter 1) does not seem to show that the electoral machines were particularly effective in that area.

There are practical reasons for this. A relatively small number of people in the total population get into situations where they need the services of a broker and the influence of a boss. Of those who do, many are people who need this once or twice in their lifetime. I have no means of measuring this frequency, but even if it is greater than this, their needs do not give rise to a permanent and lasting moral tie with the man who intervenes for them. Services paid for do not give rise to the same sentiments of loyalty as do services given by a man who has the status of leader; people do not respect brokers and bosses. In other words, while the machine seems to be an effective way of recruiting workers for an election, it does not seem to influence voters effectively. A symptom of this is the widespread belief that the funds which candidates are supposed to disburse to bribe voters are siphoned off by a succession of middlemen and never reach the voter. The atmosphere of self-interest and downright hypocrisy which surrounds the brokers and machine workers effectively prevents them from having a moral influence over the ordinary voter. It does not, of course, prevent them from sticking up posters, spreading rumours, creating disorder at rival political meetings, and doing other practical work of this kind which may, indeed, have an influence on the ordinary voter.

Finally, there are structural reasons which limit the machine's effectiveness. Since it is based on patronage, and since patronage is limited, some people are bound to be disappointed. Since, in addition to this, the bosses are not permanent officials in the employment of a party but rather politically free-lance businessmen, or interested politicians, the disappointed people turn and fight on the other side, or engineer a civil war within the party. Therefore, much of the machine's energy is lost in internal frictions.

Again, the fact that the party machine is composed of many relatively autonomous parts in the control of individuals, is not an accident. A structure of relationships based on self-interest and calculation cannot exceed a limited size; every link, so to speak, has to be forged by hand, and cannot be mass-produced in the manner of links in a movement which is based on moral considerations. The machine is a network of relationships between leading individuals and not a group in the true sense. Finally this network cannot itself be transformed into a coherent group, until the role of broker and boss is professionalized—that is, until the link-man is made into a career administrator within the party, paid and controlled by the party, and ceases to be a businessman freelancing in politics in order to expand his business. If that happened, although the basic units of the machine would still be small, they would no longer be autonomous to the same degree. Furthermore, there would then be a chance that in time such coördinated units would eventually emerge as new groups, transcending the tiny groups of traditional society, and better adapted to the tasks of educating the voter and of representing general interests in the new society that is emerging.

At this point the main operational question which we have been pursuing—the relationship between politician and voter —ceases to be useful, for in the following section I describe State politics. In order to do this, I have to begin by outlining not so much groups or roles, as in the earlier sections, but issues and policies. After I have made clear what people were fighting about, I can more clearly say who were the protagonists, and, in the end, partially account for the course of the conflict by the analysis which has occupied the first two sections.

I begin with a discussion of Oriya Nationalism, an issue which has, so to speak, defined the boundaries of the arena in which Orissa politicians come to grips with one another.

III. STATE POLITICS

7

ORIYA NATIONALISM

Orissa—in those days Cuttack, Puri, and Balasore—was taken by the British in 1803 and governed from Calcutta in Bengal.

Bengal already had long experience of British rule and provided many officials for the newly annexed areas. They became, as Oriyas later said, "an intermediary ruling race." Bengali was the language of the courts. The lawyers were Bengalis. If an Oriya wanted responsible employment in the Administration, he had to turn himself into a Bengali, because no educational institutions in Orissa, using the Oriya language, could give him the required qualifications.

It is ironical that the founder of the Utkal (Orissa) Union Conference, Madhusudan Das, went to Calcutta for higher education. To the end of his life, one man told me, he spoke not "chaste and elegant" Oriya, but Oriya with many Bengali corruptions. A fragment of autobiography by this man illustrates the feelings of ambitious Oriyas in the last two decades of the nineteenth century.

My admission into the English School brought me into contact with Bengali boys and Bengali teachers—I was the target. All my Bengali class comrades everlastingly fired their volley of sarcasm and ridicule at me . . . I had long hair which was tied at the back. This my Bengali friends considered a sign of my being a girl not a boy, for in Bengal by that time short-cropped hair was in fashion. One day one of my Bengali friends cut it off with a pair of sharp scissors . . . During the years of Bengali persecutions at school I looked back with a sigh, a regret sometimes with tears, on the days I spent in my village before I was transported to Cuttack for English education. I thought of the days when I was loved, respected, and blessed as the scion of an old family of zemindars. I was reconciled to a life where contempt and insult would be my share . . .[1]

Oriya culture was despised. Bengalis even attempted to prove that Oriya was a mere dialect of Bengali, whereas, Oriyas pointed out, Bengali with equal justification could be considered a corrupted form of Oriya.

Many Oriyas lost their land to Bengalis. Estates were sold to meet arrears of tax, and the sale took place in Calcutta, often without the knowledge of the Oriya owner.

In the second and third years after the extension of the Bengal regulations to Cuttack, estates paying a *jumma* of 4½ lakhs of rupees out of a jumma of Rs1,200,000 were sold at public auction for arrears of revenue . . . The inadequate value at which these lands were sold also immensely aggravated the hardships of the measure, and has been termed by the Collector (in his report) little better than downright robbery.[2]

All this happened in the heartland of Orissa in which Oriyas were a clear majority. Worse was happening in those tracts where they were in a minority. To the south, Ganjam Oriyas were administered from Madras by Telugu-speaking officials; to the west and northwest Oriyas had to deal with Hindi

---

[1] N. Das, 1958: 3.
[2] "Two Bachelors of Arts," 1919: 7.

speakers; to the north there were large groups of Oriya-speakers in the districts of what is now West Bengal.

In these areas Oriya language and culture was maintained with difficulty. Oriya children were educated through the medium of Bengali or Telugu or Hindi. A process, illustrated by the census return for Midnapore district in Bengal, must have been going on in all the outlying Oriya tracts. The totals of Oriya speakers in Midnapore were returned thus:

1891 572,789
1901 270,495
1911 181,801

Census figures, on issues like this, are notoriously fallible. But whether they indicated a true diminishing of Oriya-speakers, or whether they were the result of falsification by enumerators, the figures were equally disturbing to those who valued Oriya culture and the Oriya language.

Many petitions and memorials were submitted to the Government in the last two decades of the nineteenth century, but a systematic campaign for Oriya rights began only in 1903, when Madhusudan Das organized the Utkal Union Conference (*Utkal Sammilani*). The president (on that occasion) was the Raja of Mayurbhanj, and the chairman of the reception committee was the Raja of Kanika. In the succeeding years the conference met annually, usually under the presidentship of one of the Orissa Rajas. Branches were organized throughout the Oriya-speaking areas; paid propagandists ("missionaries") were employed; schools where Oriya children could be taught in their own language were opened in the outlying tracts. Oriya students taking courses of higher education outside Orissa were given grants. Memorials were submitted to various provincial administrations about the use of Oriya as a court language, about the founding of an Oriya university, about the teaching of Oriya in schools and universities, and, as a main aim, about uniting all Oriya-speakers into a single administrative unit. The Conference also interested itself in cottage industries and improved methods of agriculture.

The long and persistent agitation of the Utkal Union Conference was met halfway by the uneasiness of British administrators. They knew that Oriyas in outlying tracts—in Madras and Bengal and other areas—did suffer severe disadvantages through not speaking the same language as the Administrators. The British were also influenced by administrative difficulties. Existing provinces were large, and communications were poor. There was, for instance, a belief that the horrors of the 1866 famine could have been averted had Orissa not been so far from the eyes of the Government in Calcutta.

As far back as 1875 memorials had been submitted to the Bengal Government asking that all the Oriya tracts should be united under one administration. At first Utkal Sammilani agitated, as a minimum aim, for the inclusion of all the Oriya areas within one province, either the Central Provinces or Bengal. They were content to see this as a step on the way to a separate Orissa province. Yet the first change was concerned not so much with uniting Oriyas, but rather with relieving the Bengal Government of some of its burdens. In 1911 Bihar and Orissa were formed into a separate province. Sambalpur district became part of the Orissa section of the new province.

Oriya agitation continued, and there was a regular complaint that Bihar received the first share of what was to be had, and Orissa got only what was left. In 1936, after protracted negotiations in the course of which some Oriya leaders went to London to argue their case, Orissa became a separate province. The outlying tracts to the south (parts of the district of Ganjam and the Koraput Agency in Madras) were taken into the new Orissa province. Orissa then consisted of the following districts: Cuttack, Puri, Balasore, Ganjam, Koraput, and Sambalpur. This was an area of 32,198 square miles, and in 1941 it had a population of 8,728,544.

When the province was created the main aims of the Utkal Union Conference were accomplished. Not that there was universal satisfaction: parts of Ganjam, the whole of Singbhum and Midnapore, and other areas to which the Union Movement had laid claim were not included in the new province. Even now there is a steady trickle of literature complaining of trickery, of the falsification of census returns, of the use of double standards to prevent Orissa from getting all the territory demanded, of bad faith in other ways, of victimization, and so forth. But, by and large, the Movement subsided between 1936 and 1947, because it had achieved its main aim and because the energies of that articulate class which had organized the Union Movement were taken up by the struggle for or against Independence.

8

THE FREEDOM FIGHTERS

In Orissa the Indian Independence Movement was initiated by a section of the middle class. They were interested in social reform; they picketed "foreign cloth" shops and drink shops; they carried on educational work and attempted to foster political consciousness through meetings, discussions, pamphlets, newspapers, and so forth. This kind of work went on continuously, but three main periods of effort stand out: the Non-Coöperation Movement in the twenties, the Civil Disobedience Movement in the thirties, and the agitation against India's involvement in the Second World War culminating in the Quit India Movement of 1942.

Any national movement, particularly if successful, is remembered for its glories, and with the passage of time it becomes a great and ennobling adventure. When carried away by their own rhetoric, politicians sometimes speak as if the Independence Movement were a tidal wave, rushing forward uncheckable, irresistible, a genuine mass movement commanding everyone's loyalty, when all were comrades, when no one thought of himself, when betrayals were few and therefore more heinous, and when personal ambitions, rivalries, and jealousies were submerged in the common disciplined struggle to win freedom.

THE FREEDOM FIGHTERS

167

This picture is oversimplified; the urgencies of propaganda have obscured both the element of disharmony within the Independence Movement itself and the ambivalence, indifference, or even disapproval with which it was regarded by a large and influential section of the Indian population. It is only by examining these cleavages within the movement, and by looking at the people who for a long time supported the British against the Congress, that Orissa politics in the decade since Independence become comprehensible.

THE CONGRESS

Throughout its history the Indian National Movement was concerned not only with independence but also with social and economic reform.

Such reform movements existed in Orissa before the Congress came on the scene. Their inspiration, I was told, derived from similar movements in Bengal. There were attacks upon the caste system, and upon the custom of paying dowries, and symbolic reforms "such as introducing the social innovation of retaining moustaches alone and shaving off the beard—an innovation which was a red tag to the bull in the then conservative Brahmin Sasans in the Puri district and elsewhere in Orissa." (Mahtab, 1957, vol. III, App. B. pp. 23–24.) But in the main these reformers worked through two means: they started vernacular newspapers, and they opened schools. An example is the Satyabadi school in Puri district, opened by Gopabandhu Das in 1909. Many of those who supported these schools and who taught in them were also active members of the Utkal Sammilani. For example, the Oriya school at Chakradharpur in Singbhum district was started by the same Gopabandhu Das.

These reformers became involved in Independence politics. Gopabandhu Das "brought the Congress to Orissa." The Satyabadi School became a "National" school. Das himself was elected a member of the Bihar and Orissa Legislative Council, and the latter part of his life (he died in 1928) was spent in activities typical of a Congress politician in those days: educational work, publishing a vernacular newspaper, organizing flood relief, leading protest meetings against various Government measures, and from time to time defying the law and going to prison.

The cleavages in the Orissa Congress, speaking broadly, reflected the same divisions within the parent Indian Congress: the Swaraj group, the orthodox Congressmen sometimes called "Gandhians," and, thirdly, the Communists and Socialists. Each of these groups has a distinct history in Orissa's Independence struggle.

From the 1920's onwards the Swaraj group and the Gandhians fought a prolonged battle for control of the Utkal Congress. The Swaraj group accepted office in 1923 in the Bihar and Orissa Legislative Council, whereas the Gandhians remained outside. The Swaraj group supported the war effort and helped to form a Coalition Ministry, which held office between 1941 and 1944 in defiance of the Congress. Their leaders were expelled from the Congress. The Gandhians boycotted the Assemblies in 1923, took office together with their Swaraj opponents in 1936, resigned from the Ministry in 1939 in protest against India's participation in the war, and, for the most part, went to gaol as security prisoners between 1942 and 1945. Both groups had taken part in the Non-Coöperation Movement of the 1920's and the Salt Campaigns of the 1930's, but the Swaraj group abstained from the Individual Satyagraha of 1940 and from the Quit India Movement of 1942.

The conflict between the Swaraj group and the Gandhians was for control of the Utkal Congress. The survivors deplore it as a faction fight and say it arose from the ambitions of powerful individuals.

But the final break between the two groups, over the issue of support for the war, can be construed as a genuine difference of judgement; the Swaraj group believed that to lose the war would be to lose any prospect whatsoever of Indian independence. Earlier differences, too, to a lesser extent, were differences over tactics: for example, whether independence was best forwarded by joining or abstaining from legislative bodies.

But, to a degree which no outsider can possibly judge, these differences were also based upon communal and local loyalties. The leaders of the Gandhian group were mostly Karans (Writer caste) from the northern districts of Cuttack and Balasore. Swaraj leaders were mainly Brahmins from Puri district, trained by service in the Satyabadi School, an intellectual elite associated with the Utkal Sammilani. Occasionally one finds references to this conflict in print:

Puri being the stronghold of the Brahmans and Cuttack of Karans their differences (over the Satyabadi School) quietly ushered in the noxious Brahman-Karan problem . . . it is extremely sad to watch the two communities flying at each others' throats to secure jobs for their own kind, setting at naught all the canons of justice and fair play. In the silent wrangle . . . merit is often sacrificed on the communal fire. Even in the press . . . the dexterous attempt by certain editors at advertizing persons of one community to the exclusion of people of the other, is a direct issue of class jealousy and acrimony . . . It is a tragic experience to come across leaders confessing deep dislike for the sinister sentiment and yet succumbing to its evil influence in the actual field of action. . . . These are more dangerous than those who boldly take sides and hotly contest. . . . This caste or class feeling figures prominently among many of the educated in Orissa. They seem to be more susceptible to its seductive influence than the masses of the countryside . . . (Lal Mohan Patnaik, 1941: 252–253).

The third group, the left wing, first became distinct within the Congress about the mid-1930's. They differed from the rest over tactics and in having a positive and clearly defined political ideology, apart from and distinct from their desire for Independence. They were Marxists and were disliked both by the bourgeois groups from which they were themselves recruited, and by the other two Congress groups, who looked with disfavour on "foreign" ideologies. In tactics they inclined towards violence, and it was mainly (but not entirely) the Socialist left wing in Orissa which carried out sabotage in the war years. This group split. When the war was declared a "Peoples' War," the Communists lent their support to the Coalition Government of Swarajists and landlords. The Socialists continued to oppose the war and identified themselves with their less radical comrades within the Congress.

These are the main divisions in the Congress platform in the decades leading up to Independence in 1947. Mainly they reflect the same differences in the All-India Congress, and in the case of the division between the left wing and the rest, this seems to be the whole story. But in Orissa the difference between the Swarajists and the Gandhians also corresponded to an existing division of caste and locality.

ORIYA NATIONALISM

Early relations between the Congress and the Oriya Movement were amicable. Those who interested themselves in public affairs were jacks-of-all-trades. The leaders of the Oriya Movement were interested in social reform and economic betterment; leaders of social reform movements were also active in the Oriya Movement. From among their number also came men like Gopabandhu Das, who brought Congress to Orissa.

But soon conflicting loyalties forced a division. Social reform caused no difficulty since it was consistent both with Oriya Nationalism and the Independence Movement (which, of course, was Indian Nationalism). But between the two forms of nationalism there is a fundamental political in-

THE FREEDOM FIGHTERS

171

compatibility, and, in the last sixty years, when one waxed the other waned.

Some Oriyas chose sides. The founder of the Utkal Sammilani, although later enrolled in the Congress, resisted attempts by Congressmen to shepherd his organization into the Congress fold. Furthermore the Raj families and the bigger zemindars were opposed to the Congress and had suffered at its hands. These men had devoted their political energies to the Utkal Sammilani, and they naturally resisted attempts to have it incorporated in the Congress. In 1936 the Utkal Union Conference at Puri passed a resolution expressing loyalty to the crown. Thereupon the Congress denounced the Conference as a British device to "divide and rule."

Congress hostility towards Oriya Nationalism cost it the wholehearted support of a section of the Oriya middle classes. Many continued to work within the framework of Congress for independence, but they did so with reservations, and, from time to time, when Congress unity was weak and its aims uncertain, they broke away. A non-Congress Ministry, which had a short spell of life in 1936, and the longer Coalition Ministry, which was in office during the war years, were composed of men who were prominent in the cause of Oriya Nationalism.

Finally, when Independence was achieved, most people in this category either retired from politics or resumed Oriya nationalism in a militant form and became opponents of the Congress party.

THE LANDLORDS

The division in Orissa between the freedom fighters and their opponents resembles the same division in other parts of India. By and large the struggle went on over the heads of ordinary people and involved them only on specific occasions. The protagonists belonged to the middle class. On one side was the

Congress; on the other the Government and administrative services, supported by the landlords.

Individual landlords helped the police and the administration to suppress Congress agitations. Moreover, in the Orissa plains, the landlords were corporately active in politics, had their own party, published newspapers, and in general offered a coördinated opposition to the Congress. In the Legislative Assembly of 1936, 24 members in a House of 60 opposed the Congress. They were joined in 1941 by eight members from the Congress benches and formed the Coalition Ministry which held office until 1944.

Agrarian matters lay at the root of the hostility between the landlords and the Congress.

There had been sporadic agrarian disorders in Orissa since the beginning of the nineteenth century. These risings were against individual landlords, or sometimes against particular actions of the Government. No coördinated agitation against the landlord system itself began until the advent of the Congress Socialist Party in 1934. In that year the first meeting of the Orissa section of this organization was held, and during the next two years Peasant Councils (*Kisan Sabha*) were organized throughout the province. The Orissa Congress Socialist Party was dissolved in 1938 because the Communists had captured it, but the work of opposing the landlords and wrecking the landlord system went on. The Congress Government, then briefly in office, passed various measures to improve the position of tenants. Agitations against the landlords, illegal crop cutting, no-rent campaigns, and so forth continued and reached their climax in the '42 Movement.

From one point of view this was an attempt to broaden the base of Congress support and to involve the common people of the countryside in the Independence Movement. A campaign against the local landlord, and those of his privileges which fell most heavily on the tenants, had a much more direct appeal than "Independence." "We noticed," I was told by a leader in this campaign, "that our Kisan rallies were getting much bigger attendances than the ordinary Congress meetings. Then we knew we were on the right track."

Hill and Coast

Along the coast of Orissa there is a narrow strip of low-lying land affected by saline deposits and unfit for cultivation. Behind this lies a wide fertile plain, much of it alluvial. At the western extremities of the coastal districts rise the foothills of the Ghats. This upland region consists of jungle-covered mountains, between which lie extensive plateaux of rich agricultural land. The wealth of the coastal plain is in its agricultural land, highly fertile, but subjected to disastrous floods in the three northern districts of Cuttack, Puri, and Balasore. Some hill districts also produce surpluses of paddy, and all contain rich forests. In the northern half of the hill area, power supplied from the Hirakud dam in Sambalpur district is making possible the development of industries extracting and processing minerals.

TABLE 9

Population, Area, and Density of Hill and Coast Divisions of Orissa in 1951

	Population	Area	Density
Hill	7,813,617 (54%)	44,652	175
Plains	6,832,347 (46%)	15,475	441

At the 1951 Census the population of Orissa was fourteen and one-half million. The area of the province, in round numbers, is 60,000 square miles and the census figure of population density in 1951 was 244. But this figure conceals a difference between hill and coast, shown in Table 9.

A further difference lies in the distribution of towns (settlements of more than 5,000 people). Orissa's population is overwhelmingly rural, fourteen million countrymen and only 594,000 town-dwellers. Of these, 368,000 live in the four coastal districts. Koraput and Sambalpur account for a further 106,000. The remaining six districts in the hill division contain only 120,000 people living in towns.

There is also a difference in the proportion of "backward" to total population. In Cuttack, Puri, Balasore, and Ganjam, the four coastal districts, the backward classes are 47 per cent, 51 per cent, 53 per cent, and 45 per cent respectively. Of the remaining districts the percentage in all but Dhenkanal lies between 80 and 90. The figure for Dhenkanal is 58.

The same difference appears in the literacy rate. For Cuttack, Puri, and Balasore the figures are 23 per cent, 21 per cent, and 23 per cent respectively. Ganjam has 16 per cent. Of the remaining districts the highest is Dhenkanal with 18 per cent; Sambalpur has 16 per cent; Keonjhar has 12 per cent; and the rest are all 10 per cent or below, down to 5 per cent in the case of Koraput. Literacy in the whole State is 15 per cent.

There are, then, some basic geographic, demographic, and cultural differences between hill and coast. The hill areas are more sparsely populated; they are rich in forest and mineral wealth; fewer people live in towns; fewer are literate; more are classified as backward; and, finally, communications within the hill areas are poorer than in the coast. These characteristics are not, of course, isolated from one another. Illiteracy and "backwardness" are in part the result of poor communications and poverty. But they are also connected with certain historical differences.

For about a century and a half—and in some areas longer —the people of the two divisions had quite different experiences of government.

The coastal districts and Sambalpur, and to a lesser extent

Koraput and parts of Phulbani and Dhenkanal, have a long acquaintance with bureaucratic administration, having been governed directly by the British. Bureaucratic rule favours the growth of a professional middle class: teachers, doctors, lawyers, and government servants. These professions require a heavy investment in education, and for many years educational opportunities were restricted in Orissa. Those who were able to qualify for professional jobs came usually from a relatively wealthy background, in most cases from the smaller landlord families. These people played a leading part in government and the administration, in the Independence Movement, and in politics since 1947.

The remaining areas were Feudatory States, twenty-six of them, governed by a system closer to the feudal than the bureaucratic model. Government was likely to be more arbitrary than in the coast, and in the hands of a bad ruler the people had no constitutional redress. But government was also closer to the people, less remote and impersonal than in the British districts. Justice might be capricious, but relatively it was swift. Power was not divided among many specialists but concentrated in relatively few persons. In times of distress, aid, if it was to be given at all, was given quickly. Between the people and their ruler stood relatively few intermediaries, and, even when the ruler was harsh and exacting, inefficient administration sometimes saved his subjects from the full force of his impositions. Even in those larger States which had full-fledged bureaucracies staffed by ICS men, the distance between the people and the ultimate seat of power was much less than in British districts.

Direct and simple government made life easier for the peasants, in that the smaller benefits could easily and quickly be obtained. But the same was not true of the large public welfare activities. Some Feudatory States had enlightened and progressive rulers, who established schools and hospitals. But, by and large, there were few facilities for higher education, and little encouragement to pursue it. Relatively few of the subjects in the Feudatory States could carry their education far enough to qualify for the administrative services. There were, of course, some exceptions, but, by and large, the Rajas' administrative staffs were recruited from the coastal districts, or were not Oriyas.

The main reason was that few local people were qualified, but, this apart, absolute rulers often prefer to recruit aliens for their administration. Outsiders are more amenable to the Raja's discipline. Their security is entirely in his hands since they have no backing in the country. They are unlikely to carve out for themselves positions from which they may challenge the Raja's authority, as a local man might be able to do. They can be dismissed at will, and the people of the country remain indifferent to their fate, or may be glad that they have gone. Finally, aliens shield the ruler from unpopularity. They are scapegoats when things go wrong, and the blame falls not on the ruler, but on those who advise him, or who fail to carry out his orders and intentions, or who misinform him about the true state of things.

This type of government in the Feudatory States has had two consequences. Firstly in those areas there are few indigenous members of the professional middle classes. There is a relatively small equivalent—with the partial exception of Koraput and Sambalpur—of that articulate and self-confident class which guided the Independence Movement in the coastal districts. Such people do exist, but they are few in number. This is one reason why the people of the Feudatory States played a small part in the Independence Movement. It is also a reason why national political parties—the Congress, the Communists, and the Praja Socialists—find it difficult to build up an organization in the area, for they depend upon finding organizers and leaders from the middle classes.

Secondly, the odium which alien administrators incurred was extended to anyone who came from the same area. *Kataki*, strictly a man from Cuttack district but in most of the hill areas applying to anyone from the coast, is a term of abuse. The leaders of Congress and of the other national parties are virtually all *Katakis*, and they start with this handicap when they try to win popularity in the hill areas. This odium derives also from traders and merchants, many of whom are either Marwaris from western India, or are *Katakis*.

Not to put too fine a point upon it, the people of the hills think they have been exploited and misgoverned by people from the coast.

PRAJAMANDALS

As the Independence Movement became more forceful and aggressive, Congressmen in the coastal districts turned their attention to the Feudatory States. They had two aims: one to subvert the authority of the Rajas, who supported the British; the other to bring about social and agrarian reform and ultimately to set up representative government in the States.

Agitations in the States were organized not by Congress but by bodies called Prajamandals. The Congress advised and trained leaders and in some cases provided them from its own ranks.

The movement began in earnest in 1937 when the Orissa States Peoples Conference was convened in Cuttack. In 1938 Congress organized a States Enquiry Committee and in the following year published a report which detailed the excesses of the rulers and the burdens of their subjects. "No-Tax" campaigns were organized; people were urged to refuse their labour; meetings and processions were held. In areas where Prajamandals gained control they set up panchayats, heard cases, and fined people, exactly as if they had become the Government.

But the Princes, in defending themselves, were not always bothered by the due and sometimes lengthy processes of law. Agitators found their work in the States more perilous than in the British districts. In some States the movement collapsed. In others the people fled in large numbers to camps organized for them in British territory by the Congress. In Rampur the Political Agent was murdered; and, here and there, the movement seems to have lost sight of its nonviolent intentions and becomes a form of guerilla warfare.

The agitation continued until 1939, when there seems to have been a period of compromise, the agitations ceasing, and some of the rulers in the states most affected by the disturbances announcing constitutional reforms. The lull ended in the 1942 movement, when violence broke out again. But it was short-lived. Most of the leaders were arrested and gaoled as security prisoners; others became fugitives, and the agitation died down.

This ended the first phase of direct hostility between the princes and the Congress. Neither side was efficiently organized. From time to time directives on strategy and policy came down to Prajamandals from the States' Peoples Conference or the Congress. But, for the most part, in each state a separate Prajamandal fought its separate fight.

Nor do the rulers seem to have coöperated with one another. Each ruler fought the battle on his own. When parleys took place, they were often between a leading Congressman from the coast (seeking, usually without success, to assume the role of mediator), the British Political Agent, and the ruler of the state concerned. Nor was the movement widespread. Although there were Prajamandals throughout the hills, they were strong only in some states which bordered on the coastal districts. British territory provided a base and a training ground, and a refuge when the Raja reacted too strongly.

In both its aims the agitation of 1937–1942 failed. No social reforms were brought about in the states, none at least of any importance, and, when the agitation was suppressed in 1942, some rulers who had made concessions withdrew them again.

THE FREEDOM FIGHTERS
179

Secondly, as a part of the struggle for Independence, the agitations in the Feudatory States collapsed with the general failure of the Quit India Movement when its leaders were interned. On the credit side the Congress gained some experience of agitation in the Feudatory States, and recruited some members from those areas; and it was able to make use both of the experience and the personnel when the struggle was resumed after Independence.

By 1947 both sides had reorganized. Bigger armies, so to speak, were in the field. The rulers were attempting to combine in a Union of the Eastern States, to include the Chota Nagpur States, the Orissa States, and some Chattisgarh States. Their opponents worked at two levels. An Orissa and Chattisgarh States Regional Council reorganized the Prajamandals and directed their agitations. "Veterans" from the coast, now out of prison, were available for the job. But the battle was also fought at the higher level of diplomacy, between the consortium of rulers and the Government of Orissa, backed by the Union Government. The scale of the struggle on the eve of Independence, and afterwards, was larger than it had been before the war. It took place between two relatively large integrated forces and was no longer an affair of piecemeal harassment and counterharassment.

The merging of the Feudatory States with Orissa had been advocated in the report of the Congress States Enquiry Committee in 1929 and was no doubt in the minds of some of those who led the prewar Prajamandal agitations. But at that time the issue seemed remote; it took second place to Independence.

By 1946, with the arrival of the Cabinet Mission, it was clear that the British were about to leave, and that this was the time to stake out claims in the area of power left vacant. The rulers of the Eastern States Union were attempting to form a unit big enough to exist as a separate state within the

Indian Union. Such a state, although backward in every respect, had potential forest and mineral wealth. But, if the state came into existence, Orissa would consist only of the four coastal districts and some enclaves in the hills, and it would be without the forest and mineral wealth of the hill areas. Much of the industrial belt now being developed in northern Orissa lies in the former Feudatory State areas. To the leaders of the Congress it must have seemed that they were fighting for the very existence of their Orissa as a viable state in the new Indian Union.

Both sides made appeals to the Union Government in Delhi. The rulers who appealed for protection received bland and unhelpful advice. The Union, with an eye on the bigger problem of Princely India, stood behind the Congress Government in Orissa.

It is not easy to discover how extensive were the 1947 Prajamandalist agitations. Those I have interviewed on this subject have been interested parties and their accounts conflict. Nor have I been able to find any detailed written account of what went on.

The disorders seem to have been strongest in those same states, neighbouring on the coastal districts, which had been most affected in the period 1937–1942. Some rulers handed government over to Prajamandal organizations. In others the Prajamandal set up parallel governments in defiance of the ruler. In other places Adibasis (tribal people) were "deserting the Prajamandals and joining their own communal organizations." (This account is drawn from H. K. Mahtab, 1957, Vols. IV and V.) Nilgiri, the first state taken over by the Orissa Government in November, 1947, capitulated not because the Prajamandalists had won their battle with the ruler, but because the local Adibasis, taking advantage of the prevalent disorders (it is alleged that they were encouraged by the ruler) began to seize the property of Hindus in the area, and to redress a long-standing economic grievance by direct action.

The Orissa Government intervened and the Collector of Balasore was ordered to take over the administration of the state. A month later the rulers of the remaining states capitulated and signed the Merger Document. On January 1, 1948, the Congress Government of Orissa assumed responsibility for the government of all the former Feudatory States, with the exception of Mayurbhanj, Saraikella, and Kharsawan. The rulers lost all their powers, but retained some personal privileges and received pensions.

There are many aspects to this struggle: social and agrarian reform, the independence of India, the contest of an old aristocracy with a middle class, the creation of a viable Orissa State in the Indian Union, and so forth. But they all exhibit the cleavage between the hill areas and the coastal plains.

The merger of 1948 put an end to an administrative division which had existed for a century and a half. But a merger, although it could change the holders of power, could not change the attitudes which had become ingrained in the people both of the hills and the coast. There remained a legacy of suspicion on the one side and contempt on the other.

The rulers were fighting to protect the institutions which gave them eminence, and without a doubt they lost the battle. In 1948 princely rule had gone, and by 1959 the Orissa Government was busy rooting out the last remnants of feudal institutions. In so far as the merger put an end to conflict between the middle class and the aristocracy, or between feudalism on the one side and representative institutions combined with a bureaucracy on the other side, then there is no question but that feudalism and the aristocracy were annihilated.

But the conflict was also between the hill and the coast, and this continued after Independence in the arena of democratic politics.

9

ORISSA POLITICS 1947–1959

CONGRESS AND ORIYA NATIONALISM

The Feudatory States had been merged in 1948 with the old British province to form the new Orissa State. But one state, Mayurbhanj, did not accede to Orissa at that time. Mayurbhanj lay between the new Orissa and two small states which had been within the jurisdiction of the British Political Agent for the Orissa Feudatory States. These were Saraikella and Kharsawan. At first they were allotted to Orissa with the rest of the Feudatory States. But when Oriya officials arrived, they were met with demonstrations of hostility, organized, so it is alleged, not by local people but by outsiders who wanted Saraikella and Kharsawan in Bihar.

Whatever their origin, the disorders were considerable. The police opened fire, and people were killed. The Union Government intervened and gave the two states temporarily to Bihar, until the question could be considered again in more settled times. This decision was prompted both by the disorders and by the fact that, until Mayurbhanj acceded, Orissa had no territorial boundary with Saraikella and Kharsawan.

Mayurbhanj joined Orissa the following year, but, so far as I could discover, the question of Saraikella and Kharsawan did not come up again until the States Reorganization Commission of 1956. The Oriyas were confident that Saraikella and Kharsawan (and possibly some other outlying tracts) would come to Orissa. Some propaganda was carried on to strengthen the Oriya case, both in those two states and elsewhere. But Saraikella and Kharsawan remained with Bihar.

It was also believed that the Orissa Congress Ministry would resign if the two states were not made part of Orissa. But, presumably on advice from the Union Government, the Orissa Congress remained in office. Demonstrations erupted throughout Orissa, directed both against the State Ministry and against the Union Government. There was a general strike. Shops were closed. Transport was blocked. The agitators concentrated upon Union institutions: the railways, the post office, and the All-India Radio. At Bhadrak trains were held up for a week and the picketers (mostly students) organized canteens to feed the stranded passengers. At Puri the railway station was burned and the houses of some officials attacked. The police opened fire, and one person was killed. Union troops were flown to Cuttack to protect Government installations, and a section of these forces, guarding the radio station, opened fire, wounded some members of the crowd, and killed a youth. This youth became a martyr, and his name was used in the 1957 elections by parties opposed to the Congress.

Public meetings were forbidden. But the leaders of the Ganatantra party courted arrest by defying the ban. Later they, with some members of other parties and Independents, resigned from the Assembly and the Parliament in protest both against the decision of the States Reorganization Commission and against the manner in which the disorders had been suppressed.

Orissa now has its University, and the greater number of people in regular administrative service are Oriyas. There are still many people of Bengali descent in Orissa, but this issue is no longer alive. From time to time a domiciled Bengali politician may have to put up with the gibes of his opponents, but few of them have connections with Bengal proper, and most of them are solidly identified with Orissa. Nor is the language issue any longer of importance.

But there are still fields in which "Orissa for the Oriyas" is a compelling slogan. Oriyas complain that some areas of commerce—the *kendu*[1] leaf contracts and the mines, for example—are in the hands of outsiders, and that sufficient profits from them do not accrue to Orissa but go outside. There is also a popular distrust of non-Oriya commercial people—the Marwari businessmen and shopkeepers, for example.

Projects under the control of the Union Government are a particular target for Oriya Nationalists. They complain that Oriyas are displaced from their homes (as at Rourkhella or at the Hirakud dam) to make room for these projects and are not properly compensated. They also complain that local people cannot get jobs and that the benefits to be got from the new concerns go mainly to non-Oriyas. The presence of Union officials, who may not be Oriyas, is also resented. A "closed shop" mentality exists from the level of the politicians and officials down to the ordinary worker. Orissa, of course, is not unique in this.

Nor is Orissa unique in the complaint that the State gives too much to the Union and gets too little in return. Whether or not such complaints are based upon accurate information, and just what constitutes a "fair" proportion of Oriyas in the employment of Union projects in Orissa, are questions which cannot be answered here, for they depend upon many variables: the balancing of State interests against Union interests, the demands of economic efficiency, and so forth. But what matters in this analysis is not the correctness or falsity of Oriya

---

[1] A leaf gathered from the jungle and used for the outer wrapping of the Indian cigarette.

beliefs about present or past injustices, but the fact that these beliefs are held, and that action springs from them.

With such a history behind them, Oriyas are not thick-skinned. Gossip and rumours of adverse opinions fall upon sensitive ears. A distinguished Indian leader is said to have described Oriyas, during the 1956 troubles, as *"goondas"* (hooligans). "Would he have dared to say that about Andhras?" one man asked. Another elder statesman is alleged to have sent a telegram of congratulation to Mayurbhanj when it refused to join Orissa along with the other Feudatory States in 1947. It is also said that when the States Reorganization Commission decided to leave Saraikella and Kharsawan with Bihar, they did so because they thought that "there would be no trouble," whereas presumably Biharis would make trouble if those two states were taken away. During the debate in the House of Lords on the Government of India Bill in 1911, when Bihar and Orissa became a separate province, Lord Curzon said, "The interests of the Oriyas have been sacrificed without compunction . . . because the Oriyas are a nonagitating people."

It seems that in 1956 the Oriyas were determined to prove that this was no longer the case.

The Congress party takes the strain of this conflict of loyalties. The Orissa Congress has two masters: its Oriya electorate and the All-India party. Theoretically the other All-India parties working in Orissa, the Praja Socialists and the Communists, face the same dilemma, but not being in office they can more freely speak up for Oriya rights. The Ganatantra, a state party, and the Independents, have no difficulties since they do not have to calculate whether their actions will damage the unity of the party at a national level.

When Saraikella and Kharsawan first went to Bihar in 1948, people said that the Orissa Congress leaders were weak in the face of central pressure, and naive in failing to counter the manoeuvres and intrigues of Congressmen in other states. In 1956 the failure of the Orissa Congress Government to resign in protest against the award of the States Reorganization Commission, after the general expectation that they would make this gesture, and the subsequent firings, did considerable damage to the party's prestige in Orissa. In the elections of 1957 there was a large protest vote against the Congress in the coastal area. In the Chief Minister's own constituency a Ganatantra candidate polled over 19,000 votes in an area where the Ganatantra at that time had virtually no organization: these can only have been votes in protest against what had been done in 1956. A candidate who stood as an Independent told me that one reason why he had defeated an old and respected Congress leader was that he had been imprisoned for his part in the 1956 agitations, and it was generally believed that his Congress opponent, at that time the MLA, was concerned in this arrest. The same candidate issued a pamphlet with a photograph on the cover of a youth who had been killed in the police firing in 1956 and the caption "Why you should give me your vote."

But Congress difficulties are not to be attributed merely to "want of strength in face of the Centre," nor to baser motives which are sometimes suggested as explanations of their behaviour in 1956. The point is that they were faced, in a very acute form, with the politician's dilemma: his loyalties upwards and to the wider group—in this case to the party and to India as a nation—conflict inevitably with his loyalties downwards, in this case to the State.

SOCIAL AND ECONOMIC REFORM IN THE ORISSA PLAINS

Among the middle classes, particularly the intelligentsia (but not, in my experience, among the peasants) there is a radical outlook: an assumption that change is good and that it is the duty of the middle classes to improve the lot of the poor. There are, no doubt, variations in the sincerity with which these opinions are held: but there was no one among those I met (apart from some officials letting their hair down) who disputed the rightness of this attitude. In Orissa to be called a "do-gooder" would not be considered slighting.

There are conservatives. But their conservatism appears more in deeds than in words, and no one has appeared on the post-Independence stage in Orissa with a manifesto proclaiming the rightness of the present state of society and deploring change. The Ganatantra Parishad is commonly labelled "feudal reactionary," but the programme which that party put out, at the time when it was in alliance with the Praja Socialists in the Orissa Assembly, was more radical than that of the Congress. Manifestos, the cynics say, are merely words on paper. But that is another question and does not alter the fact that the climate of political opinion in 1959 did not permit open opposition to change. If there were conservatives, they objected not to change itself, but to the pace of change; or they argued that certain elements in the radical programme, such as "social justice" and "economic development" might at that time be incompatible with one another.

Reformist activities in Orissa fall into two main categories: material and moral. These poles are represented in contemporary India by the Five Year Plans at one end and at the other by the work of Vinoba Bhave. One is concerned with man's virtue, the other with his material well-being. The "moral" reformers are, on the whole, not a success in party politics. Certain "moral" reforms—for instance, the abolition of untouchability and the introduction of prohibition—have been attempted through legislative means. But on the whole men of this inclination work lower in the power hierarchy: they are fieldworkers, and their techniques are precept, example, and preaching. In day-to-day politics, in the field of manipulation and bargaining, they tend to be helpless and are sometimes used by those who are more skilled at manoeuvring. But even by those who think that such work is a waste of time, they are held in great respect as individuals.

The other reformers do not attempt to change society by working only on individual minds, but attack the structure of social relations through legislation. Their assault is upon institutions, or privileged classes, and they seek to bring about a more equitable distribution of wealth and at the same time to increase the total wealth.

Between these extremes is a type of activity, the primary aim of which is economic development, but not by means of centrally directed projects involving heavy expenditure of capital. Examples would be the work of institutions like the Khadi and Village Industries Board, and, at an earlier date, some items on the Congress list of "constructive work."

These categories refer to activities rather than to persons. Every senior Congress politician has had experience of all three types of work. But differences arise over which type of activity is the more fundamental.

There is a conflict between those who believe in a planned socialist economy and those who do not. Some think that structural reform toward socialism is ineffective because it does not touch the moral problem and because it sometimes violates traditional values. Others say that although such measures might satisfy the dictates of social justice, they ignore economic realities and in the end would lower production and would merely result in the sharing out of greater and greater poverty. For them the first requirement is to increase production; distribution logically came afterwards, and if increased production could only be bought with some increase in social inequality, then that could be remedied later.

This opposition was spasmodic, ill-organized, and usually voiced as private misgivings. By 1959 no group in Orissa had put forward a programme openly opposed to socialism. The Gandhians went their own way, keeping mostly outside the arena of party politics. Those who placed production first functioned as a pressure group behind the scenes, only occasionally emerging into the light of public debate. But they were not an organized group openly opposed to the socialist principles advocated by Congress.

These were the main cleavages among social and economic reformers: the socialists believed in a planned economy, and their first aim was social justice; others may or may not have believed in planning, but they did think that the first need was to raise production; finally, the Gandhians had their own economic ideas and considered a moral reformation more important than—indeed, a prior necessity to—economic betterment.

The Congress Government did not always find it easy to satisfy all these different pressure groups.

The professed politicians were not the only persons concerned with social reforms and economic development. There were innumerable societies and official or semiofficial organizations whose purpose was social work. Few were mere charitable bodies concerned with palliating distress: they aimed at reform and education. What was their relation to the Government?

In some cases the reformers opposed the ruling power, just as the Congress social workers themselves did before 1947. The politician, particularly the small man in his own locality, who went on hunger strike to draw attention to the government's scandalous neglect of the plight of agricultural labourers, or the distress of displaced persons, or even the need to have a new roof on the local school, would describe himself as a social worker. Sometimes more serious and responsible persons resorted to the same tactics and ran the risk of being labelled "agitators," particularly if they were known to be sympathizers of a party in opposition, just as they were labelled by the British in the days before Independence. Again, when there was some crisis with which the official agencies could not fully cope, as when there was a flood, then hosts of individual social workers came forward to help in the distribution of relief. Finally there were a few individuals or small groups who went about exhorting and setting an example and pioneering, on a small scale, education or hygiene or some other form of socially beneficial work.

But by and large in 1959 the day of the private person or small group of such persons was past. Firstly, this happened because the Government accepted a much wider responsibility for social welfare than did its British predecessor. If a man wanted to start a school, or build a hospital, or dig a well, then sooner or later he went to the Government or to one of the bigger social work societies to get money. The initiative still often came from private sources: but the organizers could usually count on Government assistance to keep their project running.

Consequently the attitude of such persons towards the Government came more and more to resemble that of, in the old days, the Utkal Sammilani than that of the social reform groups which later merged with the Congress. Their tactic was diplomacy; they were prepared to argue their case, and to lobby, but they did not want to make themselves such an embarrassment that the Government would not help them. They were, so to speak, loyal subjects and their claims to assistance rested on this fact.

The Government reciprocated this attitude. Congress was committed to a welfare policy and was prepared to help private organizations. There were official and semiofficial bodies like the Khadi and Village Industries Board, or the Depressed Classes League, which existed to foster and encourage local self-help. Nonofficial groups, like the A.B. Sarva Seva Sangh, were usually looked upon with favour, although, in the case of this particular organization, relations with the Orissa Government were not always happy.

The two left-wing parties consistently tried to force social and economic reforms more rapidly than the Congress Government was able to grant them. The following quotations, taken from *Orissa 1949*, issued by the Public Relations Department, are some examples of what was going on in the areas where Congress had dominated the 1946 elections.

(1947) In Puri district the Communist-instigated tenants of Malipara were prosecuted for forcibly entering upon the land of the local zemindar. In Kakatpur and Minapara areas the agrarian agitation was more widespread, and several cases were instituted against the raiyats for indulging in assaults and preventing landowners from cultivating their lands. (p. 27)

(1948) The Communists intensified their activities in the districts of Cuttack, Puri, Ganjam and parts of Sambalpur and Balasore. In Cuttack they incited the raiyats of Patia to undertake repair of the Domuhin embankment in spite of prohibitory orders with the result that several arrests had to be made to maintain law and order. In Puri district, particularly in Gop and Kakatpur areas, the agitation among the raiyats led to several instances of forcible cultivation of lands of zemindars for which specific cases were instituted. The situation deteriorated in Shergada (Ganjam) in May when a large mob armed with *lathis* and other weapons attacked a Police search party with the result that firing had to be opened resulting in 5 dead and 16 injured. In Sambalpur district the Communist leaders were rounded up and proceeded against. The Communists established a firm hold over the sweepers in Puri and successfully instigated them to launch a strike. The Communists also instigated the workers of the Ib river colliery who formed an unlawful assembly and had to be dispersed after a *lathi* charge ... Section 144, Cr.P.C. had to be promulgated in the Tirthol and Ersama areas of Cuttack district and Mangalpur of Puri district to check the Socialist-sponsored agrarian agitation. (p. 29)

(1949) In the beginning of the year the Communists concentrated on the railway employees to bring about a strike which was averted by the arrest and detention of the main instigators. They turned their attention towards the forcible removal of paddy, usurpation of land, and intimidation of local land-owners and zemindars at Ardhaulia (Cuttack), in Shergada area in Ganjam, Chandka, Kakatpur, Tangi, and Begunia in Puri, and Rasam and Kandeikela in Sambalpur. (p. 31)

The troubles continued in 1950, as the following excerpt from *Orissa 1950–51* (p. 5) shows:

The Socialists organized two labour strikes—one at the Textile Mills at Chowdwar and the other in a colliery at Talcher in Dhenkanal District. The Bhagchas law also afforded them a wide opportunity to foment agrarian disputes in many parts of the State. The scarcity of essential commodities and the necessary tightening of control was taken advantage of by all these reactionary parties including a few Congress malcontents, in making propaganda against the Government. This propaganda put a premium on criminal tendencies and led to the unauthorized demolition of reserved forests in Sundargarh and Nilgiri, in looting of ride-carts in Ganjam and obstructing movement of rice in Cuttack, where Supply officials were intimidated and obstructed in the discharge of their duties. Thanks to the vigilance of the Police, the troubles were everywhere localized and brought under control with comparative ease.

The 1952 Congress Government, under the leadership of a former Congress Socialist, made a serious and determined effort to bring about agrarian reform. To some extent this countered the left-wing campaign within the Legislative Assembly. But delays and the difficulties of implementation gave plenty of scope for continuing agitations outside.

A series of connected agrarian reforms had passed or were passing through the Orissa Legislative Assembly by 1959. These measures were intended to eliminate rent receivers intermediate between tillers of the land and the Government, and to establish the cultivators as small landowning farmers. Sharecroppers were given security of tenure, and the size of the landlord's share was cut down. Agricultural income tax was raised to make the position of the big landlords less desirable, and, since compensation was to be based on net income from estates, this measure had the bonus for the Government of reducing the cost of compensating zemindars. Then the big zemindari estates were taken over and vested in the Government. In the session of the Assembly which met between February and April, 1959, a bill was introduced, in conformity with the decisions of the Nagpur meeting of the All India Congress, to fix a ceiling on land and to encourage coöperative activities in farming. In short, and employing the familiar jargon, the intention was to eliminate the "feudal" elements in the countryside and to bring about a socialist pattern of society.

The Minister who piloted the Zemindari Abolition measures through the Assembly told me that two years later a fellow Congress politician said to him, "Well, my friend, you see now that people were not happy about the abolition of zemindari." When one considers that Zemindari Abolition was designed to relieve poor people of a large number of exactions, this is a surprising statement. It is worth examining what it means.

There are horrifying accounts of the brutality and avarice of some of the zemindars. But, even if they were all bad, nevertheless they performed a service for their tenants which the bureaucracy, by its very nature, found it difficult to provide. The essence of their role was that it was personal and direct and paternal. A good zemindar could remit the rent, if he wished, without looking up the regulations to see if that was permissible. He lent money and grain. He was not surrounded by a host of clerks and intermediaries, through whom the peasant had to find his way to reach the source of power. He was not an impersonal regular machine; he was a man, and he was accessible. In other words, though the peasant undoubtedly paid through the nose for the services he got, he did get something.

The persons who drafted the various zemindari restriction and abolition bills were aware that when they took over the estates they would have to provide comparable services. As an interim measure officials called Adhikari were appointed. But these officials were members of the bureaucracy and bound by its rules and accustomed to its ways of dealing with peasants. Difficulties and frictions were bound to ensue. Ties which had existed for generations were broken up, for it was impossible to replace every zemindar by an Adhikari. For some people the change meant that they now had to go longer distances to pay their rents or to make their petitions. It is not surprising, therefore, that the concrete economic benefits which the measures brought to the peasants were sometimes forgotten in the welter of administrative difficulties.

But this was not the only reason that those same Congress members who supported the Zemindari Abolition measures were pessimistic about its effects. Many felt that the measures might endanger their electoral chances, because they harmed persons of power and influence in the countryside. It was generally believed that the peasants did not vote according to their own convictions, but on the instructions of their masters. A rich man's support was believed to be worth many votes. One MLA said, "The rich will always be having their power. You can hate the moneylender, but you have to do what he says. Even the secret ballot isn't really much protection, because the moneylender or zemindar soon finds out how people voted, because often they themselves can't keep quiet about it."

Zemindari Abolition was followed by an act designed to set up Local Government institutions to replace the Adhikaris, and to fill the gap left by zemindars in zemindari areas, and elsewhere to decentralize government and make its services more accessible to the ordinary people. This was the Anchal Sasan Act, the story of which illustrates one of the main difficulties of social reformers—legislation has to be implemented, and this has to be done by the bureaucracy.

The individuals who had promoted the Anchal Sasan bill, for various reasons happened to retire from cabinet before the Act was implemented. The successor cabinet, the bill having already been ratified by the legislature, convened a committee of administrators to recommend ways and means of implementing the bill, and the timing of its introduction. After two years this committee reported that in the present circumstances the bill was unworkable and recommended that it be implemented some time in the course of the third Five Year Plan.

I need not here go into the reasons why the Committee thought the measure impracticable, still less can I take sides and try from my very limited knowledge to say whether in fact the measure could have been implemented then. Our interest lies in the attitude of politicians towards the executive services.

Various comments on the bill not being implemented were given to me in conversation with politicians. Some said that their fellow MLAs were pleased with the outcome, because if an adequate system of Local Government came into being, their constituents would no longer be bringing every little grievance to their MLA and so feeling dependent on him. But others denied this and said that they themselves would be pleased to be relieved of the burden of dealing with these trifles and have time to get on with their proper business. ("They come to me with every conceivable kind of demand, from one who wants a power station built in his village to one who wants me to find a bride for his son.") Others claimed that the majority of the MLAs were distressed at the shelving of a measure which had been passed in the Legislature and said that this was typical of the cautious and negative attitude of the bureaucracy. The more thoughtful informants made it clear that the civil servants were not reluctant to devolve power because they were personally interested in retaining it, but because they feared that the institutions which would take their place would not function efficiently. "What they're saying, in fact, is what the British said of us, 'They're not ripe for self-government.'"

The executive comes under hostile criticism from all sides. The Opposition parties accuse it of being unduly subservient to the party in power, and of allowing itself to be used for party purposes. Both sides are loud in their accusations of inefficiency and corruption and delay. Members of the Government party attribute the difficulties and frictions which have resulted from agrarian reform to the incompetence of administrators. Others consider that the fault lies rather with the institutional arrangement than with individuals, and that the bureaucracy, as at present constituted, is not adapted to implementing measures of social reform and economic development.

There is everywhere an antipathy between the civil servant and the legislator who in a fever of enthusiasm brings in a new measure and then runs his head against a brick wall of cold practical objections: "X, which you have passed, will not be effective unless you also do p, q, and r: and the cost of this will be . . ." But in India this feeling must be heightened by the way in which the Civil Services are associated, in their origin and form and in men's memories, with the British regime in India. They are thought to be cautious and conservative, negative and unadventurous. They are thought to look down upon the legislators, and there are frequent rumours, current among the politicians themselves, of how this or that Minister was snubbed by this or that Secretary.

One must not make too much of this. But it would be a mistake to forget that the reforms which go through the Legislature and which, as they are written down on paper, might be expected to rally voters to the side of the party in power have to be implemented; and the popularity of the party in power depends not on its legislative intentions, but on their implementation.

In short, social and agrarian reforms only redound to the credit of the party in power in the eyes of the common man if they measure up to his expectations and to the promises made to him, or at least if he does not feel worse off after them than he did before. These are two-edged weapons, and if they are not handled carefully, they can do more damage to the wielder than to his opponent. Frictions and difficulties, downright bungling and corruption, have given the Opposition parties powerful electoral weapons to turn against the Congress.

There are two difficulties. Firstly, it is impossible to please everyone all the time, and a redistribution of privileges means that some people feel themselves dispossessed. Secondly, the promise is not always the same as the fulfilment, and the reforms may bring in their train all kinds of unexpected difficulties.

THE ORISSAN HILLS

The returns of the 1957 general elections for the Legislative Assembly showed clearly that Congress had failed to win support in the ex-state areas of the western hills. The votes polled by Congress and its main opponent, the Ganatantra Parishad, are given in Table 10. In each of the four coastal districts Congress polled roughly four times as many votes as did Ganatantra. In seven of the remaining nine districts Ganatantra collected between one-and-a-half and three times as many votes as the Congress. In the remaining two districts, Koraput and Mayurbhanj, the voting figures were near parity.

There were 66 seats in the four coastal districts; of these, Congress obtained 42, and Ganatantra won two. In the remaining districts there are 74 seats, of which Congress won 14, and Ganatantra won 49.

Why did Congress fail in the hill areas?

TABLE 10

VOTES POLLED IN EACH DISTRICT IN THE 1957 ELECTIONS TO THE ORISSA LEGISLATIVE ASSEMBLY BY THE GANATANTRA PARISHAD AND THE CONGRESS PARTY [a]

District	Congress votes	Ganatantra votes
Cuttack	441,434	100,664
Puri	216,363	49,108
Balasore	203,487	41,106
Ganjam	199,659	41,219
Koraput	99,639	84,019
Mayurbhanj	47,293	49,540
Bolangir	65,998	200,896
Dhenkanal	60,337	122,298
Kalahandi	77,823	172,612
Keonjhar	37,907	61,705
Phulbani	21,660	46,100
Sundargarh	53,575	107,752
Sambalpur	102,965	148,558
Total	1,628,180	1,225,577

SOURCE: *Statistical Outline of Orissa*, 1957.
[a] The remaining contestants, Communists, Praja Socialists, Independents, and others, not shown in this table, polled between them roughly 1,400,000 votes.

India in 1948 was fighting a desperate struggle against anarchy. There was the crisis in Kashmir, there were refugee problems, and there was the struggle over the Princely States.

The Orissa Government had won its battle against the rulers of the Feudatory States, and it took over the administration of these areas on January 1, 1948. The rulers were granted a privy purse, based on their state's income, an allowance to meet religious obligations, and certain tax concessions. At the higher level of policy-making there is discernible a distinct effort to be conciliatory, or at least to avoid vindictiveness. But at the same time the climate of 1948 was not suited to gentle and subtle handling of opponents who showed even the least sign of recalcitrance. Disorders were suppressed with a heavy hand.

The need for peace and order in the country was never felt so keenly as after the war. As always happens after wars, anti-social elements, who were drafted into the war or had been suppressed by it, find free play for their activities when the Government is war-weary and the people faced with various privations, the fruits of war. Then came the partition of the country and brought in its wake carnage, loot, and mass movement of population. The sanctity of life and property was lost, the Father of the nation fell a victim to the mad orgy of hatred and violence. It was at this time that the Orissa States lost their identity and merged in Orissa. The Rulers of the States who were dreaming of sovereignty after the withdrawal of the British awoke from the helplessness which had led them to agree to the merger. Some of them misused the privileges guaranteed to them by the Government of India and like the traditional "Bhasmasur" attempted to use these privileges to weaken the Power that granted them the same. The rulers were joined by self-seekers whose ambition could not be fulfilled with the assumption of power by the Congress. Many of those Congressmen who had outlived the patriotic fervour of the thirties and whose political ambition had got the better of their good sense, cut themselves from the Congress as Socialists and Communists, to preach discontent and disaffection. Independence brought freedom of thought in a degree which never existed in the country before and this freedom was unscrupulously used for subversive activities. A weak-kneed administration would certainly have fallen a prey in Orissa to the forces of disorder and disturbance which raised their head in the first years of the present regime. The big plans of development which the Government launched upon at the very beginning of their regime afforded the Socialists, the Communists, and the feudal rulers an opportunity to launch their attacks against the Government at Hirakud and among the Adibasis of Bamra and Mayurbhanj. The Government of Orissa boldly faced the attack and used the very force which had been so long used against themselves by the British, to establish order in the State. For over a century the Police had been used by the British to suppress popular movements to keep the people in abject bondage. Now they served as guardians of peace, engaged by a democratic Government, so that revolutionary administrative changes and the bold development plans might proceed unhampered. Naturally both the Government and their agents were misrepresented and mis-judged . . .

Towards the end of the year (1950) the activities of Hon'ble Ranjit Singh Bariha and other Hon'ble Ministers among the Adibasi population, contributed to a very great degree by easing the Adibasi situation by bringing about a broad outlook of unity among them. The foundation of the Nikhil Utkal Adibasi Congress was laid which in the succeeding year was to give the Jharkhand movement of Orissa a go-by. (*Orissa 1950–51* Public Relations Department. pp. 4–5.)

There were Adibasi risings in 1948 in Bamra, Gangpur, Bonai, and Pal-Lahara. These were put down by the Armed Police, some people were killed, others were detained, and collective fines were imposed on villages. In Kharsawan there was a particularly unpleasant outbreak, resulting, according to the official enquiry, in fourteen deaths, and according to an unofficial estimate, in several hundred. (R. Ghosh, 1948, pp. 1–6.)

There is a neat summary in *Orissa 1949* of the events of 1948 and 1949, showing how the political developments in the ex-states appeared to the Orissa Government.

In Gangpur the Bihar Adibasi leaders had a hand. At about this time some Rulers started an agitation for a State Union. Demonstrations were arranged in Kalahandi, Bolangir-Patna, Keonjhar, and Bamra, and extensive leafleteering urging the masses to nullify the merger was indulged in. The centres of activity were shifted to Calcutta, Chaibassa and Monoharpur (Singbhum) to avoid legal action by the Provincial Government. Adibasis in Keonjhar, Gangpur, Bonai, Bamra and Kalahandi were regularly contacted and incited to violence. In spite of the arrest and externment of prominent agitators, the Royalists continued to excite the Adibasis of Bamra, who were worked up to demand an immediate transfer of power to them. Mob lawlessness broke out with the result that at Deogarh (Bamra) on 26th July firing had to be resorted to resulting in 3 dead and 13 injured. The situation was soon brought under control. The Union movement continued with the financial backing of the Rulers, but in October, 1948, the Rulers agreed to accept the merger, and the movement died out.

The next phase in the integrated States started with the Maharajas of Kalahandi and Bolangir-Patna aided by the Rajas of Gangpur, Sonepur, and Bamra sponsoring a new political organization called the "Khoshal-Utkal Praja Parishad," the members of which consisted chiefly of Prajamandal seceders and anti-merger agitators with headquarters at Bolangir (Patna). Branches of the Parishad were opened in Kalahandi, Sonepur, Gangpur, Bonai, Keonjhar, Athmallick and Boudh and paid workers were busy propagating the party's ideals vilifying the Congress Government and Government employees, and canvassing support from the States people who were advised to vote for the Parishad candidates in the next general election.

(1949) Following the merger of Mayurbhanj the leaders of the Adibasi Mahasabha and the antimergerists incited the Adibasis to widespread defiance of law and order. With the arrest of some of their leaders the agitation took a more violent form and felling of Reserve forests started on a large scale. Armed Adibasi mobs moved about in the interior and threatened non-Adibasis, two of whom were killed. They damaged *ghat* roads and telegraph communications in their attempt to march upon Rairangpur and Baripada. To check lawlessness fire had to be opened on a few occasions and the movement gradually died out with the quartering of detachments of the Military Police Force, rounding up of agitators in specific cases, a few detentions, and the imposition of collective fines. (pp. 30–31)

There are several strands discernible in these disorders and, although I can disentangle them, I am not competent to discuss all of them, nor are they all relevant to the present theme.

One element which I will notice but not enlarge upon is the role of the Adibasis, the Jharkhand party, and the neighbouring state of Bihar. It will be noticed that the major disorders took place in the northern hill areas. This area, which is now part of Orissa's "Ruhr," has a large proportion of tribals in its population, and it is here that the Jharkhand has its support in Orissa. There are frequent allegations that people from Bihar and the Jharkhand were concerned in fomenting Adibasi disorders. Particularly is this said to be true of Saraikella and Kharsawan. But this is perhaps too delicate a subject to analyse, and in any case it is not my intention to describe particular historical events. I merely notice that these Adibasi movements occurred, and remark that if in the beginning they were connected with the formation of the Ganatantra Parishad, there was soon a parting of the ways. The Ganatantra is staunchly Oriya Nationalist, and it has been a constant opponent of the Jharkhand, particularly since, between 1957 and 1959, Congress was kept in power by the five Jharkhand voters in the Orissa Legislative Assembly.

The main lesson to be drawn from the events of 1948 and 1949 was that the Orissa Congress Government was not welcomed into the hill areas.

There were many reasons for this. Firstly, and fundamentally, there was the long-established antipathy between the hill and the coastal areas—the feeling against *Katakis*. This meant that not only the ex-rulers, who had their own particular grievance and reason for being "disgruntled," but also the small middle class and the common people of the hill areas looked with alarm on the new incursion of *Katakis*. Nor, so it seems, was much attempt made to win them over. The officials and the police descended upon the ex-state areas looking for trouble, as they could hardly have done otherwise in 1948. They came, as one of the Ganatantra MLA said, "with the mentality of conquerors." Complaints and protests were treated as "subversion." It need not be assumed that all the administrators had this outlook, but the many accounts I have had of highhandedness are, to say the least, not rendered unlikely by the attitude revealed in the quotations from *Orissa 1950–51*. People were imprisoned or "externed" from their home areas, and the ordinary mechanisms of democratic protest did not exist.

Secondly, there were certain administrative discomforts following the merger. A startling and immediate one was the price of rice. The ex-states were, in many respects, closed economies and shielded from the market prices ruling elsewhere in Orissa. I have been told that the price of rice increased fourfold overnight in some states, although I can find no published figures to substantiate this. In addition came the inconveniences of a large-scale bureaucracy. The personal rule of the Raja vanished and in its place came an organization which could be moved to action only by unfamiliar, lengthy, and complicated procedures, and often located many miles further away. It would have been miraculous if the take-over had occurred without friction, and whatever went wrong was naturally blamed upon the administrators who had been sent up from the coast by the Congress Government. In their turn the administrators blamed their difficulties on local "subversive" elements and "agitators."

The Ganatantra grew strong, for one reason, because it had the support of the local intelligentsia, and I will summarize the background in 1948 from which the Ganatantra emerged by quoting at length from an interview which I had with a man from one of the ex-states.

After the merger things were bad, as you know. We had to do something. The people could not swallow the merger: they were never consulted.

There was a difference in the Administration after '48 too. Petty officials stayed. But they did not believe in our officers and all the high officials came from outside. It was just like a military occupation. Our civil servants were transferred to other districts. The ruler had no hand in the administration. We were handed over to the State Ministry of India, and they handed us over to the Orissa Government.

There were all kinds of difficulties. For example, up to 31.12.47 rice was selling at 8 seers to the rupee. On the next day it was 2 seers to the rupee, due to the control price and fair price throughout Orissa. Then the medical facilities were free before the merger and the people were even being supplied with proprietary medicines. The institution was closed. There was a good X-ray equipment, Siemens, one of the only three in India, got during the Jubilee celebrations, and that was left uncared-for and other equipment was taken away. The administration did not care for the people. They behaved like victors over vanquished. After all, we are Indian too, aren't we?

This, all this, moulded the mind of the intelligentsia. Previously we had direct approach to the Raja, and we could get our remedy. But the remedy was now too far away. All educated people felt something had to be done. We could not undo the merger. But bribery and corruption became so rampant and so vivid. Bribery was there before in the state time, but it was not in broad daylight. Nor was there any punishment for it.

Everyone thought that something must be done. So we must have a party. Some of us went to the ruler and wanted him to start a party, since he had plenty of administrative and political experience. That was in 1949.

There was firing in Saraikella and Kharsawan and Bamra and Mayurbhanj; that all led to a cumulative effect. Our people were actually being killed.

We wanted everyone in the party, officials, everyone, so that we could end the misrule: We had to take everyone: there was a great shortage of people with administrative and political experience. We asked the Ruler to participate and we went to other states to ask other people to take part.

First we started a party that was called Khoshal-Utkal Praja Parishad. We established headquarters at Sambalpur, after the firing at Bamra. Prior to that we were all taken to prison. I was in Cuttack gaol for a month, but they could not make any charge against me except that I opposed the Government. They could not produce us in court; it was just preventive detention. Then I was interned in my district. Then I was served with an externment notice. So I went to Chaibassa in Bihar. I had headquarters there. I went there because we wanted an Eastern States Union. One thing we considered was that they had not taken the consent of the people, but only of the rulers, in getting us merged with Orissa. Secondly we had lost our own administration and were being ruled by outsiders in the name of democracy and self-rule. We wanted the right of self-determination. Patel [2] never con-

---

[2] Sardar Vallabhai Patel, the Union Government Minister in charge of the States Department.

sulted anyone except the rulers in merging the states—not the people. The people were active in politics in the Garjhat areas [Feudatory States]. We had our own Prajamandal Movements for getting popular rule in the states, and we had succeeded and we didn't want the Congress Prajamandal. We were getting self-rule by our own efforts. We did not want to be dictated to by outsider Congress Prajamandalists.

At the beginning of its life in 1948, while it was still called the Khoshal-Utkal Praja Parishad, the Ganatantra party had the inestimable advantage of being persecuted. What the Congress gained in 1921 and 1930 and between 1939 and 1942, the Ganatantra gained in 1948–1949. Leaders were externed or interned, public meetings were forbidden, the police broke up meetings, there were firings and arrests, and the people who witnessed these events or took part in them no doubt were too excited to perceive that the police were not suppressing "popular movements to keep the people in abject bondage" but were "guardians of the peace, engaged by a democratic government."

A broken head is equally painful, whoever wields the *lathi*.

FROM MOVEMENT TO PARTY

The story so far is one of difficulties for the Congress: Oriya Nationalism, conflicting ideas about the direction and pace of social reform and difficulties of implementation, and the legacy of suspicion and hostility between the coast and the hill peoples. What effect did these forces have upon the Congress up to 1959? The answer, in brief, is that Congress ceased to be a movement and became a party.

On March 29, 1959, a conference of "political sufferers" (those who suffered hardship as a result of their part in the Freedom Fight) met in Cuttack. The meeting was reported in the *Amrita Bazar Patrika* of April 2, 1959. Several public men, including MLAs, spoke to the gathering. The Deputy Speaker of the Legislative Assembly "deplored that certain new types of persons, who were veering round the present-day Ministry, had styled themselves political workers. Ministers should not expect any sort of flattery from these people." The meaning of this last sentence is obscure, but the general trend of the remarks is clear: some persons, not genuine political sufferers, were trying to gain positions of influence by posing as such. A later speaker, the leader of the Communists in the Orissa Assembly, put a similar point more clearly. "[He] commented on the attitude of those at the helm of administration of free India and said that some of them unfortunately were those who had taken pleasure in suppressing Freedom Movement."

An Independent MLA, making a different point, asked the political sufferers "to be above present-day politics and not to be a wing of the party-in-power."

From the first two of these quotations it appears that those who took part and suffered in the Independence Movement are thought to have a superior right to hold power to-day. From the last quotation one would conclude that the Congress party in 1959 was not the same body as the Congress which fought for Independence. I now describe this change.

The reasons for the 1947 victory, when Congress won 45 seats in a house of 60 (37 seats uncontested), are clear. Congress was virtually the only party in the field. Its candidates consisted largely of "martyrs," men who had a few months before been released from security prisons. Independence was just around the corner, and the credit for this seemed to lie with the Gandhian wing of the Congress. Congress was clearly about to become the Government. This accounts for the 37 uncontested seats: few people could be found who would risk branding themselves as the implacable opponents of a party that was about to assume power. The same fact testifies to party discipline. At that time those Congressmen who were not given a ticket could be persuaded not to try their luck as Independents, in opposition to the Congress.

After the merger of the Feudatory States, 31 people were nominated by the Government to form an Orissa State Assembly. A year later this was dissolved and members were nominated to sit in the regular Legislative Assembly which then used to meet at Cuttack. Since these members were nominated by the Congress, their presence made no difference to that party's hold upon the Legislative Assembly.

There was a cabinet, initially of six members. Four of these came from the two northern districts of the coast, one from Puri, and one from Koraput. All six cabinet members were exemplary Freedom Fighters, and at least five of them had been security prisoners. Later three persons were nominated from the ex-state areas and given cabinet rank; all three were leaders of the Prajamandal Movement.

In 1948 two of the original members of the cabinet resigned. One, who sat for a Koraput constituency, was replaced by another man from Koraput. The portfolios were reshuffled and one was given to a member (since dead) who was both a Raja and a member of a Scheduled tribe. This gentleman's success in giving "the Jharkhand movement of Orissa a go-by" was mentioned earlier. He came from Sambalpur, and it may be assumed that he was taken into the cabinet both in order to give that area some representation and because he was especially qualified, as a tribal chief, to counter the growing menace of the Jharkhand in the northern hills of Orissa. He, alone in the cabinet, did not have a record as a Freedom Fighter.

The 1952 election covered the whole of the State and was held on a universal adult franchise. There were 140 seats in the new house. Of these Congress won 67: in the coastal districts 41 out of a possible 68, and in the hills 26 out of a possible 72.

I shall analyse Congress membership in the 1952 and the 1957 houses and in some of the cabinets, using three categories. The first are Freedom Fighters (FF), whom I define as those people who gained an Orissa-wide reputation for their part in the Independence Movement, and I take as a criterion of this the mention of their names, as leaders, in the third, fourth, or fifth volumes of the official *History of the Freedom Movement in Orissa* (Mahtab, 1957). The second category consists of Congress workers and sympathizers (W&S), people who are not mentioned in the *History*, but who were active or passive sympathizers of the Movement and who certainly never opposed it. This category includes a few junior men who came to the Congress after 1947, having been too young to play any serious part in the Independence Movement. The third category are the opponents of the Congress, and this includes those who actively opposed it in the period before Independence, those who at some time left the Congress and opposed it (e.g., the Swarajists), those who were won over from opposition parties after 1947, and finally those who, while not themselves active opponents of the Congress, belonged to groups or categories which were ranged against the Congress (e.g. some zemindars, rajas, and administrators).

These three categories of FF, W&S, and Opponents are not entirely satisfactory. The *History* certainly overestimates the work of some individuals and probably undervalues the significant part played by others, and it is possible that the W&S category is a very broad one and may include some persons whose Congress sympathies only became apparent after 1946 —"new types of persons, who . . . had styled themselves political workers." In short, the categories are somewhat arbitrary, but they are the best that the limited material will allow, and, crude though they are, they meet the present purpose, which is to trace the progressive dilution of Congress "purity" in Orissa—its transformation from "movement" to "party." According to these categories the Congress members of the 1952 house are as follows:

Of the 26 members from the hill districts,
  4 were FF (two coming from British districts)
  20 were W&S, and
  2 were Opponents, both Raj (princely) family, one being the ex-minister from Sambalpur.
Of the 41 members from the four coastal districts
  18 were FF,
  21 were W&S, and
  2 were Opponents, both from Raj families.
The cabinet in 1952 included 13 Ministers. Of these
  5 were FF, 3 being Ministers and 2 Deputy Ministers,
  5 were W&S, 2 being Ministers and 3 Deputy Ministers, and
  3 were Opponents, all Raj family, one Minister, and two Deputy Ministers.

In the 1947 House both the Government and Congress were still narrowly based on "orthodox" Congressmen, and had a dominant number of FF. Eight of the nine members of the 1948 cabinet were in that category. But in the 1952 House there are clear signs that the cleavage between the FF and their erstwhile opponents was beginning to close. The Congress Assembly Party included four members from Raj families, three in the 1952 cabinet and one who had previously held a portfolio. One other member of a Raj family had been given the Congress ticket, but was not elected. The 1948 cabinet of nine men included one person (11 per cent) from the Opponent category: the 1952 cabinet of thirteen men included three persons (23 per cent) from that category.

Five of the 1952 Congressmen in the cabinet were in the W&S category. This partly reflects the passing of time and the promotion of earlier leaders to the higher realms of politics. But it also, perhaps, indicates that some of those who had not the gifts to lead an agitation did have the skills required for orderly government, and that it was becoming clear that the FF badge alone was not a sufficient qualification for political leadership after 1947.

But the gap was as yet far from being closed. By and large the Congress tickets were still being given to old Congress workers. The Swarajists were still outside the fold. Nor was the Congress leadership happy about taking in members of Raj families. I have been told that as many as eighteen members of Raj families would have accepted the Congress ticket had it been offered to them. But it was not. The Congress preferred their own men, and the Rajas threw their influence against these candidates and most of them were defeated.

The 1952 elections demonstrated that the appeal which the party seemed to have in 1946 had not lasted until 1952 and had not spread outside the coastal plain. Congress was returned in 1952 on a minority vote. Even on the coastal plain, out of 68 Congress candidates 27 had been defeated. Twelve of these fell to other parties (one Ganatantra, five Communists, five Socialists, and one Marxist Forward Block) and no less than fifteen seats were taken by Independents. Seven of these Independents were Rajas or zemindars and two were Swarajists; another Swarajist was the Forward Block member. Fifteen individuals showed that they could win seats without the official backing of any party. If some of these and some other persons had been given the Congress ticket, then the party might have come in with a majority. At least it must have occurred to the party managers then that one day they might be faced with the choice of compromising on Congress "purity" or being entirely defeated.

Although the 1952 Congress was elected with a minority, it did not have such a difficult time in the House as one might expect. Some Independents joined the party soon after the election; others, who were not permitted to join the party, nevertheless voted consistently with the Government. Again, many of the measures which Congress introduced—particularly agrarian reform—had the support of the left-wing parties, and these bills went through with majorities far in excess of the paper majority commanded by the Government.

But by 1956 the Congress was in difficulties. For personal reasons the Minister from Koraput, who had piloted through the Zemindari Abolition measure, resigned his portfolio. The Chief Minister, who was the mainspring behind the agrarian reforms and the attempt to introduce local self-government through the Anchal Sasan bill, and who before the war had been the leader of the Congress Socialist Party, resigned to join the Bhoodan Movement. At the same time there was the grave embarrassment of the States Reorganization Commission's report and the subsequent disorders. Within the Congress there was a deep cleavage between those who supported the Chief Minister, approved of Zemindari Abolition, and admired his refusal to compromise on ideological issues, including Congress "purity" and those who believed that a more "realistic" policy must be adopted if Congress was to remain a power within the State. These were the people who noticed that Zemindari Abolition was "not popular" and who considered it right to take in former opponents of the Congress in order to meet the growing threat of the Ganatantra Parishad in the hills and of the left-wing parties on the plains.

An analysis of Congress membership of the 1957 House and the cabinets shows quite clearly that "realistic" thinking had prevailed in the party's councils. Congress had 56 members, eleven less than after the 1952 election. Of these 42 (out of a possible 66) were in the four coastal districts, and 14 in the hill districts. Thus they gained one seat in the coastal districts and lost 13 in the hills.

Of the 42 members for constituencies in the coastal districts

17 had held Congress seats in the 1952 House, of whom
   7 were FF,

8 were W&S, and
2 were Opponents, both Raj family: and
25 were new members, of whom
  3 were Congressmen who had failed to be elected in 1952,
    2 being FF, and
    1 was W&S,
  2 were FF who had not stood in the 1952 election, and
10 were W&S newcomers. But against this there were as many as
10 Opponents returned on the Congress ticket, of whom
  2 were ex-Swaraj, one an Independent in the 1952 House and one who had narrowly failed to be elected to that House on a non-Congress ticket,
  1 had been a Communist in the 1952 House,
  4 were Raj family, three of whom had been Independents in the 1952 House, two of them being the leaders of the prewar rentier Opposition in the Assembly,
  1 had been an Independent MLA in the 1952 House in a reserved seat, and
  2 had been officials, one of whom was an old enemy of the Congress.

In this way no less than 6 of these 10 Opponents had defeated Congress candidates in the 1952 general elections.

Of the 14 members in the hill districts,
  5 had held seats in the 1952 House, of whom
    3 were FF,
    1 was W&S, and
    1 was an Opponent, a member of a Raj family: and
  9 were newcomers, of whom
    7 were W&S, and
    2 were Opponents, both Raj family, one of whom was unseated by an election tribunal and lost the subsequent bye-election to a Ganatantra commoner candidate a few weeks before the Coalition came about.

There were thus fifteen Opponents within the ranks of the Congress when the election results were announced. But even then the Congress was able to achieve a precarious majority only by taking in Independents and deserters from other parties, and by relying on the support of five Jharkhand members. Congress support, according to the "purist" way of thinking, was down to 41 persons, and that must have included a number of bandwaggoners in the W&S category. This was in a House of 140 persons.

Just prior to the Coalition in 1959 (that is, after the scandals of April and May, 1958, and the dismissal of one of the Congress Deputy Ministers) the cabinet numbered 14, 10 being Ministers and 4 Deputy Ministers. Of these 14

6 had held portfolios in the previous cabinet, of whom
   3 were FF,
   2 were W&S, and
   1 was Raj family: and
8 were newcomers, of whom
   2 were Congressmen, both members of previous cabinets,
      1 being FF, and
      1 W&S; and
   6 were Opponents, of whom
      1 was a Raja,
      3 were prominent enemies of the Congress before 1947
         2 being Rajas, and
         1 an official, and
      2 were people who had defeated Congress candidates in the 1957 election,
         1 Raj family, standing as an Independent, and
         1 elected on a Ganatantra ticket.

Thus in the fourteen member cabinet, seven members came from the Opponent category, four were FF, and three were W&S.

The broadening of the base of Congress, culminating in the

closing of the breach between it and its pre-1947 opponents on the Orissa plains, is summarized in Table 11 and Table 12.

TABLE 11
CONGRESS MEMBERSHIP IN THE ORISSA LEGISLATIVE ASSEMBLY
1952–1957

Year	Seats won	FF	W&S	Opponents
1952	67	22 (33%)	41 (61%)	4 (6%)
1957	56	15 (27%)	26 (46%)	15 (27%)

From these tables it is clear that the pre-1947 opposition to the Congress on the coastal plains after 1957 found its political representation within the Congress. By 1957 the social base of the Orissa Congress was entirely changed from what it had been before 1947. By 1957 its membership cut across the former cleavage of Congress and landlords on the plains, and this cleavage, on the surface at least, disappeared.

TABLE 12
SOME CONGRESS CABINETS IN ORISSA, 1946–1959

Year	Members	FF	W&S	Opponents
1946	6	6 (100%)	–	–
1948	9	8 (89%)	–	1 (11%)
1952	13	5 (38%)	5 (38%)	3 (24%)
1959	14	4 (29%)	3 (21%)	7 (50%)
Coalition (July, 1959)	11	3 (27%)	2 (18%)	6 (55%)

Seen against this background, the coalition formed in 1959 was an extension of the policy already followed in dealing with the landlord interest in the plains. There was a technical difference in form, in that this was a coalition of two parties, and not merely the absorbing of individuals from the opposing interest into the Congress. But from a structural point of view the two processes were identical; a new group was formed by cutting across groups which previously opposed one another.

These events were a godsend to the propagandists of the opposition parties, and a source of dissension within the Congress. The left-wing parties argued that the Congress could no longer pretend to socialism. Whatever the Congress or the Coalition Government had to say about their intentions, it was unlikely (the left-wing argued) that men who were not only born into an aristocracy but also had fought a long and bitter fight to maintain their way of life would overnight become enthusiastic proponents of socialism.

Congress paid a price for thus diluting its "purity." By strengthening the party on one wing, it lost members on the other. Most of the leading figures in the left wing had already resigned from the Congress before the 1952 elections and were not there to dispute the evident change of outlook and policy in 1956. But the adoption of former Opponents caused some demoralization in the Congress at district and constituency level. The allocation of tickets is always a delicate operation and at the best of times puts a strain on the unity of the local organization. But when the ticket goes to someone who has no record of service to the party, but may even have a record of active opposition, then old Congressmen who wanted the ticket feel free to try their luck as Independents. (But, if the party has judged correctly, they do not succeed.)

Persons adopted into the Congress from the Opponent category were in a peculiarly strong position, since the Government had a very narrow majority. Their strength did not rest on party backing; they were persons of influence in their own right; and they were sometimes persons of ability. This was one reason why seven members of the 1959 cabinet came from the Opponent category.

This resulted in a further demoralization of the "pure" Congressmen, when they saw that some of those "at the helm of administration of free India" were "unfortunately those who had taken pleasure in suppressing Freedom Movement." In this category of dissidents are to be included both those who felt that the prizes of victory had been given to the wrong persons and those more idealistic persons who felt that with such new members the party would no longer follow the policies in approval of which they had given it their allegiance.

POLITICIANS AND VOTERS

Out of this short narrative of events in Orissa since the turn of the century, I direct attention at two things. One is the change in the style of politics, most clearly typified by the change in Congress. Congress was a movement; after 1947, by degrees it became a party. Before Independence the members of the movement were united by a common moral purpose. They were moved by an ideology, the rightness of which none of them questioned, although they might from time to time fall out over tactics. After Independence—the fulfilment of their purpose—no new moral focus, none at least of the same power, was found. From 1947 to 1959 Congress came more and more to be held together by a very delicate balancing of interests. Moral action tended to be replaced by expedient action.

The other topic—they are related—is the participation of ordinary people in politics. "Independence" had to be given a parochial twist before it became an effective rallying cry for the peasants. Oriya Nationalism, in the early days, concerned them hardly at all. The message had to be carried to them by "missionaries," and the main task—that of uniting the Oriya-speaking tracts—was performed by professional men and aristocrats, using the methods of round-the-table diplomacy. Politics, up to 1947, went on over the heads of the ordinary people.

The problem of politics in the years between 1947 and 1959 was that politics still went on over the heads of the ordinary people—except in one vital respect: politicians needed votes.

What are the steps in this argument? Oriya politicians in 1959 said that their trouble had been "instability." No party had an effective majority; too much time and energy went into balancing the narrow interests that kept the majority intact or in trying to upset them. One explanation for this is the removal of the mainspring—the quest for Independence. Other explanations lie in the realm of accident: for example, Congress might have done better in the 1957 election, if the report of the States Reorganization Commission had not at that particular time detonated Oriya Nationalism. Equally it is an accident that the two halves of Orissa are approximately equal in voting strength. Had the hill area and the former Feudatory States been smaller, then the Orissa Congress might have won the comfortable majorities that the party commanded in other States in the Indian Union.

But we are still left with a question. Why was the Congress unable to make effective contact with the electorate in the hill areas? Why could it not dispossess the coastal landlords of their popularity, as it took away their estates? Why, indeed, did all parties fail to break into the narrow bastions of parochial loyalty?

I have given descriptive answers to these questions in the two first parts of the book. In my final chapter I discuss them again, from a more analytical point of view.

CONCLUSION.
POLITICS AND SOCIAL CHANGE

The three parts of this book appear to be integrated with one another in a far from satisfactory way. The first resembles social anthropology; the second looks like political science; and the third part might have been written by a somewhat hasty historian with sociological leanings. Is there a single conceptual framework into which the three parts fit?

One difficulty is that Orissa is not a unity. It is not yet a single complex society, but an aggregate of many simple societies, imperfectly linked into what may be a cultural and linguistic whole, but is hardly yet a social whole. Clearly "simple" and "complex" are important concepts. What do they mean?

The distinction resembles that between segmentary and organic types of society. Orissa is segmentary insofar as it consists of many self-contained units, able to carry on political life without concern for other units. It is for this reason that politicians have to devise approaches tailor-made for the particular community whose support they are trying to enlist.

When social anthropologists analyse simple societies, they are, as I understand the process, demonstrating an ultimate

CONCLUSION

consistency not only between sets of activities, but also between types of activities: for example, they show that a man's economic roles are systematically linked not only with the economic roles of other people but also with his (and other peoples') political roles, kinship roles, religious roles, and so forth. These different roles sometimes appear to be one single role, albeit consisting of interwoven strands of conceptually separable activities. The values (and sometimes the terminology) of one set of activities may dominate the rest, as when kinship is the master principle of one type of society or religion (so it is claimed) underwrites the Indian caste system.

In this context the word simple does not refer immediately to cultural or technical achievements, but to a pattern of relationships. Simple societies are those in which the same set of people interact with one another in politics, in ritual, in making a living, and so forth. People in such societies are related to one another by "multiplex" ties, that is, by ties woven from all the different kinds of social activity.

Conversely, complex societies are those characterized by single-interest relationships, where a man interacts with one set of people in politics, another in his religious activities, a third in economic affairs, and a fourth set of people make up his kinsmen. These different sets of people may have no direct connection with one another. Relationships are specialized, and in such societies it is easier to describe one type of activity (e.g., politics) without having to introduce others (e.g., religion or kinship). On the other hand that form of analysis which consists in demonstrating the multiplex nature of relationships, will clearly not be effective in a complex society, insofar as single-interest relationships are prevalent.

This crude opposition of two ideal types of society—the simple and the complex—removes some of the vagueness of the confrontation, made at the beginning of this book, between "traditional society" and "representative institutions."

The rules and conventions under which parliamentary institutions operate presuppose a complex society and not an aggregate of simple societies. Accordingly, where difficulties arise, it will be seen that people are continuing to work within the framework of their own simple society, in situations which demand single-interest relationships. For example, the legitimate forms of electioneering are suited to a complex society where politics are accepted as a specialized activity. In Orissa, on the other hand, effective vote-catching can only be done by establishing a more-than-political, that is, a multiplex relationship with the villagers.

Our problem, then, is to find a conceptual framework into which both the specialized political roles of representative institutions and the undifferentiated roles of traditional society (whether at the elite or the village level) will fit.

I have analysed political activity at three levels: the State, the constituencies, and the villages. These are only three among many possible levels. Furthermore, within the lower levels, there are many fields; there is one Orissa State, but in 1959 there were 101 constituencies, and (to go by the 1951 Census) 51,000 villages. There are also such non-localized fields of political activity as castes and caste associations, trade unions, and countless other associations.

Such a wide field must be arbitrarily cut down to make discussion possible. I shall stay with the three already used (village, constituency, and State) in the hope that, if these three can be satisfactorily handled, this will provide a method of handling other arenas as well.

The most intractable difficulty—for practical but not theoretical reasons—is sampling. In a universe of 51,000 villages a sample of about 2,500 would not by any means be extravagantly large. No anthropologist has the resources for work on this scale. I do not know how many Orissa villages more closely resemble Bisipara than they do Mohanpur. I can argue

CONCLUSION

deductively that Bisipara must be the more typical, but I have not done the counting, and no one ever will do the counting, to prove that this is so. Perhaps there is no need, because the statements towards which we aim are logical: statements of what must be, given certain conditions, and not descriptions of what exists.

Leaving aside the problem of sampling, one may either handle the several fields of political activity as if they were joined systematically to one another, or as if they were separate units which are considered together only because they fall into the same logical category. The first is an interactional approach; the second may be called cultural, or attributional.

The second approach seems to me to be the less fruitful, although it is easier to use and may give results which seem to be less fogged by doubts and qualifications than the interactional approach. This cultural approach can give a quite spurious air of profundity and insight. To invent an example, one may say that leadership in the Indian political parties can best be understood in the light of attitudes in the Indian joint family towards the family head. The same value is thus found in two different fields, and we are on the way to discovering the distinctive "style" of Indian politics. But are we really so much further when, in a flash of inspiration, we remember that Gandhi is called by the villagers their "mother and father"? Not all the endeavours to find traits and values and sentiments which appear to be common to the different political fields are so superficial as this one, but they all involve the same weakness; they fail to ask whether the fields of political activity, both at the same and at different levels, are connected with one another through social interaction. This is to me the more interesting question, and the one which I shall pursue in the remainder of this chapter.

To summarize so far. Out of the many possible fields I have

CONCLUSION
223

chosen those of the village, the constituency, and the State. Our postulate is that there may be some kind of framework into which all three of these can be fitted, and we hope that the exercise of constructing this framework will also help to include fields of different levels (e.g. the districts) and of different kinds (e.g. castes, associations, and so forth). The search is not so much to find similarities and differences between the different arenas, with the intention of establishing a "style" or "idiom" of Indian politics, but to discover how the different arenas are connected through interaction. In other words, if such a framework is found, it would enable us to include not only fields at different levels, and of different types, but also the many examples of fields within one level (e.g. the 101 constituencies) as a single sociopolitical system.

Having decided on an interactional approach, the next step is to define "political." The political is that aspect of any act which concerns the distribution of power, providing that there is competition for this power, and provided, secondly, that the competition takes place under a set of rules which the competitors observe and which ensure that the competition is orderly. Insofar as there may be no competition, then the action ceases to be political and becomes merely administrative. If the competitors do not agree upon rules and institutions which make for orderly competition and resort to violence, then their actions are warlike and not political.

A definition of this kind clearly has a wider reference than merely to the activities of those who are ordinarily considered politicians. Anthropologists, having been long in contact with societies which are orderly and yet have no government, have ceased to limit their definition of political to such institutions as kings and parliaments and political parties. Almost every social act may have its political aspect, whether this act takes place within a family, or in a religious congregation, or in the world of business. We talk of "University politics" or "Church

CONCLUSION

politics." These are not metaphors. We are talking on these occasions of people competing for power or preferment, and this is no less political than what goes on in parliaments and council chambers.

I have used the word institution, as well as the word rule, in order to make clear that there does not have to be a codified and published set of rules (such as those put out by the Election Commissioners and contained in the various statutes governing free elections) before political activity can exist. There is no comparable body of rules which directly and explicitly regulate politics in the villages. This competition—as that between castes in Bisipara—is, of course, restrained and limited by the general laws governing violence and disorders, but these are of general application and not designed to umpire village conflicts alone. Nor is there any statute laying down, for instance, that it shall be caste groups which are eligible to compete. Nevertheless the village arena is clearly governed by institutions—by conventions and customs—whatever is the appropriate word. It must be understood, therefore, that although I continue to use the word rules for the sake of simplicity, I do not necessarily mean codified legal rules and statutes. I mean also customs and conventions.

These rules, customs, and conventions define political arenas. They regulate political conflict by laying down who is eligible to compete, what are the prizes for the winner, and what the competitors may do and what they must not do in their efforts to gain the prizes.

It is clear that what I have called arenas can on other occasions or from a different point of view be called groups. For example, a constituency is an arena when an election is held. In theory, once the representative is elected, the constituency becomes a group for whose interests the representative works. Similarly the village arena may, in opposition to a rival village or an administrator, become a group. Likewise

CONCLUSION

Oriya Nationalism is an indication that the State has for the time being ceased to be an arena and itself entered the all-India arena as a group. The process is called "fission and fusion" in the segmentary political systems described by anthropologists. What from below appears as an arena, from above seems to be a group.

If we are satisfied with this model, then we need look no further for a systematic account of political activity in Orissa. If we begin with the State, we can say that this is a group on some occasions, but on others it segments into competing districts or constituencies. Each of these are groups when in competition with one another, but when they are not in competition a process of fission takes place and they become arenas, and so forth down to the village. We can sketch out the same framework from the bottom upwards. Villages are arenas until they come into competition with one another, when a process of fusion takes place and they become groups, and so on, up to State politics and beyond.

Yet this does not seem to be a satisfactory framework within which to make sense of Orissa politics at all levels. It is, of course, true that the village, for example, is sometimes a group and sometimes an arena. But it is not true, as the fission and fusion model implies, that an interfering hand from outside will cause the village to close its ranks. Often the result is quite the reverse, and the villagers may take the opportunity to intensify their fissile activity and try to use the interfering hand to do one another down. This is the way the Bisipara villagers used the 1957 General Election.

The fission and fusion model fails to account for the internecine qualities of villages like Bisipara, because it assumes a consistency of rules at all levels. In fact, in the three levels which I have described in this book, there is an evident conflict of rules between the village arenas and arenas at higher levels. If I may reify, the rules of representative democracy, as applied at State and constituency levels, are trying to put the

CONCLUSION

village rules out of business and to "digest" and transform the village arenas. The situation is one of potential change, and a plain "fission and fusion" model must be discarded because it does not allow for a contradiction of rules at different levels and consequently it does not allow for change.

I am not, of course, dispensing with the concept of "group." To do so would be absurd, for it would not be possible to describe an arena without identifying the groups which compete within it. Perhaps I am saying no more than a sociologist's *memento mori*: groups are liable not just to fission but to permanent fission, to disintegration. Indeed some, like the machines and brokerage networks described earlier, seem to have within them the seeds of their own destruction; like Mr. Cornford's medlar, they have the knack of going rotten before they ever become ripe.

Arena, rather than group, must be a key concept, because group has too many connotations of permanence and stability. Even the most superficial survey of the fate of parliamentary democracy in the new nations steers one away from words which suggest permanence and stability.

In theory, through free elections, every adult in Orissa is potentially an actor in the arena of State politics. In practice, this arena is much narrower. Firstly, in Orissa between 50 and 60 per cent of the electorate do not avail themselves of the right to vote. Secondly, voting and elections are far from being the only activity in this arena. The voters are like the crowd at a football match—their cheers may influence the course of the game, but the game itself is played by the men on the field. The protagonists in the arena of State politics are an elite of professional politicians and some other persons. To emphasize this fact, I shall from this point onwards call this the "elite arena."

It would, of course, be unrealistic to attempt to draw a sharp boundary around this arena, in terms of the protagonists. It is clear than an MLA is in and that a village headman is out, *ex officio* so to speak. But a businessman or a contractor may be in or out, depending on the scale of his operations, and upon the people with whom he is connected.

The word "connected" suggests another characteristic of this arena. In my third section I briefly outlined three main conflicts which have taken place in State politics: Oriya Nationalism, the Independence Movement, and the Hill against Coast struggle since Independence. Speaking roughly, in Oriya Nationalism the teams were an association against a ruling bureaucracy; the same description would fit the Independence struggle; in the third case there are several associations (the political parties) in competition with one another. An association is by definition a group of people coöperating to pursue a common interest, and it is this interest which defines the group. In other words, the relationships which make up such a group are single-interest.

But we may also attempt to define any kind of group socially—that is to say, in the case of an association, by asking whether the members have any ties with one another besides their common interest. How do the protagonists appear in this form?

In the case of Oriya Nationalism, it becomes a team of princes, landlords, and professional middle class against the British and non-Oriyas; in the Independence Movement it becomes a section of the landlord and professional middle class (i.e. the Congress) against the British, the Princes, and the bigger landlords; in the post-Independence conflict the sides are princes and landlords against Congress politicians and some landlords, with professional people found on both sides.

The striking thing about this list is that in all three episodes we seem to be dealing with the same set of people, except that in the last the British have dropped out. Defined as associations, the protagonists in Oriya Nationalism, in the Free-

CONCLUSION

dom Fight, and in the post-Independence Hill against Coast struggle are separate groups. Sociologically identified they are the same set of people; they are an elite or an "establishment." More than this, these people interact with one another not merely by coöperating and competing for political ends. They also know one another socially; they are drawn from a limited number of castes; and many of them are kinsmen. I do not mean that everyone in the arena of elite politics knows everyone else, still less that they can all trace links of kinship. But I do mean that the links of kinship, and of personal face-to-face acquaintances are so numerous that they must be taken into account if we are to understand the behaviour of the contestants in elite politics. Political conflict or coöperation is only one among many ways in which these people interact with one another.

There is a temptation here to reintroduce the word "group." When, for example, we notice that in two of the contests there are landlords on both sides, and when we further discover that some of these landlords are related to one another, or when we learn that leaders of opposing parties may come from the same caste and be related to one another, we must conclude that these crosscutting ties will tend to prevent out-and-out conflict. When we further establish that such crosscutting ties are ubiquitous, should we then say that they must lead to a degree of integration and that the elite is in fact a group and not an arena?

There is some truth in this. When all the elite coöperate, as they tend to do over Oriya Nationalism, then undoubtedly the mesh of crosscutting ties is one of the mechanisms which makes this coöperation possible.

But can we take the further step and say that this is a middle class, a group to be set in opposition to the peasants or the landless labourers or the industrial workers of Orissa? If we can do so, then we are on the way to setting up another framework within which to understand Orissa politics.

CONCLUSION

229

Once we have further established that peasants or workers are similarly to be considered groups, then Orissa politics can be envisaged as the conflict of economic classes; we have one arena in which the different classes fight it out with one another.

But this will not do. Firstly there is no corporate group of peasants or of workers. Secondly, when the arena of elite politics does undergo a process of fusion and the establishment closes its ranks, it is not in opposition to those whom they rule and perhaps exploit, but in opposition to establishments elsewhere—to other States or the Delhi Government. In relation to its own subjects, the establishment becomes most internecine.

A last point about the elite can be most briefly made by a metaphor: the members of the elite are not squires married to the daughters of their tenant farmers, hunting with their tenants, spending their lives on their estates. They are more like absentee landlords, making a five-yearly descent to collect rent in the form of votes. This does not, I repeat, make the elite a group in conflict with the mass; it merely reflects the fact that most of their time is spent as protagonists in the arena of elite politics, and that most of their social interaction is with their enemies and allies in that arena.

From the point of view of politics regarded as a system of single-interest relationships, the constituency is the easiest arena to comprehend. The prize is quite clear—a seat in the Legislative Assembly. The rules of the competition are not only explicitly stated—who may take part, what they may and may not do in order to win—but they are relatively rigorously enforced. But when we begin to identify the protagonists, the picture becomes more complicated, and this is true whether we identify them through political relationships, or socially.

When we try to identify constituency politicians through political links alone, it becomes clear that at least some of

CONCLUSION

them are in this arena only, so to speak, as members of an expedition to collect votes. Their constituency activities are simply a means of qualifying themselves to enter the struggle in the elite arena. They are, as I have said, like absentee landlords come down to collect the rent.

Conversely, other protagonists in the constituency arena are on an expedition up from the villages, entering this arena to better qualify themselves or better train and arm themselves for the village arenas. I am not saying that they are all doing this consciously—only that people like the untouchable candidates in Bisipara (see Chapter 1), although their foray into constituency politics may be a total fiasco, nevertheless are bigger men in the village after the experience. Just as the upper half of the constituency protagonists really belong, so to speak, in the elite arena, so the lower half really belong in the village arenas.

In other words, no one belongs socially to a constituency arena. In respect of nonpolitical interaction, they belong either with the elite or with the villages. The constituency does not have an "establishment" as the State does.

This is another way of saying, as I did in Part II, that the constituency is an "artificial" unit, and does not correspond to any social unit.

The social interaction which underlies political interaction in the elite arena makes it easier for us to conceive of that arena as a bounded universe. The same is true, to an even greater extent, of many village arenas. I do not need to expand on this point, since the account in Chapter 1 of the attitudes of the people of Bisipara towards outsiders make this fact clear.

We can treat either the elite or the villages as relatively closed systems of sociopolitical interaction. We know that they are not in fact closed; but relationships which intrude from outside and affect the working of the system we can re-

CONCLUSION

gard as accidents, the effects of which we notice, but the genesis of which need not be explained within our system.[1]

These outside relationships are clearly important in the present analysis, for it is through them, if anything, that the different arenas are linked into a single system.

There was a time when a village like Bisipara could have been regarded, without reservations, as a simple society based upon a system of multiplex relationships. For example, the Warriors were connected with their untouchables, as their rulers, their employers, and their ritual superiors. Insofar as this system was an arena, competition lay not between castes but between descent groups within the dominant caste of Warriors, sometimes within the village and sometimes between the Warriors of Bisipara and the Warriors of other villages. Nowadays Bisipara is different; the main cleavage, as Chapter 1 shows, lies between the untouchables and the clean castes.

This change has come about because the Bisipara untouchables have been able to establish outside relationships, both economic and political, and have used these relationships to enter into competition with their former masters. In effect, the "village establishment"—that is, the dominant caste of Warriors—had had to close its ranks in order to meet the threat from its former subjects.

The important fact about this development is that the untouchables invest, so to speak, the political and social resources which they gain from outside in the village arena. Because they do this, the village continues to be an arena; the villagers still interact for the most part with one another. The pattern

---

[1] In another book (1957) I have done this with Bisipara, where I discussed the effect of ties which untouchables have with outsiders upon their conflict with the clean castes within the village; and I have discussed this procedure, from a more theoretical point of view, in a collection of essays to be published under the editorship of Gluckman and Devons.

CONCLUSION

of interaction has changed from vertical to horizontal cleavages, but by and large the boundary of interaction has remained the same, except for those fragmentary outside interactions which have caused this change.

At first sight we could arrange all three arenas (village, constituency, and State) as a system of nesting units within one framework, thus: so many villages make up a constituency, and so many constituencies make up the State. The same general principles regulate competition at all three levels; the prize of victory is the same—control of the State; the protagonists are the political parties, exemplified at their various levels from Mandal committee to State committee. This scheme has the merit of simplicity. Its drawback is that it gives us very little understanding of actual behaviour. The point is, as I have said before, that there is not homogeneity at all levels; the issues which are at stake in State politics have to be translated into something else at constituency level and have to be translated yet again at village level. For example, the Ganatantra-Congress conflict at State level appears in the guise of rival policies (or, in another form, of regional rivalries—Hill against Coast); in the constituencies of Kalahandi district it appeared as a dynastic dispute; in Bisipara it was translated into caste conflict. We will not understand why these translations have to take place if we keep our eyes only on the rules which govern representative democracy and free elections. These rules do no more than set a wide limit around a variety of possible actual behaviour. We begin to discern regularities within this wide field of possible behaviour when we take into account the social interactions of those whose political interactions we are surveying.

When we do take the social dimension into account, it becomes clear at once that the nesting model may fit the rules of representative democracy, but does not fit the facts of political behaviour. The homogeneity between the three levels,

CONCLUSION

233

which appears to accord with the design of free elections and representative democracy, vanishes when we take into account the social relationships which political actors have in different arenas. In particular, in the present context, the constituency arena differs from the other two in that it does not have—speaking relatively—a field of social interaction corresponding to political action.

I do not mean by this that constituency politics can be understood in themselves, purely as political action, without taking into account the social rights and obligations which the political protagonists have. But I do mean that the social interaction which must be considered to understand constituency politics is either that of the elite or of the villages.

The constituency, in other words, has a different quality from the other two arenas. The elite and the village are arenas in which political interaction and social interaction overlap with one another. The elite is not, it is true, a structure in the anthropologist's sense of multiplex ties and consistent statuses, but it is a field in which the same set of people are found whether we are dealing with politics or economics or kinship or anything else. But in both cases the boundaries around a field of interaction enclose more than just political interaction. But the same is not true of the constituency—this is an arena specialized in political interaction.

It follows from this that the constituency is a meeting place between the two sociopolitical arenas of village and elite. But what does "meeting-place" mean?

The first meaning is the literal one of communication. The two halves must communicate—the elite in order to get votes, and the ordinary people in order to make their wishes known. These ties are instrumental; they are used by the villagers to gain their ends in the village arena and by the elite to gain their ends in the elite arena. The elite arena and the village arena are more important and more valued, have a legitimacy and a moral quality, which relatively is lacking in the constituency arena. They have this quality because they involve not merely political interaction, but also social interaction. If we may risk so vague a phrase, the elite arena and the village arena are, for their respective protagonists, ways of life; the constituency is merely an instrument for the preservation of those ways of life.

"Preservation" is used advisedly, since it is clear that representative politics threaten the integrity both of the elite and of the villages. The rules of representative politics harmonize with neither. If we take our stand beside the villagers, every time the issues of State politics have to be translated into a village idiom, then the village arenas have won a victory and vindicated their existence. This is the story of Bisipara. When, on the other hand, as in Mohanpur, the villagers treat State politics as a system of relationships in its own right, and when village politics are unconnected with State politics, then this is a victory for representative institutions, for, to continue using metaphors, those institutions have successfully broken into the tight circle of parochial loyalties and succeeded in differentiating their kind of political interaction from social interaction.

A similar threat hangs over the elite. The more effectively representative institutions bring the elite into contact with the villagers, the more must the elite too lose their "parochial" qualities, cease to operate so much within the unspecialized highly personal relationships which they have with one another, and make more effective use of specialized impersonal political links with the mass.

Neither process has yet gone very far in Orissa. But this is the direction in which new political institutions are leading social change.

REFERENCES

Official Publications

Census of India, 1891, 1901, 1911, 1951
Report on the First General Elections in India 1951–1952 (2 vols) Election Commission, Delhi
Report on the Second General Elections in India 1957 (2 vols) Election Commission, Delhi
The Orissa Gazette (for reports on Election Tribunals). Cuttack
Orissa 1949 Public Relations Department, Cuttack
Orissa 1950–51 Public Relations Department, Cuttack
Statistical Outline of Orissa, 1957 Finance Department, Bhubaneswar
List of Members of the Orissa Legislative Assembly, 1952 Assembly Secretariat, Cuttack
List of Members of the Orissa Legislative Assembly, 1958 Assembly Secretariat, Bhubaneswar

Others

Amrita Bazar Patrika, Calcutta
Anonymous ("Two Bachelors of Arts"), 1919, *The Oriya Movement*, Ganjam
Bailey, F. G., 1957, *Caste and the Economic Frontier*, Manchester
1960, *Tribe Caste and Nation*, Manchester

REFERENCES

Bose, N. K., Patnaik, N., Ray, A. K., "The Organization of the Oilman or Teli caste in Orissa," unpublished essay
Das, N., 1958, *Madhusudan's Immortal Words*, Cuttack
Ghosh, R., 1958, "The 1948 Blood Bath in Kharswan" in *Mankind* Vol. 3, No. 1, Hyderabad
Ghurye, G. S., 1950, *Caste and Class in India*, Bombay
Gluckman, Max and Devons, E. (Editors), *Closed Systems and Open Minds* (in preparation)
Lipset, S. M., 1960, *Political Man*, London
Mackenzie, W. J. M., 1958, *Free Elections*, London
Mahtab, H. K. (Editor), 1957, *History of the Freedom Movement in Orissa* (5 vols), Cuttack
Marriott, McKim (Editor), 1955, *Village India*, Chicago
Miller, E. J., 1954, "Caste and territory in Malabar" in the *American Anthropologist*, Vol. 56, No. 3
Patnaik, L. M., 1941, *Resurrected Orissa*, Cuttack
Philips, C. H. (Editor), 1963, *Politics and Society in South Asia*, London

INDEX

Adhikari, 194
Adibasis: agitations, 200, 201, 202; in Independence Movement, 180. *See also* Scheduled tribes
Administration: and politicians, 195–197; in Feudatory States, 118 ff., 175 ff.
Agitation, 149, 191 ff., 200; and social work, 189; in Jaipatna, 120
All-India Radio, 183
Amrita Bazar Patrika, 7, 207, 235
Arenas, 224–226; and social change, 231–234

Balimendi, 55
Bengalis, 161 ff., 183–184
Besringia, 55
Bhadrak, 183
Bhave, Vinoba, 187
Bhoodan, 212
Bihar, 139, 164, 183, 202
Bisipara, Ch. 1 *passim*; caste conflict in, 49 ff., 231, 232; community development in, 56; contrasted with Mohanpur, 99 ff., 234; degree of typicality, 67; Distillers, 40, 42–43, 59, 61; dominant caste in, 48; elections in, 13, 16, 36, 71; Government employees in, 37, 38, 42; Independents, 18, 26; Potters, 40; statutory panchayat, 55; traditional social organization, 48; Untouchables, 36 ff., 44, 48, 50; Warriors, 40, 48, 94; women, 37, 40. *See also* Government
Bisoi, of Bisipara, 57. *See also* Headman; Sirdar
Boad, 15; status of Untouchables in, 52; status of Washermen in, 129. *See also* Districts: Phulbani
Bose, N. K., 130, 133
Boudh. *See* Boad
Bribery. *See* Electoral malpractices
Broker: ambiguous position of in Bisipara, 62; distinguished from touter and agitator, 149; function of in Bisipara, 60, 66; in Mohanpur, 101–102; role of Ind 4 as, 60

Cabinet Mission, 179
Cabinets in Orissa, 170, 171, 208, 210, 215, 216
Candidates: importance of personal qualities, 24 ff., 45 ff.; in Mohanpur election, 81–85

INDEX

Caste associations, 128–133; and politics, 133 ff.; function of ritual in, 131; moral appeal of, 135; Orissa Oilmen, 130, 133
Caste system, 122–126; and Ganatantra Parishad, 21; and politics, 126–128; and territory, 132
Castes, Ch. 5 *passim*; and voting in Bisipara, 41; caste assemblies, 125, 127; in Mohanpur, 86; organization of, 124–125:
Bauri, 127–128
Brahmin: as dominant caste, 90; in Mohanpur, 90; leadership in political parties, 90; rivalry with Karans, 92; women not voting in Bisipara, 40
Cultivator: and politics, 92; caste in Mohanpur, 91
Distiller, 127; biography of *Ind 4*, 59; caste assembly, 125; status in Bisipara, 61; voting in Bisipara, 42–43; women voting in Bisipara, 40
Harijan, 48 ff. *See also* Castes: Untouchables
Herdsman, 52; caste assemblies, 125, 129
Karan: as dominant caste, 90; in Mohanpur, 90; rivalry with Brahmins, 92, 169
Kond, 37, 67; and forest restrictions, 28
Marwari, 177, 184
Nair, 134
Oilman, 130, 134
Potter, 40
Untouchable: advancement in Bisipara, 48 ff.; and access to Bisipara temples, 36, 50; in Bisipara elections, 36 ff.; in Boad, 52; in Mohanpur, 87 ff.; privileges of, 38; voting in Bisipara, 48 ff. *See also* Scheduled Castes
Warrior, 231; as dominant caste in Bisipara, 48, 94; caste assembly, 125; women voters in Bisipara, 40
Washerman, 81, 129
Writer. *See* Castes: Karan
Census of India, 163
Chief Minister, 7, 54, 186, 212
Coalition, viii, 7, 8, 172, 214
Communist Party, viii, ix, xi; agitations, 191, 200; agrarian reforms, 75; campaign in Mohanpur, 80, 90; candidates in Cuttack Rural, 82 ff.; organization, 137; origins, 170
Community development: and political machines. 148; in Bisipara, 56
Congress: and hill areas, 198, 203 ff.; and Oriya Nationalism, 170–171, 181–186; and Untouchables in Bisipara, 51; change of leadership, 76, 212; movement becomes party, 206–218; 1957 election campaign in Mohanpur, 76; party organization, xi, 137–140; Rajas in, 210 ff.; regional support, viii, 198; socialist wing, 170, 216; success in 1947 elections, 207 ff.
Congress Socialist Party, 172, 212
Constituencies: as "artificial" units, 111, 229–230; delimitation of, 111 ff.; double-member, 15, 44–45, 47; size of, 108. *See also* Elections

Das, Gopabandhu, 167, 170
Das, Madhusudan, 161, 163
Das, Nabakishore, 162
Depressed Classes League, 21, 190; in Mohanpur, 80
Devons, E., 231
Districts, 174. *See also* Elections
Balasore, 161, 181, 191
Bolangir, 139, 201
Cuttack, 161, 191, 192; influence in Mohanpur, 70, 93

INDEX

Dhenkanal, 174, 175, 192
Ganjam, 6, 7, 129, 162, 164, 191, 192
Kalahandi, Ch. 4 *passim*, 139, 201, 232. *See also* Rajas: of Kalahandi
Keonjhar, 174, 201
Koraput, 139, 164, 174
Mayurbhanj, 139, 181, 182, 200, 202
Midnapore, 163, 165
Phulbani, Ch. 1 *passim*
Puri, 161, 167, 191, 192
Sambalpur, 6, 139, 174, 191
Singhbhum, 165, 167
Sundargarh, 192
Division of Labour: in Bisipara, 48; in the caste system, 122
Dominant caste, in Bisipara, 48, 124. *See also* Castes

Eastern States Union, 179
Education: and prestige, 62; valued in Mohanpur, 97
Election Commission, 15, 33
Election Reports, x, 14, 34, 235
Election Tribunals, x, 31, 143, 235
Elections: communication difficulties, 107, 136, 154; Congress success in 1947, 207 ff.; contrasted attitudes 1952 and 1957 in Mohanpur, 71; headmen in, 119; issues in Bisipara, 36 ff.; issues of policy in Phulbani, 27; Kalahandi 1952 and 1957, Ch. 4 *passim*; mass contact, 107, 111; 1957 campaign in Mohanpur, 78; 1957 in Bisipara, 13 ff.; 1957 in Kalahandi Parliamentary constituency, 17; 1957 in Phulbani Assembly constituency, 16; 1957 Orissa Legislative Assembly, 5; 1952 Orissa Legislative Assembly, 4; vote banks, 109-111. *See also* Agitation; Constituencies
Electoral malpractices, 143 ff.; and parochial loyalties, 32, 35; cumulative voting, 43; in Mohanpur, 79; in Phulbani, 29 ff.; safeguards against corruption and intimidation, 33 ff., 111. *See also* Free elections
Elite, 226-229

Feudatory States, viii, 3; administration in, 118, 175 ff.; merger of, 179 ff., 199, 203 ff.
Fission and fusion, 225-226
Flood relief, an issue in Mohanpur elections, 77
Free elections, 1; corruption and intimidation, 33; not valued, 32. *See also* Electoral malpractices
Freedom Fighters, 207 ff.; defined, 209

Ganatantra Parishad: and Oriya Nationalism, 183, 202; and Rajas, 26; in coastal plain, 186; in hill areas, viii, 198 ff.; origins of, 201 ff.; party organization, xi, 139; policy of, 187
Gandhi, 21, 26; and Untouchables, 50
Gandhians, 168 ff., 188
Ghosh, R., 201
Ghurye, G. S., 133
Gluckman, M., 231
Government: a "vote for the Raj," 23 ff., 85; employees as voters in Bisipara, 37, 38, 42
Gujarat, 134

Headman: chiefs in hill areas, 118 ff.; in Bisipara. *See* Bisoi. *See also* Sirdar
Hirakud, 184, 200

Independence Movement, ix, 83, Ch. 8 *passim*; and middle classes, 166, 172 ff., 227; as an ideology, 217, 218; as a qualification for leadership, 84; caste and locality

INDEX

Independence Movement (*continued*) in, 169; cleavages in, 168; ideological cleavages, 170; in Mohanpur, 73; landlords, 171–173; main periods of, 166; Oriya Nationalism, 170–171; Prajamandals, 177–181; social and economic reform, 167
Independents, 3, 4, 16, 183, 211; in Bisipara, 18, 26
Instability, 8

Jeypore, 116, 117
Jharkhand Party, viii, 6, 139, 200, 202, 208

Katakis, 176, 203
Kendu, 184
Kerala, 132, 134
Kharsawan, 200–201. See *also* Saraikella and Kharsawan
Kinship, in the caste system, 124–125
KMPP, 72
Kondmals, 15, 31, 48, 49, 67
Kui, 49, 51

Landlords, 192; and Independence Movement, 171 *ff.*; reaction to Tenant Relief Acts, 75
Leadership: and the Administration, 65; brokers and "real" leaders, 63; in political parties, 90; of Congress, 76
Lipsett, S. M., 136
Literacy rates, 108
Local Government: Anchal Sasan Act, 195; Statutory panchayat in Bisipara, 55 *ff.*; Statutory panchayat in Mohanpur, 95 *ff.*

Mackenzie, W. J. M., 1
Madras, 162, 164
Mahtab, H. K., 167, 180, 209
Marriott, McKim, 125
Members of the Legislative Assembly, vii, viii, ix, x; parochial loyalties of, 25

Middle class: attitude towards change, 186 *ff.*; in Mohanpur, 102
Miller, E. J., 132
"Missionaries," 163, 217
Mohanpur, Ch. 2 *passim*; attitudes of villagers to 1952 and 1957 elections compared, 71; brokers, 101; castes, 86; characteristics of candidates in 1957 election, 82–85; contrasted with Bisipara, 99, 234; election workers, 80–81; experience of representative democracy, 73; issues in 1957 election, 74–78; lack of caste conflict, 90–93; middle class, 102; 1957 election meetings, 79; political prisoners, 73; schools, 97; size and situation, 69–70; Statutory panchayat, 96; traditional village council, 95; Untouchables, 87
Mutha: Balimendi, 55; Besringia, 55

National Movement. See Independence Movement
Newspapers: in Mohanpur, 73; readers, 108–109
Nilgiri, 180, 192

Officials, and villagers, 58 *ff.*
Opposition, 6, 7
Orissa States Assembly, 208
Oriya, viii; language of administration, 49
Oriya Nationalism, 9, Ch. 7 *passim*, 217, 227; and Congress, 170, 181–186; and Ganatantra Parishad, 183, 202. See *also* Saraikella and Kharsawan; States Reorganization Commission

Panchayat: in Mohanpur, 95. See *also* Bisipara; Local Government; Mohanpur
Parliamentary democracy, 1; and complex society, 221
Parties: categories of, 136–137; ma-

INDEX

chines and movements distinguished, 141; machine structure in, 151, 156, Ch. 6 *passim*. See also Congress; Communist; Ganatantra Parishad; Jharkhand; Praja Socialist
Patnaik, L. M., 169
Police, 192, 200, 202
Political prisoners, 83, 206, 207, 208; in Mohanpur, 73
Politicians: distinguished from brokers, 149; professional politicians as candidates in Mohanpur, 83
Politics, defined, 223
Poverty: and electoral honesty, 32; and party organization, 140
Prajamandals, 177 ff., 208
Praja Socialist Party, viii, ix; party organization, xi, 139

Rajas: and Ganatantra Parishad, 26; as candidates, 46, 114; in Congress, 210 ff.; in opposition to Prajamandals, 177 ff.; in the Oriya Movement, 163 ff., 171
of Bastar, 116
of Boad, 20, 25, 26, 46
of Jeypore, 116
of Kalahandi, 17, 18, 26, 30 ff., 46 ff., 114 ff.
of Kanika, 163
of Mayurbhanj, 163
of Talcher, 114
Ritual, function in caste associations and the caste system compared, 131
Rourkhella, 6, 184

Sampling, problems of, 221–222
Saraikella and Kharsawan, 181, 182, 185, 202; an issue in 1957 election, 76, 186
Satyabadi school, 167, 169
Scheduled castes: candidates in Bisipara, 14; privileges of, 38

Scheduled tribes: candidates in Kalahandi, 14; privileges of, 38
Schoolmaster: Communist in Mohanpur, 97; Untouchable in Bisipara, 49. See also Education; Schools
Schools: in Jaipatna, 121; in Mohanpur, 97; in politics, 97. See also Education; Schoolmaster
Share-cropping, 192; an issue in Mohanpur election, 74
Sirdar: influence in elections, 37, 118–119. See also Bisoi; Headman
Socialists, 5; agitations, 191, 200. See also Praja Socialist Party
Society: complex and simple, vii, 219–220; interactional and cultural approach to, 222
States Peoples Conference, 177, 178
States Reorganization Commission, 3, 183, 185 ff.; an issue in Mohanpur election, 76
Swaraj, 168 ff., 213

Taxes, an issue in elections, 28, 31, 47
Temple, in Bisipara. See Castes: Untouchable
"Touters," 63, 149
Tributary States. See Feudatory States

Village Level Worker, 57
Villagers: Mohanpur and Administration, 93–103; relations with outsiders in Bisipara, 54, 58 ff., 62; sophistication of Mohanpur, 71, 73, 93

Women: as voters in Bisipara, 37, 40; canvassing in Mohanpur, 80

Zemindar: of Jaipatna, 115 ff., 120; of Kasipur, 115 ff.; of Nawapara, 115 ff.
Zemindari Abolition, 3, 193 ff., 212; an issue in Mohanpur election, 75

www.ingramcontent.com/pod-product-compliance
Lightning Source LLC
Chambersburg PA
CBHW021700230426
43668CB00008B/681

BIBLIOGRAPHY

(confined to works cited more than once)

Bogner, Hans. *Der Tragische Gegensatz* (Heidelberg 1947), pp. 104-39.

Croiset, Maurice. *Eschyle* (Paris 1928), pp. 43-71.

Hiltbrunner, Otto. *Wiederholungs- und Motivtechnik bei Aischylos* (Bern 1950).

Korte, Alfred. "Die Entstehungszeit der Hiketiden des Aischylus," *Mélanges Nicole* (Geneva 1905), pp. 289-300.

Macurdy, Grace M. "Had the Danaid Trilogy a Social Problem?", *Classical Philology 39* (1944), pp. 95-100.

Mazon, Paul. *Eschyle* (Paris 1920).

Méautis, Georges. *Eschyle et la Trilogie* (Paris 1936).

Murray, Gilbert. *Aeschylus, the Creator of Tragedy* (Oxford 1940).

Owen, E. T. *The Harmony of Aeschylus* (Toronto 1952).

Richter, Paul. *Zur Dramaturgie des Aeschylus* (Leipzig 1892).

Ridgeway, William. *The Origin of Tragedy* (Cambridge 1910).

Robertson, D. S. "The End of the Supplices Trilogy of Aeschylus," *Classical Review 38* (1924), pp. 51-3.

Bibliography

Sheppard, J. T. "The First Scene of the Suppliants of Aeschylus," *Classical Quarterly* 5 (1911), pp. 220-9.

Smyth, Herbert W. *Aeschylean Tragedy* (Berkeley 1924).

Stanford, William B. *Aeschylus in his Style* (Dublin 1942).

Stoessl, Franz. *Die Trilogie des Aischylos* (Baden bei Wien 1937).

Thomson, George. *Aeschylus and Athens* (London 1946).

von Fritz, Kurt. "Die Danaiden Trilogie des Aeschylus," *Philologus* 91 (1936), pp. 121-36 and 249-69.

Vürtheim, J. *Aischylos' Schutzflehende* (Amsterdam 1928).

Wilamowitz-Moellendorff, Ulrich von. *Aischylos Interpretationen* (Berlin 1914).

GPSR Authorized Representative: Easy Access System Europe - Mustamäe tee 50, 10621 Tallinn, Estonia, gpsr.requests@easproject.com

www.ingramcontent.com/pod-product-compliance
Lightning Source LLC
Chambersburg PA
CBHW051529230426
43668CB00012B/1787